Engaging Play

Engaging Play

Edited by

Liz Brooker and Susan Edwards

 Open University Press

Open University Press
McGraw-Hill Education
McGraw-Hill House
Shoppenhangers Road
Maidenhead
Berkshire
England
SL6 2QL

email: enquiries@openup.co.uk
world wide web: www.openup.co.uk

First published 2010

Copyright © Liz Brooker and Susan Edwards 2010

A catalogue record of this book is available from the British Library

ISBN-13: 978-0-335-23586-5   978-0-335-23585-8
ISBN-10: 0-335-23586-7   0-335-23585-9

Library of Congress Cataloging-in-Publication Data
CIP data applied for

Typeset by Aptara, Inc.
Printed in the UK by Bell and Bain Ltd., Glasgow

Fictitious names of companies, products, people, characters and/or data that
may be used herein (in case studies or in examples) are not intended to
represent any real individual, company, product or event.

McGraw-Hill books are available at special quantity discounts to use as premiums
and sales promotions, or for use in corporate training programmes. To contact a
representative, please e-mail us at bulksales@mcgraw-hill.com.

Mixed Sources
Product group from well-managed
forests and other controlled sources
www.fsc.org Cert no. TT-COC-002769
© 1996 Forest Stewardship Council

FSC

The **McGraw·Hill** Companies

Contents

Notes on contributors

Jo Ailwood has taught early years both in Queensland, Australia, and in the UK. Her research interests focus on the educational experiences of children in the year before compulsory schooling. She has pursued historical analyses of pre-school education in Queensland government schools, making use of developments of Foucault's notion of governmentality. She has also published in the areas of gender, play, pedagogy and policy. Her current research focus is on children's participation, rights and citizenship. Jo teaches on the Childhood Studies and Initial Teacher Education programmes at the University of Edinburgh, and is Adjunct Associate Professor in the Centre for Learning Innovation, Queensland University of Technology.

Jo Ailwood
The University of Edinburgh, Scotland
jo.ailwood@ed.ac.uk

Mindy Blaise's interests include utilizing queer and poststructuralist perspectives in ways that assist her feminist, theoretical and methodological project of disrupting the status quo in the field of early childhood education.

Mindy Blaise
Monash University, Australia
mindy.blaise@education.monash.edu.au

Liz Brooker moved into research and teaching at the Institute of Education in London, where she is now involved in doctoral training in research methods, after a career spent working with young children. Her research has focused on the transitions made by young children and their families as they move from the home and community environment into pre-school settings and then into formal schooling, with a special emphasis on the experiences of children from disadvantaged backgrounds. Her interpretation of these experiences employs perspectives from cultural-historical theory and from the sociology of childhood, but is also informed by the sociological theories of Bernstein and Bourdieu, and the explanations these offer for the persistence of inequalities.

Liz Brooker
Institute of Education, England
E.Brooker@ioe.ac.uk

Joy Cullen was foundation Professor of Early Years Education (birth–eight) at Massey University, New Zealand. Following retirement she now lives in Australia where she continues to undertake doctoral supervision and publish in early years education. Her research interests reflect many of the issues that confronted New Zealand's early childhood educators as they worked with the national early childhood curriculum, *Te Whāriki*, including: sociocultural pedagogy for an inclusive curriculum, the ethics of research in early childhood settings, and teacher-research as a form of professional learning. She is co-editor with Angela Anning, UK, and Marilyn Fleer, Australia, of a cross-national book, *Early Childhood Education: Society and Culture* (2004, 2008) which explores sociocultural-historical perspectives in early childhood research. Research contracts include evaluation of early intervention services for young children; research support for teacher research in NZ's Centre of Innovation programme, and literacy continuity across early childhood and junior primary.

Joy Cullen
Massey University, New Zealand
joy.l.cullen@gmail.com

Amy Cutter-Mackenzie's broad research interests are situated within environmental education and sustainability. She has a clear interest in teachers' and children's environmental thinking (ecoliteracy) and experiences, together with research-led teaching practices and methodologies in environmental education and sustainability. Amy's interests also extend to: early childhood education; research methodologies involving children as researchers; environmental philosophy; human and other-than-human relations; social ecology; experiential education; teachers' knowledge; science education; and professional practice. Amy is a recipient of the Monash University Vice-Chancellor's Teaching Excellence Award (September 2009); and a prestigious Australian Learning and Teaching Council Citation for Outstanding Contributions to Student Learning (August 2008).

Amy Cutter-Mackenzie
Monash University, Australia
Amy.cuttermackenzie@education.monash.edu.au

Brian Edmiston is an Associate Professor of Teaching and Learning at the Ohio State University. A former primary teacher in the US and a secondary teacher in the UK, Brian is the recipient of both research and teaching awards. His research interests focus on the overlap between play, drama and education in contexts where adults and young people collaboratively create imagined worlds. He is the author or co-author of three books and many articles. *Imagining to Learn: Inquiry, Ethics, and Integration through Drama* is a practical and theoretical analysis of classroom drama as education. *Forming Ethical Identities in Early Childhood Play* (Routledge, 2008) breaks new ground in early childhood moral education by providing a dialogic theory for adult–child play and by exploring the mythic dimensions of superhero play. *Bring Literacy to Life: Transforming Classroom Lives* includes an analysis of how dramatic inquiry affects space, identify formation and power.

Brian Edmiston
Ohio State University, United States of America
edmiston.1@osu.edu

Susan Edwards has taught in early childhood settings and in higher education in Australia. Her research interests include examining how teachers perceive different dimensions of the early childhood curriculum, including their understandings of development, learning and play from a cultural historical perspective. Susan is interested in examining how these dimensions of curriculum relate to teacher pedagogy and professional learning in early childhood education. Additional areas of research interest include the role of ICTs in early learning and higher education. Susan has won national and university awards for teaching excellence for the development of innovative approaches to teacher education which inspire and motivate student learning.

Susan Edwards
Monash University, Australia
susan.edwards@education.monash.edu.au

Marilyn Fleer holds the Foundation Chair of Early Childhood Education at Monash University, Australia, and is the President of the International Society for Cultural Activity Research (ISCAR). Her research interests focus on early years learning and development, with special attention on pedagogy, culture, science and technology. More recently she has investigated child development in the contexts of home and school.

Marilyn Fleer
Monash University, Australia
marilyn.fleer@education.monash.edu.au

Helen Hedges' teaching and research interests focus on children's and teachers' knowledge and interests, and teachers' professional learning. She has also published on ethical considerations related to the involvement of children aged under 5 years in research activity. Theoretical frameworks of interest at present are funds of knowledge and communities of inquiry. Her current research includes investigating, through narrative interviews with young adults, the long-term outcomes of their interests as children, in order to consider evidence-based policies and practices for early childhood education.

Helen Hedges
Assistant Dean (Research)
University of Auckland, New Zealand
h.hedges@auckland.ac.nz

Elizabeth Hunt is interested in using a cultural-historical approach as an informant to her pedagogy and is currently enrolled in a higher degree by research studies at Monash University. She is particularly interested in looking at how a teacher can use Vygotsky's theory of the Zone of Proximal Development to support children's learning and development within a play-based programme. She is also drawing on the newer work of E. Kravtsova on play to extend and reinforce the teacher's position within the kindergarten programme.

Elizabeth Hunt
Director
Timbarra Kindergarten, Australia
timbarra@kindergarten.vic.gov.au

Barbara Jordan is especially interested in research related to the professional development of teachers, both pre-service and in-service. Preferred methodologies of research are qualitative, collaborative and empowering, in order to maximize the sharing of expertise of university lecturers and practising teachers, for mutual learning. The core of her work is the development of understandings in the early childhood field of the implications and possibilities of socio-cultural-historical theory in holistic and authentic learning programmes. Particular subject areas include: understanding, articulating and celebrating leadership; integrating the curriculum, especially science, numeracy and literacy; and incorporating children's home funds of knowledge into the ECE curriculum, alongside the involvement of parents and the community in co-constructing the curriculum.

Barbara Jordan
Massey University, New Zealand
B.J.Jordan@massey.ac.nz

Anna Kilderry is a Senior Lecturer in Early Years at the University of Greenwich, London, where part of her role has been to develop Early Years undergraduate programmes and manage Early Years Professional Status (EYPS). Previously Anna was a pre-school teacher, a TAFE (Technical and Further Education) teacher and a university lecturer in early childhood education in Victoria, Australia. It is through her involvement in teacher education that she has developed her research interests in curriculum and pedagogy, professional learning and educational policy.

Anna Kilderry
University of Greenwich, England
A.Kilderry@greenwich.ac.uk

Annica Löfdahl is an Associate Professor in Educational Work at Karlstad University, Sweden. She is actively involved in teacher education and as director of the postgraduate school in educational work. She has previously worked as a pre-school teacher in various areas of the Swedish childcare system. Her current research interests include educational policy, research ethics in educational studies, pre-school children's play, peer cultures and interactions and social processes among children in the pre-school.

Annica Löfdahl
Karlstad University, Sweden
annica.lofdahl@kau.se

Andrea Nolan is an Associate Professor in Early Childhood in the School of Education, Victoria University, Melbourne. She has conducted research in both schools and kindergartens and has worked on a number of state, national and international projects concerning literacy development, programme evaluation, and professional learning for teachers. Andrea's research interests include the use of reflective practice as a way to enhance teachers' professional growth and development, children's play and learning, and early childhood pedagogy. Her current projects include a large-scale longitudinal study that aims to identify factors including the role of the teacher, home life and child characteristics, which are positively associated with high outcomes in literacy in the first year of schooling and a study focusing on resilient students, families, schools and inter-agency collaboration in disadvantaged communities.

Andrea Nolan
Victoria University, Australia
Andrea.Nolan@vu.edu.au

Leigh O'Brien has presented papers nationally and internationally and has published numerous articles, several chapters and one co-edited book. She has also served in many editorial positions and has been chair of committees at the local, state and national levels. Her research interests include early care and education, inclusive education for young children with disabilities, women in education, critical theory and education, and teacher education.

Leigh O'Brien
Ella Cline Shear School of Education
State University of New York at Geneseo, United States of America
obrienL@geneseo.edu

Bert van Oers' research interests are in the areas of play, emergent literacy and mathematics, and developmental education, studied from a cultural-historical (Vygotskian) point of view.

Bert van Oers
Professor of Cultural-historical Theory of Education
VU University Amsterdam, the Netherlands
HJM.van.Oers@psy.vu.nl

Sue Rogers, formerly an early childhood teacher and researcher, has worked in higher education since 1995. Her research interests include play, curriculum and pedagogy in early childhood, young children's perspectives and identity formation. She has published widely in the field of early childhood education and play, including most recently *Inside Role Play in Early Childhood Education: researching children's perspectives* (2008, with Julie Evans). She is the editor of a forthcoming collection on play entitled *Rethinking Play and Pedagogy: Concepts, Contexts and Cultures*.

Sue Rogers
Department of Learning Curriculum and Communication
Institute of Education, England
S.Rogers@ioe.ac.uk

Anette Sandberg has several ongoing research projects such as 'Teacher Competence in Change: A Study of Teacher Competence in Pre-school'; 'A Day in the Life of an Early Years Practitioner'; 'Pre-school as the Context for Language Development in Children'; and 'Practicum and Praxis in Teacher Education'. Her interest in play can be traced in most of them, but there are also some projects that focus on other fascinating areas of education.

Anette Sandberg
Mälardalen University, Sweden
anette.sandberg@mdh.se

Tim Taylor has been a classroom teacher for 15 years and currently teaches a class of 8- and 9-year-old children at a school in Norfolk. Tim uses dramatic play within the 'mantle-of-the-expert' approach to teaching and learning, a pedagogy that he has promoted and researched as an Advanced Skills Teacher, a freelance consultant, a presenter at national and international conferences, and as a visiting lecturer at Newcastle University. He has published several articles including one in collaboration with Brian Edmiston; they are currently writing a book on the 'mantle-of-the-expert' approach.

Tim Taylor
Assistant Head Teacher
Surlingham Community Primary School
Norfolk, England

Tuula Vuorinen is a PhD student in Didactics, and a Lecturer in Early Childhood Education, Mälardalen University, School of Education, Culture and Communication, Sweden. Her research interests concern mainly the co-operation between home and pre-school, teacher competence in pre-school, children's play and learning from a gender perspective and equality work in pre-school and school.

Tuula Vuorinen
Mälardalen University, Sweden
tuula.vuorinen@mdh.se

Elizabeth Wood has carried out research in the areas of play, learning and pedagogy in early childhood education; children's choices in free choice time; teachers' thinking and classroom practice; and gender and achievement. She has worked with the National Union of Teachers and with policy-makers on developing play within and beyond early childhood.

Elizabeth Wood
University of Exeter, England
E.A.Wood@exeter.ac.uk

Preface

Early childhood education has many stakeholders: children, parents, teachers, academic researchers, health professionals, teacher educators and, increasingly, politicians. Notwithstanding the differing frames of reference of these diverse groups, the concept of play is typically awarded a key role in statements about the conditions deemed to be appropriate for young children's education and care in early childhood settings. The degree and nature of adult intervention in children's play may vary in different interpretations, but the notion that children learn through play has remained part of the ongoing narrative of early childhood education (albeit with the cultural overlay of different educational systems and countries). That this outcome does not automatically occur has been part of my own professional learning as teacher, academic and researcher in early years' settings, over several decades.

My background as a New Zealander has ensured the continuity of play in my perspectives on early education. New Zealand's natural environment and community-based early childhood programmes had fostered a focus on unstructured play, both indoors and outdoors, as services for young children were established and expanded. Today, the free-play ethos of my student years has been transformed into a much richer conception of play that enables adults to access children's meanings and funds of knowledge, to develop shared meanings and to co-construct new meanings. Acknowledging and working with diverse meanings and practices are integral to this process. *Engaging Play* encapsulates this approach to understanding play in early years settings, inviting the reader to participate in diverse ways of thinking about play and pedagogy.

My learning curve about the nature and functions of play draws not only on academic trends in theory and research but significantly on societal change and associated expectations for the education of young children. In New Zealand, during the 1980s, indigenous Māori began to establish language immersion early childhood programmes, which at that time appeared overly formal and lacking a play base to the eyes of mainstream early childhood educators. Learning to respect Māori views of development and learning became part of a revised early childhood narrative that did not always sit easily with established views about the primacy of play.

Expectations for the education of young children with disabilities also changed. In the late 1990s, several years after the introduction of *Te Whāriki*, New Zealand's inclusive early childhood curriculum, I directed a national research project on the inclusion of young children with special educational needs in early childhood centres. It became clear to me, as I observed these children across a range of early childhood settings, that attendance at play-based programmes did not ensure either participation or learning. Children were often on the fringes of groups of children playing together, and in the absence of teacher intervention in play episodes, they were also unable to access learning opportunities. In often stark terms the inadvertent exclusion of these children illustrated that play skills were not simply a function of the child: play partners, peers and adults were essential to inclusive practices. Further, a socio-culturally focused curriculum did not ensure inclusive teaching strategies when the long-established free play narrative continued to dominate over emerging ideas regarding the role of the adult. *Te Whāriki* is framed by a socio-cultural philosophy that acknowledges the embeddedness of children's learning in homes, communities and cultures, but it took many years for pedagogy to catch up with the new discourse. Part of my pedagogical learning occurred in response to this issue as I explored new ways of thinking about the play–pedagogy nexus with postgraduate researchers.

Internationally, the language of play has survived the increasing professionalization of early childhood education, and the associated need to upskill early childhood professionals with tertiary qualifications. The burgeoning of early childhood research by early childhood and curriculum academics, and postgraduate researchers, has been supported by governments keen to provide evidence to justify and monitor political initiatives. Today, play research may be embedded within investigations of outcomes of early childhood education and of broader topics such as literacy or environmental learning; or driven by theoretical concerns such as the feminist poststructuralist focus on power and relations, or a social constructivist focus on interactions with peers in play contexts. Such research has coincided with the increasing use and credibility of qualitative research, with innovative methodologies contributing new insights into play research. Typically, recent research has focused on aspects of play rather than embracing an all-encompassing theoretical construct.

Against this background, *Engaging Play* presents the reader with a diverse set of chapters that collectively support a conclusion that has increasingly emerged from research and reviews on young children's development, learning and education. Accordingly, the book highlights in the field of play research that diverse theoretical perspectives and methodologies are able to illuminate children's experiences of play and the learning trajectories that may, or may not, follow. The editors position the book's focus on diversity in the field of play research as a valid state in its own right, to be viewed in its own terms, rather than in relation to earlier play perspectives. This approach has several corollaries.

First, the collection parallels trends in research on children and childhood, which has moved beyond reliance on single disciplinary studies to multidisciplinary and interdisciplinary approaches. Just as research on the complexity of contemporary childhoods requires a broader lens than a psychological approach, research into children's play warrants a broader focus than a psychological or developmental perspective. This does not necessarily mean that earlier insights are rejected; rather, that multiple perspectives can sit alongside insights derived from a single theoretical lens, in much the same way as a kaleidoscope can detect patterns among discrete objects. Kaleidoscope patterns alter as objects shift; so too are commonalities identified across research chapters as they are viewed relationally. Evidence of the unevenness with which different children experience opportunities for learning within play settings supports one such insight that is strengthened when viewed across settings and across research foci.

Second, the collection includes the work of international researchers who are exploring themes related to pedagogy and play. Pedagogy can be closely linked to systems and contexts; juxtaposed across systems and countries, commonalities and differences appear, adding credence to research outcomes within research contexts and cultures. Moreover, the presence of diverse interpretations and forms of evidence about pedagogy has the potential to enrich the reader's professional knowledge base and to encourage the reader to reflect and explore new pedagogical ideas that may mesh more readily with the experiences of the diverse populations now entering early years settings. Importantly, as teachers access children's meanings and everyday practices they are provided with a means of moving children towards the more formal learning that underpins the practices of modern societies. My colleagues and I made this premise an important theoretical driver as we changed the parameters of our early childhood education course from preparing graduates to work in a range of early childhood services, to include the first years of school. We found that working with the experiential-disciplinary nexus provided considerable potential for strengthening the curriculum content components of a birth-to-8 teacher education programme, without sacrificing the concept of authentic learning which had guided curriculum studies in the birth-to-5 programme.

Third, the editors' concept of engaging play moves both researchers and professionals towards dialogue and inquiry about the role of play in early childhood education. This is a healthy process for a sector which too often has been guided by maxims, rather than evidence: 'play is the child's work', or 'children learn through play', rather than asking how children experience play in diverse settings and conditions. *Engaging Play* encourages researchers and professionals in the early childhood field to connect with ideas, theories and methodologies in order to understand children's play experiences. The collection therefore not only brings new insights to our understanding of children's play, it provides an approach to professional learning that should engage and interest the minds of the diverse stakeholders in early childhood education.

New forms of professional learning are signalled by the concept of engaging play. To me, the notion of engagement resonates with concepts of community – of learning, practice, inquiry. This was illustrated for me when I participated as a research associate in New Zealand's Centre of Innovation (COI) programme, in which academic research associates supported teacher researchers to carry out research into their teaching practices. Our COI's focus was on the inclusion of Samoan children in the kindergarten's informal play-based programme. Over the three years of the project, we examined, interpreted and revisited research data, and then reinvestigated with new ideas and questions. Over time, an explicit understanding of the processes and content of cultural learning for both children and adults gradually evolved, fostered in part by our willingness to consider alternative explanations of our early observations of teachers and children engaged in learning episodes. The participation of parents and community stakeholders informed this process, and at times dislodged academic perspectives. The teacher-researchers identified several teaching strategies that contributed to sustained and mediated learning experiences in the kindergarten, including 'Teachers and learners have[ing] fun as part of the learning process'. This notion of having fun also became a quality of our debate in research team meetings which I now recognize as a valuable aspect of our professional learning.

In retrospect, playing with ideas about teaching (or having fun) became a core of our research processes, as teacher-researchers and associates searched for new forms of understanding about learning in the context of an intercultural setting and within their expanded community of practice. Professional learning, as we discovered, was not simply a matter of imposing academic perspectives; it invited dialogue and inquiry. In other words, the theoretical drivers that we, as associates, had earlier assumed in the context of pre-service teacher education did not necessarily mesh with the teachers' everyday experience and their views about holistic learning. As I write, I recall vividly an example from an earlier professional development project in which I participated, that involved early intervention teams working with children with high and/or multiple needs, and researchers from different applied fields of practice. The project provided professional development to the hospital and special education team members who were using skills-based assessment, in order to increase their understanding of the strength-based early childhood assessment practice of narrative assessment (or learning stories). At the time, educational rhetoric was to criticize the use of the term 'need', as deficit-oriented. A hospital-based specialist was puzzled about this view and redefined a 'special' need as a constraint with which she had to work when assisting a hearing-impaired (or vision-impaired or physically-impaired) child to participate in play settings. This constructive use of constraint by the hospital specialist assisted teachers in the team to acknowledge that living with a visual or language impairment was part of the children's everyday experiences, and indeed their identities. In turn, the educators were empowered to explore new ways of thinking about inclusion in play settings. Ultimately, this project resulted in dynamic professional learning that engaged all participants and yielded new shared pedagogical perspectives, rather than being restricted by its original narrower goal of understanding narrative assessment. Playing with ideas seems a good description of the processes that occurred as the early intervention teams shared their diverse views. I now consider this notion is able to elaborate the concept of community of practice, thereby minimizing the risk that static conceptions of practice are perpetuated.

These corollaries foreground the dynamic nature of contemporary research about play. Readers of *Engaging Play* will find much to suggest diverse explanations of children's play experiences as they reflect upon interpretations and issues raised by the authors and editors, and engage in dialogue and inquiry about play. This book presents play as a 'many-splendoured thing', with all its pitfalls and possibilities, in the play narrative. I have no doubt that readers will find this book as thought-provoking and as enjoyable to read as I did.

Joy Cullen
Massey University
joy.l.cullen@gmail.com
October 2009

Acknowledgements

We would like to acknowledge the various people and institutions who have contributed to the development of this book in many different ways. First, we wish to thank the staff at Open University Press for their unfailing professionalism and support in developing the book and bringing this work to publication.

We also wish to thank Draga Tomas for her patient work in formatting the final manuscript. This is important and detailed work and we are most grateful to Draga for her contribution to this aspect of the book.

The contributing authors to this collection are also acknowledged, and we thank them for their patience, their good humour and their willingness to engage so readily with reviewer and editorial feedback. We also wish to acknowledge the contribution made to this book by Professor Joy Cullen who has so generously shared her own accumulated wisdom and knowledge about play and pedagogy by writing the Preface for this book.

To the many reviewers who contributed their time and expertise by reviewing the chapters and providing detailed and thoughtful feedback, we also offer our thanks.

Acknowledgement is also necessary of the time and finance provided by Monash University in the form of sabbatical leave for Susan. This time and monetary support enabled us to meet in London to finalize the book, and were critical to the development of our ideas and the timely completion of this work.

Finally, we would like to acknowledge the images on the cover of the book, including the photograph of the children by Polly Shields and the image of the child playing by Noah Cosgriff.

Introduction

From challenging to engaging play

Liz Brooker and Susan Edwards

For over two years this book has been known among its contributors as *Challenging Play*. As editors of this collection we have had great difficulty with the many layers of meaning embedded in such a title. Should 'Challenging Play' be taken to mean that play should be challenging for children? Should it be read as adults being challenged by children's play? Perhaps it might mean challenging the concept that there is some sort of relationship between play and pedagogy in early learning settings? To our minds, working with 'challenge' began to establish a sense of opposition in which the chapters in the book would be positioned as speaking against some existing orthodoxy, theoretical perspective or set of practices that were taken as the starting point for understanding play itself. And yet as the chapters for the book arrived, were reviewed, re-written and edited, this notion of challenging play seemed to become increasingly passé, and even irrelevant. The authors in this book have engaged with play in ways which demonstrate not only that the theory and practice of play remain a central concern for those involved in the education of young children, but also that the current status quo consists of multiple world-views and perspectives on play rather than a single consensual view. It no longer made sense to us to talk of 'challenging' play, when the authors we had invited to write for us themselves seemed so committed to 'engaging' play.

In this book, there are chapters which reflect on how play is used structurally, institutionally and pedagogically. There are chapters which consider the relationship between concepts, content, power, gender and social relationship within play. There are yet others which explore the relationships between culture, assessment, learning, thinking and play. While these descriptions might seem to reflect theoretical clusters, our engagement with the chapters made us disinclined to structure the book according to particular groupings. Instead, in developing the book, we tried to consider how the authors engaged with play, and what they felt was most important about play, rather than necessarily focusing on the particular theoretical framework they employed as our main criterion for ordering the chapters. Our focus shifted from thinking about play in terms of theoretical 'categories', to considering the central idea or 'problem situation' about play which each of the authors was engaging in their chapters. As part of this process, we stopped thinking about the book as 'individual chapters in a collection', and began to think about how the chapters were applied to understanding the various roles and interpretations about play that exist in early childhood education. As we worked, we struggled to realize the idea of 'challenging play', seeming to find that the multiple and diverse theoretical perspectives that currently inform many aspects of early childhood education represent ways of thinking that have moved not only beyond traditional models, but also beyond the need to refer to traditional perspectives as a step towards proposing newer alternatives. This seemed to indicate to us a maturing of the field of early childhood education, whereby the need to work (at least theoretically) in response to, or in tension with, traditional and more normative accounts of play has lessened. The moment for 'challenging' play, it appeared, had passed.

We could engage in debate about how and why early education has moved on from many of its historically valued perspectives, such as developmental and constructivist orientations towards play. Perhaps it has been the increased use of cultural-historical theory in the field to theorize learning, development and play in relation to children's lived social and cultural experiences? Perhaps poststructuralist accounts of power and relations and ways of viewing knowledge have allowed the field to see theoretical perspectives as holding particular potentials to determine play in dominant ways? Maybe it has been the advent of postmodernism and the realization that within this field and community of practice there is not, and cannot be, one truth which guides our thinking, theorizing and practice? Perhaps it has been the combined effect of all of these perspectives in grappling with the limitations which existing ideas might impose on children, families and communities in practice?

Engaging ideas about play

The chapters in this book lend support to all of these explanations. Many of them engage with play from a range of theoretical perspectives which exist in their own right, rather than defining themselves in relation to traditional orientations such as those represented by modernist accounts. As we continued to work with them, we began to experiment with the notion of 'engaging' play as a means to allow multiple perspectives to sit alongside one another in ways which respect the individual heritage of each, and yet allow the various shades of meaning to resonate with each other.

For example, in this book the chapter by Marilyn Fleer (Chapter 5) is followed by a contribution by Mindy Blaise (Chapter 6) which leads into the seventh chapter by Barbara Jordan. Working from distinctively different theoretical paradigms, these three chapters nonetheless ask readers to engage in questioning some deeply held assumptions about the role of play in early childhood education. Fleer's model for establishing teachers' conceptual and contextual subjectivity in relation to children's conceptual development during play disrupts conventional notions associated with children's learning through open-ended or exploratory play. Likewise, Blaise's consideration of the role of desire in relation to children's exploration of gender through play reconfigures the way adults might respond to the gendered practices enacted by children in early learning settings. Meanwhile, Jordan considers the need for teachers to draw on their own shared content knowledge in order to develop assessment practices which contribute to children's acquisition of theoretical knowledge. In each case, the chapters engage with play in ways which prompt the reader to think critically about the role of the adult in children's play – in one case, in relation to concept formation, in another, in supporting children's developing perspectives on gender and sexuality, and, in the third, according to the relationship between the role of theoretical knowledge and assessment. The question of how these ideas have been previously considered in the literature in relation to more traditional perspectives is then examined by Andrea Nolan and Anna Kilderry (Chapter 8), who draw on their own professional experience in teacher education to describe ways of thinking about play that help to articulate these considerations, and make them visible.

These counterpointed perspectives reflect a way of thinking which sees the notion of 'engaging' theories of play, not so much as engaging in a challenge (as in 'engaging battle'), but more as a process of placing ideas relationally to deepen our understandings about play. We are reminded here of the ongoing quest in early childhood education to find ways to address issues of cultural diversity: do we focus on 'difference', celebrating the existence of those aspects of our physical and cultural being which set us apart, or on 'similarity', drawing attention instead to the human characteristics we share? Both of these positions can seem to falsify the reality, which is far more complex than either implies, but a way forward can be to look not for similarity but for *commonality*, or a common cause. In the case of the diversity of perspectives on play included here, a commonality among all the authors might simply be described as a concern to understand what happens when children play in early childhood settings, whether under the direction of adults or in their own spontaneous activities. This concern may have many different motivations: a commitment to children's conceptual understanding, or to safeguarding children's rights as a minority social group, or to recognizing children's social competence. As van Oers argues, all activity arises from a motive. The thinking which lies behind each of these 15 chapters has its own motivation, but all 15 are engaged in a shared activity. Their shared concern encourages us to think of the book as a dialogue about play between different members of our community of practice.

As a result, we have tried to treat the chapters as neither competing nor complementary, but rather as mutually illuminative both in terms of their side-by-side placement, and also in terms of their overall position within the narrative of the entire book. This intention has resulted in the early placing of Helen Hedges (Chapter 2), Liz Brooker (Chapter 3) and Anette Sandberg and Tuula Vuorinen (Chapter 4) as consecutive chapters which all affirm the importance of understanding and using children's acquired funds of knowledge as a valid base for constructing pedagogy. For Hedges, this perspective informs an exploration of the ways that the concept of funds of knowledge can relate to the pedagogical use of children's interests as a basis for curriculum. For Brooker, it relates to the disjunction that can occur between the pedagogic discourses developed in homes and communities, and the enacted pedagogical approaches which children encounter in the classroom. For Sandberg and Vuorinen, this is reflected through a consideration of the playthings and preferred activities that have characterized children's funds of 'play-knowledge' across different generations and in different locations, acknowledging the contribution of time and space, history and geography, to the construction of children's cultures.

This series of chapters is also linked with chapters located further on in the book which emphasize, from various perspectives, the idea that children have a right to play that is enacted in their own terms, and achieves their own conscious or unconscious purposes. Here we see, for example, Sue Rogers (Chapter 11), Brian Edmiston and Tim Taylor (Chapter 12) and Leigh O'Brien (Chapter 13) framing perspectives that explore, respectively, how young children politicize their play actions in direct opposition to teacher intentions; how adults learn to work constructively with boys' 'aggressive' play; and how the concept of inclusion can result in exclusion from play, in the case of children with disabilities. The association of funds of knowledge derived from peer cultures (explicitly called upon by Hedges, and generally theorized from a socio-cultural orientation) with children's rights to shape their own play (foregrounded by Edmiston and Taylor, and often argued using perspectives from poststructuralism or the sociology of childhood) seems at first glance to be spurious. Yet when read relationally, these chapters suggest that children's funds of knowledge may be inextricably linked to their play rights. Otherwise why would children fight (or need to fight) for them in the ways outlined by Rogers, O'Brien and Edmiston and Taylor? And why would play-funds have such a seemingly important (if under-utilized) relationship to pedagogy, as suggested by Hedges, Brooker and Sandberg and Vuorinen?

Engaging play allows multiple perspectives to inform multiple readings of play for a whole range of different purposes. This is not to suggest that attempts to understand or research play should not utilize their own particular theoretical perspectives, as this would make a nonsense of any attempt to theorize anything. Rather, it is to highlight how the positioning of these perspectives in relation to each other can contribute to ways of thinking about play that might otherwise have remained unconsidered or invisible. Three further chapters in this collection offer an illustration of the process we have been trying to facilitate: Bert van Oers' (Chapter 14) articulation of a cultural-historical play-based pedagogy, Annica Löfdahl's (Chapter 9) investigation of how children call upon their own social knowledge domains in play-based settings, and Susan Edwards, Amy Cutter-Mackenzie and Elizabeth Hunt's exploration (in Chapter 10) of the pedagogical outcomes associated with a teacher's consideration of alternative play types as a basis for professional reflection. Like other chapters in this book, these three chapters draw on alternative theoretical frameworks to explain a particular aspect of play in early childhood education. In these cases, the concern lies in the ways in which the pedagogical use of play operates as a dynamic between the teacher and children within early childhood classrooms.

But these chapters resonate in turn with other contributions. The accounts, for instance, from Löfdahl in Sweden and from Edwards and colleagues in Australia, echo the narratives offered by Rogers, and by Edmiston and Taylor (each writing from the UK), because all four chapters focus on portraying children's responses to the enacted values and pedagogies they experience in the classroom and the playground. Thus, we see the children in Rogers' study deliberately resisting the teacher's intentions for their play; those in Edmiston and Taylor's chapter seeking ways to accommodate their play needs to the restrictions and requirements of the playground; and those in Edwards, Cutter-Mackenzie and Hunt's study expressing their preference for some 'teaching' to inform and extend their own exploratory play. Yet another important thread, among the many that we might identify, stems from Bert van Oers' account of a project which employs cultural-historical activity theory (CHAT) approaches to promote children's playful involvement in their learning in school. This chapter engages in a dialogue which runs right through the book, and especially with the accounts of Hedges, Fleer, Blaise, Jordan and Löfdahl, all of which seek to theorize children's learning and development through a reconsideration of traditional play-based provision, and of teachers' efforts to interpret its meaning for children.

Engaging change

Working with the notion of 'engaging play' was a substantial move forward in our own thinking, not only about this book, but also in relation to the multiple perspectives which characterize contemporary theorization and discussion in early childhood education. The concept of engaging play became important to us, not just because a catch-all phrase is convenient for writing, but also because it began to allow us to engage theoretically with the social, cultural, technological and economic changes that have defined much of the late twentieth and early twenty-first centuries.

In fact, this notion describes our very experience in producing the book. For the first two years of this project we had never met in person and worked exclusively with each other and the contributing authors online across timelines, countries and cultures. Finally meeting for one week in London we began to discover our own similarities, differences and above all commonalities, not simply as early childhood educators and researchers, but as parents. One of us gave birth to two sons in England in the early 1970s while the other gave birth to two sons in Australia in the early years of the new millennium. Reflecting on the play and learning experiences of these four children, and the contexts which have shaped them, has helped to give us insights, both into the changes that have taken place in children's lives over this period, even within the Western, European-heritage world, and into the underlying commonalities in these lives. We have compared notes, for instance, on taking our small children abroad while travelling for work, and the ways that each of them engaged with the experience of travel and cultural change, and of communicating with family and friends back home. Above all, the generational differences across these four childhoods have highlighted how greatly technological change has driven social and cultural change and resulted in experiences for today's children, families and communities that were once simply unimagined and unimaginable.

This was illustrated for us by memories of our own children's early engagements with the concept of a computer. In around 1974, when the oldest of our children was aged 4, his grandmother, herself an early years teacher, brought home a 'computer' from her classroom and gave it to him. The computer was actually a large cardboard carton, with two rectangular slots cut at the top and bottom so that a child or adult outside the box could post a slip of paper – a message or question – to the child sitting inside, and the computer-operator child could respond by posting another message out. The small boy soon moved from wishing to sit inside the box and 'answer the questions', to requiring his play-partner, whether his baby brother or an adult, to crawl inside and answer the questions which he devised and posted. Thirty-five years later, the youngest of our four sons was a computer-user at the age of 18 months, sitting on his mother's knee until she had finished her email and then leaning forward to select and play his favourite YouTube clips. The impact of new technologies has quite literally put power and knowledge at children's fingertips, to the extent that even a baby's small fingers have the power to summon up a world of information – sometimes intentionally, but equally often by accident. (We are reminded too of the role of 'accidents' in creating new knowledge, in human history and in the daily play experiences of each generation and individual.)

Today's parents and educators have all participated, at different ages, in different stages in this revolutionary but still ongoing transformation of human experience and understanding. We can look back, and marvel. But the harder task for all of us is trying to imagine the unimaginable that lies ahead for all of our children, and this is why an important task for educators is to solve the problem of appropriately preparing children for the lives they will lead. What unimagined knowledge and skills will have evolved in young children in another 35 years? As many authors have identified, contemporary and future times will require ways of thinking and working that allow children and adults to use knowledge and information in sophisticated ways:

> The new era gives premiums to those citizens who are able to be creative, innovative and transformative in their use of knowledge and skills in order to create new products, ideas and services. This group is able to work abstractly and efficiently and adapt to changing times with fluency.
>
> (Yelland 2007: 7)

This changing social, cultural and technological situation suggests that thinking about play and pedagogy in early childhood settings needs to encompass an understanding of the context in which play is enacted, rather than a continuing focus on the nature of play itself.

Engaging with play as knowledge production

For us, the concept of 'engaging play' requires us to situate the problem of understanding how play is used (and to what end) across many contexts, to meet the needs of children and families according to the particular communities in which they are current and future participants and contributors. Focusing on this problem places the emphasis about play on the 'context of application' (Nowotny et al. 2001), to which our understandings of how and why play is used in the early years are necessarily related.

Thinking about the 'context of application' characterizes an important shift in theories of knowledge production. In twenty-first-century contexts, it has been argued (Gibbons et al. 1994), we should be concerned not only with continually adding to the knowledge base of one discipline, but also with finding ways of responding to 'problem situations' which arise from rapidly changing and highly contextualized social, cultural and technological environments (Nowotny et al. 2003). Such environments include those manifest in attempts to understand, theorize and practise play in early childhood education. As indicated earlier, this movement towards plurality and multidisciplinarity is not intended to devalue the importance of cumulative research and knowledge within particular theoretical fields; rather, it is a way of thinking about how the social, cultural and economic changes wrought by technological innovation and globalization can be responded to most effectively, by working across or even above traditional disciplinary fields. Nowotny et al. (2001), working within the field of knowledge production in science, describe the movement towards a focus on the context of application or 'problem situation' as one important difference between what they have termed 'Mode 1' and 'Mode 2' knowledge production. Mode 1 is characterized by traditional perspectives and approaches to science which value the homogeneous nature of the disciplines as a way of building knowledge, and which works towards the continued generation of increasingly advanced knowledge within a single field. In contrast, Mode 2 knowledge production is argued to be a cause of, and response to, social, technological and cultural change, and as such is characterized by heterogeneity and a transdisciplinary approach which focuses on building knowledge which informs how a problem situation (a particular 'context of application') can be interpreted and addressed.

Within this theoretical framework, however, 'Mode 1' and 'Mode 2' do not represent opposing forces: as Gibbons et al. (1994: 14) explain, Mode 2 knowledge supplements but does not supplant Mode 1 just as, within the field of play, the theories we may describe as 'postdevelopmental' supplement rather than supplant traditional developmental perspectives. But a key idea associated with the difference between Mode 1 and Mode 2, is that the latter is positioned as generating knowledge which operates as a socially accountable and reflexive response to the problem situation, rather than to the continued accumulation of a series of tested hypotheses about a particular phenomenon. A Mode 2 perspective on play, for instance, involves thinking about the context of application in which play is used, considered and theorized. It asks, for instance: What can we learn about play that offers us new insights into understanding and responding to the complex social and technological world we inhabit now; and, which allows us to work towards what the world might look like 35 years from today?

It has been our intention to make the theme of engaging play visible throughout the book: to create a thread which links the chapters together in an informative dialogue which takes in different directions our shared interest in the role, use, status and implications of play in early childhood education. For us, this rather fragile 'Mode 2' thread is what we present in this book as the notion of engaging play; that is, the placement and reading of chapters relationally according to their intent within a particular 'context of application', whether this be thinking about how children respond to the enacted values and pedagogies of their classrooms, or thinking seriously about the role of the adult and teacher in children's conceptual, gendered or assessment-based play experiences. Notionally, the thread begins with Elizabeth Wood's insightful survey of the field in Chapter 1, which brings together understandings from the many disciplines and intellectual traditions which underpin research into play. It reaches a very provisional 'ending' with Jo Ailwood's provocative reminders, in the final chapter, of the need to continually reflect on the ways in which new or 'alternative' perspectives on play can develop into forms of regulation and conformity which are every bit as restrictive as those they were designed to challenge. Although placed as book-ends, we see these chapters as contributing to the overall dialogue of the book, helping to make it 'more than the sum of its parts'. We feel that all the contributing authors to this book have pushed boundaries in thinking about the multiple meanings and purposes of play in educational contexts, and as a result have helped us to stretch our own thinking. We thank them for the contributions, and through these, for allowing us to move from challenging to engaging play.

References

Gibbons, M., Limoges, C., Nowotny, H., Schwartzman, S., Scott, P. and Trow, M. (1994) *The New Production of Knowledge: The Dynamics of Science and Research in Contemporary Societies*. London: Sage.

Nowotny, H., Scott, P. and Gibbons, M. (2001) *Re-thinking Science: Knowledge and the Public in an Age of Uncertainty*. Cambridge: Polity Press.
Nowotny, H., Scott, P. and Gibbons, M. (2003) Introduction. Mode 2 revisited: the new production of knowledge, *Minerva*, 41(3): 179–94.
Yelland, N. (2007) *Shift to the Future: Rethinking Learning with New Technologies in Education*. New York: Routledge.

1 Reconceptualizing the play–pedagogy relationship

From control to complexity

Elizabeth Wood

Introduction

This chapter examines contemporary developments in play and pedagogy in early childhood education settings, drawing on UK policies and international play scholarship. Established principles about play and learning are reified in many curriculum guidelines, alongside recommendations for the role of adults in linking play provision with their pedagogical framing and strategies. Play is also located within contemporary discourses about quality and effectiveness, with a specific focus on 'educational' play (Wood 2009, 2010). Although policy texts and policy-oriented research have provided positive validations for play as integral to 'effective practice', there remain significant challenges in conceptualizing the play–pedagogy relationship. Linking play with defined educational outcomes and effectiveness agendas also raises questions about the regulation of play through dominant policy discourses and practices.

Drawing on critical and postdevelopmental theories, some of the key principles underpinning play and pedagogy are scrutinized here, specifically in relation to assumptions about the efficacy of play across dimensions of diversity (gender, age, ethnicity, social class, language, religious affiliation, ability/disability, sexualities). It will be argued that some of the essential truths about play can also be seen as myths, which need to be contested in the light of contemporary concerns with diversity, power, control and agency, and how these relate to social justice within educational settings. Furthermore, the early childhood community needs to question assumptions about play, by considering educational discourses and practices as well as personal beliefs and values in determining what play is (or is allowed to be), and what play means for children.

Postdevelopmental and critical perspectives on play and pedagogy

Global discourses about quality and effectiveness have drawn play into an educational and social justice remit in which pre-school provision is justified in relation to the immediate and long-term impact on children's life chances (Siraj-Blatchford and Sylva 2004). Many countries in the OECD (Organization for Economic Co-operation and Development) have developed policy frameworks that define children's entitlement to pre-school provision, and mobilize the state apparatus of quality assurance, testing and inspection regimes, and professional standards to ensure such impact (UNESCO 2007). As play has become embedded in policy frameworks, the early childhood community has been challenged to provide clear specification of how children learn through play, how play can be integrated into the curriculum through child- and adult-initiated activities, and how play-based pedagogy can be defined (Wood 2009). Such justifications typically draw on Western theories of play as progress, learning and development (Sutton-Smith 1997). However, these policy and theoretical frameworks can be seen as regimes of power, because they privilege certain ways of understanding children against a developmental continuum, typically conceptualized as stages, norms and milestones, and against curriculum goals, which can serve to position groups and individuals in deficit terms. Contemporary trends in education research and theory contest such universal assumptions, particularly from cultural-historical and postdevelopmental perspectives (Blaise 2005; Hedegaard and Fleer 2008; Edwards and Nuttall 2009), and from critical perspectives (Cannella 2005; MacNaughton 2005).

Postdevelopmental theorists contest universal concepts about learning, development and play and the ways in which these underpin institutional practices, and propose different ways of viewing children in relation to cultures, contexts and social diversity (Edwards 2003; Hedegaard and Fleer 2008). By emphasizing the socially and culturally situated nature of learning, children can be understood as active participants in cultural communities. Children's repertoires of activity and participation are culturally shaped with adults and peers, and with cultural tools and symbol systems. Thus social practices provoke qualitatively different changes in children's development, as do children's activities, including their motivation, interest, engagement and involvement. Participation also provokes situated agency – children actively engage in the social construction of their own identities and subjectivities.

In critical theory, the notion of dominant voices and regimes of power is rejected in favour of multiple narratives and multi-voiced narratives regarding educational practices and belief structures (Cannella 2005; MacNaughton 2005). Critical perspectives exemplify the ways in which different forms of disciplinary power produce different forms of knowledge, how these come to circulate within communities as truths, and the status of those who are charged with saying what counts as true (Foucault 1977). It is argued here that by taking critical perspectives on play, early childhood educators can consider whose truths and whose power are being exercised in 'outside-in' or macro-political models of education, including curriculum documents, practice guidance and policy-focused research. They can also review their personal/professional epistemologies and 'inside-out' or micro-political practices, including the ethical and political dimensions of their pedagogical choices and decisions, the ways in which children use play to establish their own agency and power and how they negotiate multiple identities. Postdevelopmental and critical perspectives thus mark a shift from the scientific search for norms and regularities, towards embracing complexity.

From a Foucauldian perspective, the ways in which power operates (at macro- and micro-levels) should not be seen as establishing inviolable truths, or as being essentially repressive or prohibiting:

> If power were never anything but repressive, if it never did anything but say no, do you really think that one would be brought to obey it? What makes power hold good, what makes it accepted, is simply the fact that it traverses and produces things, it induces pleasure, forms knowledge, produces discourse. It needs to be considered as a productive network which runs through the whole social body, much more than a negative instance whose function is repression.
>
> (Rabinow 1984: 84)

This dual conceptualization of power is used here to explore and challenge established myths and truths about play and pedagogy, particularly in the context of contemporary concerns with social justice, equity and diversity, and to highlight some of the tensions that educators grapple with in practice. Play in educational settings attempts to harness children's learning and development in line with curriculum frameworks, and wider societal expectations of schooling (Wood 2009, 2010). It is claimed that play underpins learning and development, and that both can be seen in play; therefore, play should provide evidence of children's progress and achievements along culturally defined pathways. The gaze of practitioners from a curriculum perspective typically focuses on individual activity and progress. In contrast, truly free play is open-ended and unpredictable, and is controlled and directed by the players. The gaze of practitioners from a play perspective focuses on understanding children's choices, meanings and intentions. The former gaze is regulatory, while the latter gaze is more about a hermeneutical understanding of play. Critical consideration of these competing discourses opens reflective spaces for diverse (and playful) ways of thinking about the truths and myths that surround play.

Truths and myths

Play is often claimed to be the dominant feature of early childhood, and *the* way in which children learn and develop. However, this claim is contested (Smith 2005), and there are many tensions between pragmatic and philosophical conceptualizations of play (Sutton-Smith 1997; Lytle 2003; Sluss and Jarrett 2007). From an educational/pragmatic perspective, play has always been invested with significance for children's immediate and future development, in terms of social, educational and economic goals (Sutton-Smith 1997). It is not just play, but the capacity to play that has significance for human development and learning. From a therapeutic perspective Youell (2008) states that there are huge discrepancies in children's capacity to play, according to their early life experiences:

> [C]hildren who cannot play (in the full sense of the word) are at a disadvantage when it comes to making relationships and to tackling new learning tasks. If early relationships have not introduced the child to ideas of playfulness and shared humour, these elements will be missing in later attempts to make connections with people.
>
> (2008: 125)

The 'play as progress' justification contrasts with the traditions of philosophical idealism and humanitarianism, where play is a mode of existence, a state of mind and a state of being (Sutton-Smith 1997; Henricks 2001; Steinsholt and Traasdahl 2001). Play has been credited with romantic, spiritual and existentialist dimensions: children have inner power and potential which can be realized and revealed through play. Developing the capacity to play and being in a state of play determine what players do, and enable them to be open to the spontaneous development of ideas and opportunities. Playful children develop their own play in their own ways and on their own terms. They let play happen, by becoming immersed in the mood or spirit of play. They see the world from the perspective of play, creating their own playful meanings, symbols and practices, which are imbued with cultural significance, and result in self-development and self-actualization.

These philosophical positions create an idealized version of free play as a neutral space. This is a restrictive definition because it presupposes conditions in which freedom and choice can be realized, with insufficient account of the socio-cultural-historical contexts in which play occurs, and the power relationships that are integral to play (including peer as well as child–adult relationships). The notion of play as freedom begs two questions: from what, and from whom, are children free, and what are they free to do? In the philosophical discourse, children are free to make choices and decisions, take ownership of their activities, direct and control their own learning and activity. However, free play has always been a challenge in educational settings because it can be associated with chaos, loss of adult control, and indeterminate outcomes, none of which sit comfortably within the pedagogies defined in many policy frameworks. Children's play is often constrained by adults (in both home and education settings) who see it as trivial or frivolous, or fear the 'dark side' of play which is associated with subversion of social rules and norms (Sutton-Smith 1997), or with bullying and social aggression (Wood 2008). Not all play is fun, and not all play is free, even when it is conducted beyond the gaze of adults, and is within children's control. Free choice and free play are problematic in relation to dimensions of diversity, in terms of whose choices are privileged and the extent to which children are consulted on the choice of friendship groups, play materials and activities, and their range of possible uses (Ryan 2005; Rogers and Evans 2008). Furthermore, not all children know how to play, and not all children play easily or spontaneously. Children who have not been enculturated into typically Western forms of play experience educational settings as limiting rather than enabling their participation, which can put them at a disadvantage in accessing the curriculum (Brooker 2002, 2008).

Critical theorists argue that while children do use play for their own purposes, their choices have implications for others through the ways in which they create multiple discourses, identities and power dynamics (Ryan 2005). Power may be exercised in pro-social or anti-social ways, such as including or excluding peers on the basis of perceived differences. The process of recognizing *that* power relations exist in children's play may be uncomfortable for early childhood educators, especially if they are steeped in universal certainties about the efficacy of play for children's learning and development. Recognizing *how* those power relationships are played out presents another discomfort because it requires educators to see play as a political space, and to focus on issues of power and control between adults and children, and between children. From the perspective of critical theory, these relational dynamics are central to understanding what choice means to children, and whose freedom, whose power, and whose control are exercised or marginalized. Educators need to be critically aware of how dominant discourses and practices position children in ways that may advantage some, but disadvantage others. In the following section, these issues are exemplified in two UK countries, where the early childhood community has fought long and hard to have play recognized within the curriculum.

Macro-political influences on play and pedagogy

Different models of educational play are embedded within curriculum and pedagogical processes as evidenced in position statements, social policies and practice guidance in developed and developing countries (Wood 2009). There is broad consensus that play/learning environments can be planned intentionally to achieve defined outcomes or curriculum goals. Educators can be involved in play through their pedagogical framing, decisions and actions (organizing the environment; planning play/learning activities; playing alongside children; observing and assessing play). Play is thus intrinsically bound with the contemporary politics of education, because it is subject to regulation and management through what Ball describes as 'appropriate techniques of organisation' (1995: 262). Through such techniques, macro-level policy guidance often assumes that the complexities and paradoxes of play not only can be managed, but can also be neutralized to produce defined learning outcomes. It follows that play can be aligned with other technical practices such as target setting, teacher performance, inspection, appraisal and quality assurance. From a critical perspective, such interventions beg contrasting interpretations: here we have the power of the state harnessing established (but selective) truths about the power of play, but in ways that may be circumscribed by technical and managerial approaches to education. Policy frameworks typically present a version of order, stability and agreed meanings within which certain forms of knowledge (and ways of knowing) are valued and reified in the curriculum. Thus it becomes challenging for educators to negotiate repressive and productive regimes of power, because play does not align easily with these techniques of organization.

These challenges are embedded in the Early Years Foundation Stage in England (Department for Education and Skills 2007) and the Foundation Phase in Wales (Department for Children, Education, Lifelong Learning and Skills 2008b) both of which legitimize play as a medium for teaching and learning, and for curriculum 'delivery'. Play is also linked to wider benefits, including physical and mental health, emotional well-being, creativity, positive dispositions, and social inclusion. In the English

Foundation Stage (birth to 5), the emphasis is on planned and purposeful play: 'Play underpins all development and learning for young children. Most children play spontaneously, although some may need adult support, and it is through play that they develop intellectually, creatively, physically, socially and emotionally' (Department for Education and Skills 2007: 7, para. 1.17).

Similarly, the Wales Foundation Phase (3–7) promotes play and active learning:

> There should be opportunities for children to follow their own interests and ideas through free play. Children's learning is most effective when it arises from first-hand experiences, whether spontaneous or structured, and when they are given time to play without interruptions and to reach a satisfactory conclusion.
>
> (Department for Children, Education,
> Lifelong Learning and Skills 2008a: 5)

> Play should be valued by all practitioners and structured with clear aims for children's learning. It should be structured in such a way that children have opportunities to be involved in the focus, planning and setting up of play areas both indoors and outdoors, as this will give them ownership of their learning.
>
> (Department for Children, Education,
> Lifelong Learning and Skills 2008a: 7)

In order for play to deliver educational outcomes, there are common caveats within these policy documents which state the pedagogical conditions under which play can and should happen, including informed adult involvement and intervention; planning and organization; well-resourced environments (indoors and outdoors); sustained periods of time for play; adult observation and assessment of play (DfES 2007; DCELLS 2008a). Theoretically, there is some confusion in the practice guidance documents. The Wales Foundation Phase sets out the traditional Piagetian 'developmental stages of play', but with the proviso that children develop at different rates according to their previous experience (DCELLS 2008a, 2008b). Similarly, the discourse of planning for 'individual development and needs' is embedded in the English EYFS (Department for Education and Skills 2007: 22–3). The guidelines state that practitioners should create enabling environments, that 'provide positive images that challenge children's thinking and help them to embrace differences in gender, ethnicity, language, religion, culture, special educational needs and disabilities' (2007: 22). However, children develop at different rates and in different ways, because of the culturally situated nature of development. In light of postdevelopmental theories, simplistic policy recommendations may sustain the practice of representing surface culture, such as images and artifacts, rather than engaging with deep culture, namely the ways in which children's home cultures and traditions, and dimensions of diversity influence their orientations to play.

High quality play provision is also linked to the macro-political educational effectiveness agenda, again with clear recommendations for play-based pedagogy. The findings from a British government-funded study of Effective Provision for Preschool Education (EPPE) recommend mixed or integrated pedagogical approaches, which create a balance between child- and adult-initiated activities, and the provision of freely chosen yet potentially instructive play activities (Siraj-Blatchford and Sylva 2004; www.ioe.ac.uk/projects/eppe). Within this study, play is used as an umbrella term, even though children's choices include a wide range of activities that cannot be classified as play. These recommendations skim over dimensions of diversity, by assuming that all children have (or will acquire) the necessary skills to access a 'play-based curriculum'. The emphasis on 'purposeful play' carries the opposite assumption that without pedagogical framing, play would be purposeless, and would therefore be less likely to pay into curriculum goals and outcomes. The implication here is that adults' pedagogical plans and purposes are privileged. Such a focus distorts the more complex meanings and purposes of play, including the ways in which children exercise power, agency and control, how they make and communicate meanings through symbolic activity, and the significant role of representation in play. Moreover, the concept of 'balance' between child- and adult-initiated activities may vary widely for individuals and groups of children. Wood (2009) argues that the surveillance and control that such guidance promotes are unlikely to yield the range or depth of knowledge that is needed in order to understand these complexities, particularly where pedagogical approaches are aligned with an educational effectiveness agenda.

In summary, it can be argued that play does not fit neatly into policy paradigms because it does not always 'pay into' defined learning outcomes. Moreover, the 'outcomes' focus is on the learner as an individual, and on learning as individual acquisition. In contrast, play is about collective, relational activity, which is always culturally, socially and historically situated. Corsaro argues that in attempting to make sense of the world, 'children come to *collectively produce* their own peer worlds and cultures' (1997: 24, italics in original), therefore players are always shaped by their experiences, their identities, and their abilities to understand the 'as if' and 'what if' qualities of play. These theories contest the notion of planning for individual development, needs and interests, because these may be collectively shared and culturally determined. Play is ambiguous and highly complex, in terms of the content, social interactions, symbolic meanings, communicative languages, and the environmental affordances that mediate play and playfulness. Meanings are produced dynamically, drawing on the socio-cultural-historical resources of the players, and their multiple, shifting identities. There are different interpretations of what play is, and what play does for the players, according to the perspectives of educators and children (Rogers and Evans 2008), and across dimensions of diversity (Fassler and Levin 2008; MacNaughton 2009). From children's perspectives, play is also about subversion and inversion, order and disorder, chaos and stability, inclusion and marginalization, which is where issues of power, agency and control are played out. Thus play incorporates political and ethical issues that are not addressed in the universal assumptions about educational play in policy discourses.

Edwards and Nuttall (2009) propose a more sophisticated, postdevelopmental orientation to pedagogical practices which emphasizes ethical issues, cultural contexts, and the struggle for equity in early childhood provision. They argue that early childhood educators' work has become increasingly focused on the child-in-context as the starting point of planning for learning, rather than starting from developmental norms and planning for individual developmental needs. These theories also exemplify a more productive discourse about professional knowledge in early childhood education, by challenging established truths, and arguing for pedagogies that are reciprocal, relational and inclusive. Social justice is embedded within postdevelopmental and critical praxis because pedagogical decision-making is construed as ethical and political, rather than by narrowly defined policy frameworks. However, there remain many tensions between pedagogies for complexity and pedagogies of control. The following section proposes deeper engagement with these pedagogical issues, drawing on vignettes from an action research project in a primary school.

Repressive/productive power

If we return to Foucault's dual conceptualization of power as repressive/productive, then the play–pedagogy relationship, as exemplified in these discourses, continues to pose conceptual and practical challenges. The following case study exemplifies the ways in which some of these challenges were addressed in an action research project which was instigated by teachers as they implemented the pilot stage of the Wales Foundation Phase. The teaching teams decided on their research foci, using action research cycles, including observation and documentation of play with still and video images; narrative accounts; research conversations with children; reflective team discussions; joint observations and reflective discussions with the researcher, and developing action cycles for change. In this diverse community, 87 per cent of the children came from ethnic minority groups, ranging from established second- and third-generation British Asian families, to newly arrived economic migrants from Eastern Europe, and refugees from the African and Asian continents. Around 30 community languages were spoken in the school, with English-medium assistants working alongside Learning Support Assistants and teachers.

Research conversations with the Foundation Phase team revealed their concerns about the varied starting points of the children, which reflected their prior experiences, home values and cultures, and child-rearing practices. Parents had contrasting expectations of schooling, including their understanding of play-based approaches, and relationships between children and adults. One teacher remarked that many children were 'under the radar' of the learning objectives in the Foundation Phase (DCELLS 2008b). For some children, the freedom and flexibility enshrined in a 'free play/free choice' environment were unfamiliar and difficult to negotiate without support and guidance from the adults. Therefore, play-based approaches presented many challenges to the children, their families, and the teaching teams.

The nursery team (working with 3–4/5-year-old children) voiced concerns about the involvement and participation of children from different ethnic groups in play activities. They decided to focus on the quality of language used during imaginative play, to understand whether children's interactions were better when they used their first language, and whether this influenced the quality of the play. However, many of the observations revealed little verbal communication between peers, with children often playing in parallel rather than co-operatively (even with same language speakers). Because of their beliefs in the value of free, imaginative play, the adults tended to involve themselves in table-top activities such as creative art, puzzles and games. Those children who did not enjoy (or perhaps did not understand) imaginative play tended to orientate to these activities, which, the teachers considered, reflected the more sedentary home-based activities (which were determined variously by lack of space, lack of play materials, as well as child-rearing practices). In reflecting on their data, the team realized that their interventions in play were often focused on their own, rather than the children's agendas. Therefore, they needed to take more time to ensure that their interactions, especially in imaginative play, were sensitive to the children in terms of *their* meanings, intentions and choices, as well as enabling them to understand what choices were available. The area of language and communication, especially for children with English as an additional language, influenced the extent to which the children were able to access the curriculum through play. Therefore, the team decided that adults should be able to take the lead in play (for example, through demonstrating and modelling imaginative play), as well as being led by the children. However, it was not just language differences that were problematic, but children's cultural understandings of what was expected in a play-based environment.

Observation-based assessment was considered valuable for reflective team discussions, resulting in collective decisions about 'next steps' for individual children, especially those who were 'under the radar' of the curriculum goals. The team members made a distinction between using observation as a means to understanding play in itself and for itself, and identifying learning outcomes in play activities that could be mapped against curriculum goals. The former taught them a great deal more about children's repertoires of activity and participation, and the ways in which children gradually learned to bridge their home and school cultures, which was a necessary transition process towards accessing the curriculum through play. They also reflected on their theoretical knowledge of child development, because it did not serve them well in such a culturally diverse community. As a result, they sought the help of parents and the English-medium assistants in developing culturally situated understandings of home and community beliefs and practices, which more accurately reflected diversities within the school. By viewing children's play through postdevelopmental and critical perspectives, the team members were able to review universal assumptions about play–learning and play–pedagogy relationships, and build more inclusive play environments and practices.

This vignette serves to illustrate that, from a critical perspective, culture is not seen as a coherent, integrated system, but rather as a mosaic of smaller narratives that reflect local circumstances, and their producers (Henricks 2001). In order to be truly productive, play provision needs to go beyond surface culture towards understanding deep culture, particularly children's culturally situated identities, and the complex ways in which dimensions of diversity influence children's repertoires of choice and participation. However, further detailed evidence is needed about how choice functions in play, specifically who leads or dominates particular choices, who follows, and the extent to which choices are negotiated between peers and between children and adults.

Conclusion

Policy frameworks typically present a version of order, stability and agreed meanings within which certain forms of knowledge (and ways of knowing) are valued and reified. Although play has been accorded certain authority within the discourses and practices of early childhood, it is argued here that not all children are best served by uncritical implementation of free play/free choice pedagogical approaches. At the same time, pedagogical notions about 'planned and purposeful play' demand contestation of whose plans and purposes are privileged, especially in relation to concerns with equity and diversity. Further evidence is needed of multiple versions of play and pedagogy in education settings. A productive research agenda should focus on a critical analysis of children's repertoires of activity and participation, and the ways in which peer group cultures operate across these repertoires, including the nature of power relations in play. This could usefully lead to better understanding of how curricula are constructed for, with and by children, and what pedagogical approaches might support children in connecting their diverse experiences of play in home, community and educational settings. Such research might draw on postdevelopmental perspectives (Blaise 2005; Edwards and Nuttall 2009) by enhancing knowledge and understanding of diverse socio-cultural-historical influences, and enabling educators to contest the authority of policy discourses.

Early childhood educators have an ethical responsibility to create the conditions in which different solutions to problems can be developed, tested, refined and implemented in local contexts. The ways in which such problems are formulated could create potentially productive networks of knowledge and practice that incorporate mosaics of smaller narratives. Early childhood communities can produce their own professional knowledge about the different ways in which play-based curriculum and pedagogies are conceptualized and enacted. However, the creation of productive discourses places considerable demands on educators to develop more sophisticated pedagogical repertoires, based on critical engagement with myths and truths about play.

References

Ball, S. (1995) Intellectuals or technicians? The urgent role of theory in educational studies, *British Journal of Educational Studies*, 43(3): 255–71.

Blaise, M. (2005) *Playing It Straight: Uncovering Gender Discourses in the Early Childhood Classroom*. London: Routledge.

Brooker, L. (2002) *Starting School: Young Children Learning Cultures*. Buckingham: Open University Press.

Brooker, L. (2008) *Supporting Transitions in the Early Years*. Maidenhead: Open University Press.

Cannella, G.S. (2005) Reconceptualizing the field (of early care and education): if 'western' child development is a problem, then what do we do?, in N. Yelland (ed.) *Critical Issues in Early Childhood*. Maidenhead: Open University Press, pp. 17–39.

Corsaro, W. (1997) *The Sociology of Childhood*. Thousand Oaks, CA: Pine Forge Press.

Department for Children, Education, Lifelong Learning and Skills (DCELLS) (2008a) *Play/Active Learning: Overview for 3–7 Year Olds*. Cardiff: Curriculum and Assessment Division, DCELLS.

Department for Children, Education, Lifelong Learning and Skills (DCELLS) (2008b) *Foundation Stage Framework for Children's Learning for 3–7 Year Olds in Wales*. Cardiff: Curriculum and Assessment Division, DCELLS.

Department for Education and Skills (DfES) (2007) *The Early Years Foundation Stage*. Available at: http://www.standards.dfes.gov.uk/primary/foundation_stage/eyfs/.

Edwards, S. (2003) New directions: charting the path for the role of socio–cultural theory in early childhood education and curriculum, *Contemporary Issues in Early Childhood*, 4(3): 251–66.

Edwards, S. and Nuttall, J. (eds) (2009) *Professional Learning in Early Childhood Settings*. Rotterdam: Sense Publications.

Effective Provision for Preschool Education (EPPE). Available at: www.ioe.ac.uk/projects/eppe.

Fassler, R. and Levin, D. (2008) Envisioning and supporting the play of preschoolers, in C. Genishi and A.L. Goodwin (eds) *Diversities in Early Childhood Education: Rethinking and Doing*. New York: Routledge, pp. 233–51.

Foucault, M. (1977) Truth and power, in C. Gordon (ed.) *Power/Knowledge: Selected Interviews and Other Writings, 1972–1977, Michel Foucault*. Sussex: The Harvester Press, pp. 109–33.

Hedegaard, M. and Fleer, M. (2008) *Studying Children: A Cultural–Historical Approach*. Maidenhead: McGraw-Hill.

Henricks, T. (2001) Play and postmodernism, in S. Reifel, *Theory in Context and Out. Play and Culture Studies*, vol. 3. Westport, CT: Ablex Publishing, pp. 51–71.

Lytle, D.E. (2003) *Play and Educational Theory and Practice. Play and Culture Studies*, vol. 5. Westport, CT: Praeger.

MacNaughton, G. (2005) *Doing Foucault in Early Childhood Studies: Applying Poststructural Ideas*. London: Routledge.

MacNaughton, G. (2009) Exploring critical constructivist perspectives on children's learning, in A. Anning, J. Cullen and M. Fleer (eds) *Early Childhood Education, Society and Culture*. London: Sage.

Rabinow, P. (ed.) (1984) *The Foucault Reader: An Introduction to Foucault's Thought, with Major New Unpublished Material*. London: Penguin.

Rogers, S. and Evans, J. (2008) *Inside Role Play in Early Childhood Education: Researching Young Children's Perspectives*. London: Routledge.

Ryan, S. (2005) Freedom to choose: examining children's experiences in choice time, in N. Yelland (ed.) *Critical Issues in Early Childhood*. Maidenhead: Open University Press, pp. 99–114.

Siraj-Blatchford, I. and Sylva, K. (2004) Researching pedagogy in English pre-schools, *British Educational Research Journal*, 30(5): 713–30.

Smith, P.K. (2005) Play: types and functions in human development, in B. Ellis and D. Bjorklund (eds) *Origins of the Social Mind: Evolutionary Psychology and Child Development*. New York: Guilford Press.

Sluss, D.J. and Jarrett, O.S. (2007) *Investigating Play in the 21st Century. Play and Culture Studies*, vol. 7. Lanham, MD: University Press of America.

Steinsholt, K. and Traasdahl, E. (2001) The concept of play in Hans-Georg Gadamer's hermeneutics: an educational approach, in S. Reifel, *Theory in Context and Out. Play and Culture Studies*, vol. 3. Westport, CT: Ablex Publishing, pp. 73–96.

Sutton-Smith, B. (1997) *The Ambiguity of Play*. Cambridge, MA: Harvard University Press.

UNESCO (2007) *Results from the OECD Thematic Review of Early Childhood Education and Care Policy 1998–2006*, UNESCO Policy Brief on Early Childhood No. 41, November–December 2007. New York: UN.

Wood, E. (2008) Everyday play activities as therapeutic and pedagogical encounters, *European Journal of Psychotherapy and Counselling*, 10(2): 111–20.

Wood, E. (2009) Conceptualising a pedagogy of play: international perspectives from theory, policy and practice, in D. Kuschner (ed.) *From Children to Red Hatters®: Diverse Images and Issues of Play. Play and Culture Studies*, vol. 8. Lanham, MD: University Press of America, pp. 166–89.

Wood, E. (2010) Developing integrated pedagogical approaches to play and learning, in P. Broadhead, J. Howard and E. Wood (eds) *Play and Learning in Education Settings*. London: Sage.

Youell, B. (2008) The importance of play and playfulness, *European Journal of Psychotherapy and Counselling*, 10(2): 121–9.

2 Whose goals and interests?

The interface of children's play and teachers' pedagogical practices

Helen Hedges

Introduction

Much has been written about play and pedagogy, including the ways that children engage in play in differing cultural contexts (e.g. Pramling-Samuelsson and Fleer 2008). Defying an unproblematic definition, play is both a social and cultural construct and a social practice (Wood 2009) and, thus, the literature is complex and contradictory (e.g. Brooker 2002). Moreover, the adage of learning through play has never sat comfortably alongside the notion of teaching through play, and is unlikely ever to do so. The non-compulsory, non-prescriptive, unstructured and play-based nature of Western-European early childhood education exposes it to many viewpoints and debates. For example, Youngquist and Pataray-Ching (2004) suggest that in order for curriculum to be interpreted as educational and meaningful, a distinction between 'inquiry-play' in the educational setting, and 'play-in-outside-contexts' (such as in homes and communities) is useful. However, in this chapter I argue that all contexts of play involve inquiry, and that the relationship between these types of play, through the concept of funds of knowledge, is important. Further, defining play as including inquiry provides an analytical lens with which to examine the notion of children's interests.

This chapter is structured by providing an overview of some considerations related to teachers' pedagogical goals in Aotearoa/New Zealand (NZ). Following this, I draw on my study of curriculum co-construction in early childhood education (Hedges 2008), to provide an analytical perspective of children's play and interests. Some theories resulting from contemporary socio-cultural perspectives are described and used to explain children's experiences in qualitatively different ways to developmental theories that have traditionally dominated early childhood's theoretical foundations. The chapter then proposes a continuum of children's interests and inquiries which is constructed from their funds of knowledge-based interests. The continuum represents the conceptual output derived from considering the data from my study in relation to theoretical perspectives about children's play. In this chapter, the continuum is used to raise questions about how teachers' professional knowledge, pedagogical understandings and practices are related to children's play and interests.

Whose goals?

The early childhood curriculum in NZ, *Te Whāriki* (Ministry of Education 1996), emphasizes the principles of relationships, empowerment, holistic development, and family and community. The overall aspiration for children is 'to grow up as competent and confident learners and communicators, healthy in mind, body, and spirit, secure in their sense of belonging and in the knowledge that they make a valued contribution to society' (1996: 9). Is this policy statement of teachers' pedagogical goals consistent with contemporary understandings of children's play and interests? *Te Whāriki* asserts that authentic play-based learning is situated in socially and culturally constructed settings and is mediated by 'responsive and reciprocal relationships with people, places and things' (1996: 14). If curriculum is co-constructed spontaneously during pedagogical relationships, how might these relationships impact on children's experiences? Moreover, such a pedagogical view of curriculum suggests that children might actively participate in negotiating and constructing curriculum, and draw on experiences in outside contexts to do so.

A participative and interpretive view of a curriculum for young children is apparent within *Te Whāriki*. Yet teacher curriculum decision-making is not impulsive; it is a conscious process that draws on understandings about children, curriculum, pedagogy and context (Hedges and Nuttall 2008). Moreover, the knowledge teachers draw on to inform their interpretations is crucial in determining the authenticity of children's experiences. What understandings of children's play and interests might assist teachers to work towards *Te Whāriki*'s goal and co-construct curriculum with children?

Whose interests?

'Children's interests' are commonly cited as a significant source of curriculum. Yet, little academic literature exists to guide teacher decision-making about whose and which interests might be followed in co-constructing curriculum with children in both intentional and spontaneous ways. My study of co-constructed interests-based curriculum drew on sociocultural theory and interpretivist methodology. The study took place in two early childhood settings in Auckland, NZ: one sessional public kindergarten for 3- and 4-year-olds, Takapuna Kindergarten (TK), and one full-day early education and care centre for children aged 6 months to 5 years, The No 1 Kindy (1K). Ten teachers and 35 children across both settings, along with the parents of 11 children, participated in the study.[1] During year-long fieldwork, I generated fieldnotes about children's interests and inquiries, and teachers' engagement with these, during weekly half-day attendance in each setting. Individual and teaching team interviews were undertaken, along with interviews with children and parents in family homes. Curriculum documentation was an additional source of data. In the latter part of the year, the two teaching teams met to co-analyze the data and for facilitated inquiry sessions.

Drawing on Dockett and Fleer (1999), I defined play as 'a meaningful activity that children choose to participate in, that involves children in physical, cognitive and communicative efforts in social and cultural contexts' (Hedges 2008: 10); and children's interests as 'children's spontaneous, self-motivated play, discussions, inquiry and/or investigations that derive from their social and cultural experiences' (2008: 38). I noted that children's interests, which were stimulated by their experiences, were likely to be varied and broad. Conceptualizing these might offer a framework for socio-cultural curriculum and pedagogy that would assist teacher decision-making about whose and which interests to use to co-construct curriculum.

The data were analysed through progressive focusing of categories, themes and issues. Reflection on the descriptive and theoretical analyses suggested that children's interests might reveal a deeper level of inquiry. This led to my interpretation of children's fundamental interests, which might be viewed as the inquiries they bring to the co-construction of curriculum with teachers.

From developmental to socio-cultural perspectives

Multiple theoretical perspectives can co-exist to provide coherence to curriculum. A range of perspectives are evident in *Te Whāriki*. Play as the basis of curriculum and pedagogy derives from the long-standing overarching theoretical framework of developmental psychology (Farquhar and Fleer 2007). Well-known theories such as Piaget's genetic epistemology, Erikson's theory of social and emotional development, and Bowlby's attachment theory remain important informants to early childhood curriculum and pedagogy, despite developmental theories being critiqued, from a number of perspectives, for their failure to acknowledge the social and cultural dimensions of children's experience (see Farquhar and Fleer 2007).

Contemporary interpretations view *Te Whāriki* as primarily a socio-cultural framework (Cullen 2003). Originating with the seminal ideas of Vygotsky (1978, 1986) about the learning processes that enable humans to appropriate culture, socio-cultural theory provides further insights into learning. During social and cultural interactions, knowledgeable peers and adults, in multifaceted roles, may help children to experience, explore and construct new understandings, knowledge and skills in a dialectic rather than linear process of development.

Learning through intent participation

Vygotsky (1986) believed that children's informal daily interactions in families and communities provide a bank of everyday or spontaneous experiences to draw on later to develop more formal, scientific, conceptual knowledge. Certainly, children choose to engage in many situations which are not primarily intended as educational. Learning through 'intent participation ... [is] a powerful form of learning' (Rogoff et al. 2003: 176). Rogoff et al. (2003) point out that such learning often occurs eagerly in authentic cultural situations, suggesting learners have some intrinsic interest in the activities they engage in. Moreover, collaborating in shared tasks is neither incidental nor passive. Language is a vital cultural tool employed when both information-sharing and inquiry occur to explore ideas.

From engagement in social and cultural activity, experiences are internalized by children, transformed through their participation, and represented and re-created as opportunities arise to do so, including through play in an early childhood setting. Vygotsky (1978) regarded play, particularly socio-dramatic play, as a major source of learning. He viewed imaginative and symbolic play as a way in which children acted out understandings of everyday real-life behaviours. When children engage in socio-dramatic play, they assume the actions, language, thinking and emotions of the human roles they are engaging in.

Funds of knowledge

What kinds of informal, everyday experiences and understandings might children have greatest access to? Children's foundational knowledge is based on their unique family and community experiences. A positive view of the diverse knowledge and experiences learned in families is found in studies of children's *funds of knowledge* (Moll et al. 1992; González et al. 2005).

Moll et al. (1992) define funds of knowledge as the bodies of knowledge, including information, skills and strategies, which underlie household functioning, development and well-being. These may include information, ways of thinking and learning, approaches to learning and practical skills such as meal preparation. Further examples include economics, such as budgeting, accounting and loans; repair, such as household appliances, fences and cars; and arts, such as music, painting and sculpture (Moll 2000). Funds of knowledge are derived from children's experiences of informal learning, and in turn, generate further informal learning opportunities for children. I argue that funds of knowledge provide a conceptual framework to recognize how children's interests and inquiries arise in, and are stimulated by, their intent participation in everyday activities and experiences with others.

Community of inquiry

The concept of a collaborative learning community highlights participation, intersubjectivity, shared purposes and goals, but is not unproblematic (Edwards 2005). Being specific about the kind of learning community children and teachers might be involved in is vital to extending theoretical understandings. Wells (1999, 2002) focuses the notion of participatory learning on inquiry. The concept of a community of inquiry that Wells advocates began from observing the importance of children's 'real questions' (1999: 91), and the ways that adults, in responding to these questions, co-constructed meaningful learning. This focus appears consistent with a view of learning as intent participation in everyday, funds of knowledge-based, activities and interests.

A community of inquiry is also consistent with further socio-cultural perspectives: children viewed as capable and competent, the significance of children's prior knowledge, interests and inquiry, stressing the central role of language and the intersubjective nature of the reciprocal and responsive relationships highlighted in pedagogy. Further, it enables curriculum and pedagogy to explore co-constructed, dynamic and open-ended approaches.

A continuum of children's interests

'Adults, even the most 'child-centred', tend to trivialize children's interests, making them out to be more mundane and egocentric than they really are' (Bereiter 2002: 301). One way that children's interests might be underestimated by teachers in early childhood settings is by shallow interpretations of children's interests. Cullen (2003) suggested that the

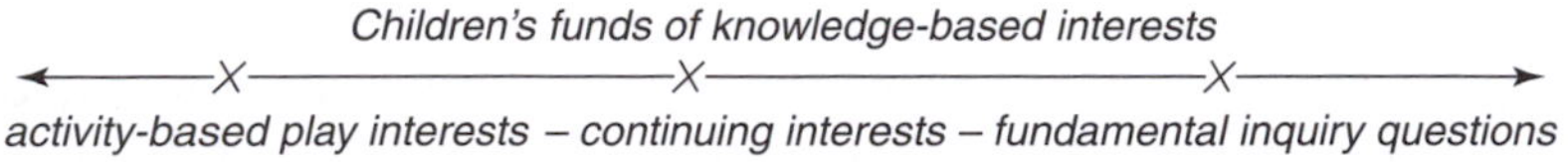

Children's funds of knowledge-based interests

←————X————————————X————————————————X————————→

activity-based play interests – continuing interests – fundamental inquiry questions

Figure 2.1 A continuum of children's interests and inquiries.

tradition of the play-based, as in activity-based, learning environment has meant that teachers have been slow to seek stronger interpretations of children's interests.

A more analytical way of interpreting children's interests was derived from the data generated during my project. These data suggested a continuum for understanding and interpreting children's interests which is linked by their funds of knowledge (Figure 2.1). The interpretation represented by this continuum is supported by Wells' (1999) notion of the genuine inquiries that ought to be addressed in a curriculum and offers a diagrammatic perspective of children's interests in a socio-cultural curriculum.

Funds of knowledge feed forward and feed back into interests at each stage of the continuum. Play is a central way in which children demonstrate, re-visit and extend interests, representing these in all points of the continuum. However, it is vital for teachers to recognize that activity-based play area interests may be responses to the environment provided in early childhood settings, and may not necessarily be representative of children's wider home and community interests. Multiple, dynamic and complex interpretations of children's play and interests are required. Further important feed-forward and feed-back along the continuum occur as children make meaning from play-based experiences, particularly socio-dramatic play.

Activity-based play interests

In relation to children's interests, in all of the individual interviews, the participating teachers first talked about the children's favourite activities in the learning environment. The teachers revealed how steeped they were in traditional views of play as a key informant to early childhood curriculum. For example, one teacher, Vicky (1K), said, 'Danyela, she comes in every day and wants to paint and that's her big thing … the same with Safiya, she loves painting as well and playdough.'

There is no doubt that the physical environment and learning resources provided in the settings offered children rich learning experiences and opportunities for experimentation, and supported their growing everyday and conceptual understandings. The equipment and resources, coupled with new physical and cognitive capabilities, supported children's continuing learning and development. However, these represent the resources and tools of curriculum, not the curriculum itself (Wright 2004). Another teacher, Christine (TK), noted:

> When I started teaching, you had the classic traditional areas of play, they called it curriculum ... which we still have today unless we make a huge big effort to change ... [our view of curriculum].

Further, these interests often appeared to be interpreted as activity or skill-based, rather than as combinations of skills, knowledge and dispositions that represented funds of knowledge-based interests. For example, Olivia and Imogen (1K) were siblings aged 4:11 and 2:4 at the time of their home interview. Their mother described how they enjoyed baking and cooking with her to prepare meals or for hosting social occasions. This interest was enacted in the sand and water resources of the centre environment with friends with shared interests, and in this context they demonstrated their current understanding and collaborated in knowledge building. However, teachers appeared to mostly attribute this interest to sand and water play itself. This demonstrated the prominence of teacher thinking about play as about activities, resources and equipment, rather than also comprising an opportunity to interpret what playing with these might represent. Similar findings in relation to other children supported that teachers' interpretation at this level sometimes impeded their understanding or investigation of deeper interests, and provided a somewhat narrow basis from which to extend curriculum experiences. Some teachers' recognition of and agreement with my interpretation led to changes in their thinking about both children's interests and curriculum.

Therefore, although the opportunities of the play environment remain essential, teachers might also organize space and equipment differently at times to recognize and respond to funds of knowledge. For example, after recognizing children's family experiences as sources of interests, TK rearranged their inside environment to represent the rooms of a home, positioning equipment and areas in a more logical manner to take account of these. One day, 1K teachers noticed Imogen clutching a 'car wash ticket', and talked with her about how important this experience with her father had been. They subsequently rearranged the water play in the outdoor environment for Imogen to direct others in cleaning the centre's wheeled equipment to assist her to represent and communicate her new understandings. While alert and sensitive teachers may do the latter spontaneously, I argue that the notion of funds of knowledge may provide a framework for understanding and choosing whose and which interests, of the myriad children have, might be selected for co-constructing curriculum.

Continuing interests

At a further point on the continuum, children revealed interests that continued over a period of time and sometimes involved them in early conceptual learning. Examples of these included children's interests in the natural, physical and material worlds. A shared interest among many children was animals and insects. Drawing on their knowledge about caring for babies and pets, their initial interests were in looking after these. The toddlers were fascinated by insects, eschewing otherwise favourite activities. For example:

> As Imogen digs, she finds something in the sandpit. It is a slug. With Barbara's [a teacher] help, she tries to put it on a leaf several times. All thoughts of 'cake baking' [a favourite activity] have disappeared as she tries to do this. Several children come out of the art room calling to her that the lion hunt [another favourite activity] is on. But she perseveres trying to get the slug on the leaf. Eventually, she gives up and puts it in her hand and takes it to show Olivia. 'Look what I found!' … [She] takes the slug to the table where she puts it on a piece of paper and draws around it … She sits and plays with it. She tells Billie and Marcella [also aged two] who are watching that it is sleeping, then puts it on her finger to show them.
>
> (1K)

This kind of response was not confined to very young children. Shannon (TK), aged nearly 5, found a spider in a tyre and made a 'home' for it that met its survival needs. While working on the spider's home, he avoided teachers' offers of conceptual information. Rather than explaining this in terms of Piaget's concept of animism (Flavell 1963), a more sophisticated interpretation consistent with socio-cultural views of children and funds of knowledge is Inagaki and Hatano's (2002: 2) notion of personification-based understandings in naïve biology which suggests 'children exploit their relatively rich knowledge about humans to make educated guesses about other entities'.

Findings also exemplified that as children grow and learn, some of these ongoing interests change focus, but remain funds of knowledge-based. For example, Jack's mother (1K) noted that boats, cars and trucks had been a major interest of his for some months. Later, while the focus on boats continued, he demonstrated an interest in language and literacy through books and visual and audio tools. This was followed by a focus on carpentry tools and activities, from which he later used the skills learned to build a small boat, revisiting and continuing his earlier interest. Much of this was prompted by intent observation and participation in home events such as a yacht restoration.

These interests were among those that could be usefully developed by project work. A notable example in both settings was children's involvement in the development of gardens, which continued throughout the year. Over the year, children were encouraged to draw on their funds of knowledge, and to actively participate and continue their exploration of interests, building everyday and conceptual knowledge:

> The garden relocation and design project is well under way and documented in the display board near the entrance ... Theresia has been out in the garden with [a girl] picking broccoli. The girl is particularly interested in this because she is growing peas in her own garden at home. They have picked the broccoli because part of their healthy heart project is about trying new foods and Theresia will have the children try the broccoli with a yogurt-based dip at morning mat time ... Theresia now has a large group of children in the garden identifying vegetables and herbs and in particular looking for silverbeet ... The scarecrow [made by Theresia and the children] is now up in the garden. I compliment Theresia on it and she comments that it's great because it's all the children's own ideas and own work. She is delighted that the project is now into its third term as different ideas evolve ...
>
> (TK)

Fundamental inquiry interests

A deeper-level interpretation of the data ascertained a further point on a continuum. Children were constantly engaged in inquiry and efforts to become 'life-theorizers' (Inagaki and Hatano 2002: 126). Underpinning the children's intent observation, participation in, and contribution to social and cultural activities in the home, centre and community settings, there appears to lie a fundamental inquiry about life as a human being. From an adult perspective, as the children did not conceptualize their inquiry in this way themselves, this might be worded as: 'How can I make sense of my world to lead an interesting, fulfilling and meaningful life as a participant in my family, community and culture?'

A link between this underlying inquiry and *Te Whāriki*'s overall pedagogical goal is evident, indicating that children may perhaps share goals with their teachers. This inquiry was represented in children's interests through repeated dialogue and actions in many different ways in a range of contexts, through efforts to engage peers and adults in play and dialogue, and appears to encompass several 'real questions': What will I do when I am bigger?, What do intelligent, responsible and caring adults do?, How can I make special connections with people I know?, How can I make and communicate meaning?, How can I understand the world I live in?, How can I develop my physical and emotional well-being?, What is special about my identity in the place I live in? While each of these questions comprised their own orientation and forms of action, two are described in more detail here.

How can I make and communicate meaning?

The ability to communicate verbally and non-verbally was a powerful stimulus to ongoing inquiry. For toddlers, expansion of their verbal language facilitated adults' ability to respond meaningfully to their ongoing interests and inquiries indicated initially through their intent participation. Vygotsky (1978, 1986) highlighted language as the most important cultural tool children develop in their quest to make meaning, understand their world and participate in it.

In relation to written communication, toddlers' interest in symbols and mark making developed into an interest in early reading and writing abilities. Both parents and teachers stimulated, encouraged and supported children's interest in literacy as a cultural tool and fund of knowledge that enabled access to meaning-making and knowledge-building. Jack's mother commented:

> He loves 'The Very Hungry Caterpillar' on DVD ... I've got *The Very Hungry Caterpillar* [book] ... It's really interesting listening to him ... he sat himself up on the couch and was reading it when the DVD wasn't on and he was reading it aloud ... and he'll correct us if we read the wrong word in the story. He just remembers it. That's quite big at the moment.

Children's interest in literacy was represented in many play experiences and formed a shared pedagogical goal with parents and teachers.

How can I understand the world I live in?

Exploration and understanding of the natural, physical and material worlds were other strong interests. On the basis of their own life experiences, the children were attracted by biological phenomena such as human bodily processes, and the lives of pets and other animals. Children's inquiries seemed to pursue questions such as: How do humans, animals, plants and trees 'get born' and/or die?, How does this work?, What are the features of the world I live in? These were most evident first of all in the domain of science, specifically naïve biology (Inagaki and Hatano 2002), with an emphasis on small animals and insects such as snails, worms, cicadas, their own pets, butterflies, sea creatures, and everyday phenomena. Second, these occurred in the domain of technology, or naïve physics (Wellman and Gel-man 1992, 1998), with interests such as cars, trucks, telephones, especially mobile telephones, cameras and computers, and batteries.

Implications for teachers' professional knowledge

I argue that it is vital teachers become more analytical about children's interests and recognize play area interests as an early point on a con-tinuum and not necessarily representative of children's underlying inter-ests: 'Children's inquiry acts provide a window to their thinking, allowing us to glimpse what they make sense of and how they are doing it, how they understand and how they use others to help them' (Lindfors 1999: 16).

In the early childhood years, children respond spontaneously to, and talk about, things that interest them, attempting to increase their under-standing during play and interactions with others. Children's inquiry emerges from everyday funds of knowledge experiences, and activities in their families and communities, the latter including their early education centre. These experiences appear to reveal some fundamental 'real ques-tions' about their humanity. As Bereiter (2002) claimed, children's inquiries are commonly about complex issues in their world. Therefore, consistent with *Te Whāriki*'s pedagogical goal, a stronger interpretation of children's interests is that of meaning-seeking about deep and serious issues of citi-zenship, culture and identity, rather than more common pedagogical interpretations which can focus on their interests using equipment or materials such as sand, paint and water. As children will find ways to rep-resent these understandings in the educational context through play, teachers can use funds of knowledge as a framework with which to iden-tify and choose interests to co-construct curriculum. As such, there is a need for teachers to access pedagogical strategies and skills to identify and support children's deep-seated interests as well as the ability to work with children's activity-based play interests.

Given that play is such a powerful way in which children represent, test and extend their interests, all three aspects (activity-based play inter-ests; continuing interests; and fundamental inquiry interests) of the con-tinuum presented in Figure 2.1 ought to be engaged with by teachers concurrently in a socio-cultural curriculum. Teachers' knowledge of chil-dren's family, centre and community funds of knowledge, along with the active involvement of families and communities in early childhood edu-cation, is vital to realizing a socio-cultural curriculum and pedagogy A funds of knowledge approach may move teachers' pedagogical thinking from having *information* about children to *knowledge* of children at a deeper level. Furthermore, the particular systems that teachers put in place to ensure all children are catered for in curriculum planning need to be flexible, and occur frequently enough to account for changes in children's interests across the continuum.

Moll et al. (1992) believed that if teachers understood local funds of knowledge as a form of professional knowledge, this could inform curriculum through teaching and learning being organized around children's interests and questions. One benefit of this approach is that it helps to build respect for diverse communities, thereby improving children's educational experiences and outcomes. Further, in order to satisfy children's fundamental inquiries, early childhood centres must not become institutions separated from the everyday worlds of families and communities. Visits from, and excursions into, the real worlds of adults that support children's current inquiries are also vital components of early childhood curriculum, particularly in terms of supporting the third aspect of the continuum – fundamental inquiry interests.

Conclusion: interfacing children's play with teachers' pedagogical practices

Defining play as involving inquiry serves to move teachers' thinking about children's play and interests from predominantly developmental perspectives to socio-cultural perspectives. Theories of learning through intent participation, funds of knowledge and a community of inquiry, become useful frameworks to identify and explain children's interests. In this chapter I have argued that children's interests and inquiries may be usefully viewed as a continuum comprising three main aspects: activity-based play interests, continuing interests and fundamental inquiry interests. The elements on this continuum feed backwards and forwards as children's experiences and interests grow and change and connect between contexts. Teachers' awareness of the deeper nature of children's interests through the framework of funds of knowledge and the notion of inquiry may enable them to co-construct curriculum and provide an environment responsive to children that is representative of their deeper interests. Teacher knowledge of this continuum may provide a sound theoretical foundation for choosing whose and which interests are followed in co-constructing meaningful curriculum.

As Wood (2009: 33) claims, 'Practitioners need a more critical understanding of the meaning of play activities to children.' The continuum proposed encourages deeper understandings of children's play and interests by teachers, and thoughtful pedagogical practices. Research on funds of knowledge present in diverse communities and cultures and the applicability of the continuum are suggested as steps towards moving early childhood education forward in the twenty-first century.

Note

1. This chapter adopts the ethical principle of credit, and uses real names to acknowledge participation.

Acknowledgements

Warm thanks to the teachers, children and families of Takapuna Kindergarten and The No 1 Kindy who generously shared their lives with me in 2005. This project was reviewed and approved by the Massey University Human Ethics Committee: reference 04/64. Sincere thanks to Joy Cullen for ongoing advice and critique.

References

Bereiter, C. (2002) *Education and Mind in the Knowledge Age*. Mahwah, NJ: Lawrence Erlbaum.

Brooker, L. (2002) *Starting School: Young Children Learning Cultures*. Buckingham: Open University Press.

Cullen, J. (2003) The challenge of *Te Whāriki*: catalyst for change?, in J. Nuttall (ed.) *Weaving Te Whāriki: Aotearoa New Zealand's Early Childhood Curriculum Document in Theory and Practice*. Wellington: New Zealand Council for Educational Research.

Dockett, S. and Fleer, M. (1999) *Play and Pedagogy in Early Childhood: Bending the Rules*. Southbank, Vic: Harcourt Brace.

Edwards, A. (2005) Let's get beyond community and practice: the many meanings of learning by participating, *The Curriculum Journal*, 16(1): 49–65.

Farquhar, S. and Fleer, M. (2007) Developmental colonisation of early childhood education in Aotearoa/New Zealand and Australia, in L. Keesing-Styles and H. Hedges (eds) *Theorising Early Childhood Practice: Emerging Dialogues*. Baulkham Hills, NSW: Pademelon Press.

Flavell, J. (1963) *The Developmental Psychology of Jean Piaget*. London: D. Van Nostrand.

González, N., Moll, L.C. and Amanti, C. (eds) (2005) *Funds of Knowledge: Theorizing Practices in Households, Communities and Classrooms*. Mahwah, NJ: Lawrence Erlbaum.

Hedges, H. (2008) *Early Childhood Communities of Inquiry: Children's and Teachers' Knowledge and Interests*. Saarbrücken: VDM Verlag.

Hedges, H. and Nuttall, J. (2008) Macropolitical forces and micropolitical realities: implementing *Te Whāriki*, in V. Carpenter, J. Jesson, P. Roberts and M. Stephenson (eds) *Ngā Kaupapa Here: Connections and Contradictions in Education*. Adelaide: Cengage.

Inagaki, K. and Hatano, G. (2002) *Young Children's Naïve Thinking about the Biological World*. Brighton: Psychology Press.

Lindfors, J.W. (1999) *Children's Inquiry: Using Language to Make Sense of the World*. New York: Teachers College Press.

Ministry of Education (1996) *Te Whāriki. He Whāriki Matauranga mō ngā Mokopuna o Aōtearoa: Early Childhood Curriculum*. Wellington: Learning Media.

Moll, L. (2000) Inspired by Vygotsky: ethnographic experiments in education, in C.D. Lee and P. Smagorinsky (eds) *Vygotskian Perspectives on Literacy Research: Constructing Meaning Through Collaborative Inquiry*. Cambridge: Cambridge University Press.

Moll, L., Amanti, C., Neff, D. and González, N. (1992) Funds of knowledge for teaching: using a qualitative approach to connect homes and classrooms, *Theory into Practice*, 31(2): 132–41.

Pramling-Samuelsson, I. and Fleer, M. (eds) (2008) *Play and Learning in Early Childhood Settings: International Perspectives on Play and Learning*. New York: Springer.

Rogoff, B., Paradise, R., Arauz, R.M., Correa-Chávez, M. and Angelillo, C. (2003) Firsthand learning through intent participation, *Annual Review of Psychology*, 54: 175–203.

Vygotsky, L.S. (1978) *Mind in Society: The Development of Higher Psychological Processes*. Cambridge, MA: Harvard University Press.

Vygotsky, L.S. (1986) *Thought and Language*. Cambridge, MA: MIT Press.

Wellman, H.M. and Gelman, S.A. (1992) Cognitive development: foundational theories of core domains, *Annual Review of Psychology*, 43: 337–75.

Wellman, H.M. and Gelman, S.A. (1998) Knowledge acquisition in foundational domains, in D. Kuhn and R. Siegler (eds) *Handbook of Child Psychology*, 5th edn, vol. 2, *Cognition, Perception and Language*. New York: John Wiley & Sons, Ltd.

Wells, G. (1999) *Dialogic Inquiry: Towards a Sociocultural Practice and Theory of Education*. New York: Cambridge University Press.

Wells, G. (2002) Inquiry as an orientation for learning, teaching and teacher education, in G. Wells and G. Claxton (eds) *Learning for Life in the 21st Century*. Oxford: Blackwell.

Wood, E. (2009) Developing a pedagogy of play, in A. Anning, J. Cullen and M. Fleer (eds) *Early Childhood Education: Society and Culture*, 2nd edn. London: Sage.

Wright, L. (2004) Spotlight on family day care: a window into home-based pedagogy, *Early Childhood Folio*, 8: 9–13.

Youngquist, J. and Pataray-Ching, J. (2004) Revisiting 'play': analyzing and articulating acts of inquiry, *Early Childhood Education Journal*, 31(3): 171–8.

3 Learning to play, or playing to learn?

Children's participation in the cultures of homes and settings

Liz Brooker

Introduction

This chapter examines the roots of two distinctively Western notions – of childhood as a time for play, and of play as a mode of learning – and the continuing meaning of these notions for current practice with children and families from diverse communities. It begins by briefly outlining the historical and cultural contexts in which discourses around play arose, and reviewing their current power and pedagogical status. It then questions the implications of these discourses for children growing up in the changing and plural world of twenty-first-century postindustrial societies: first, by exploring the alternative, socio-cultural understanding of learning as a form of apprenticeship to the cultural activities of the environments children inhabit; and then by discussing three examples of young children's learning in English schools, homes and pre-schools. Rather than trying to define play itself (a project long cherished by psychologists; Rubin et al. 1983; Smith 1994, 2006; Göncü and Gaskins 2006), the chapter focuses on the different ways that *learning through play* is understood in different cultural contexts. How is the process of learning understood by families and practitioners as they act in what they believe to be the best interests of children? How far do they agree about *what* is to be learned, as well as *how*? The chapter suggests that by adopting Rogoff's (1990) definition of learning as the transformation of participation in cultural activities, we can embrace a more inclusive understanding of learning: one which is both sensitive to the local cultural contexts in which children learn, and appreciative of their active endeavours in their own learning.

A time when play was king

> There was a time when play was king and early childhood was its
> domain.
>
> (Paley 2004: 4)

This time, like most golden-age theories, proves hard to define and
demonstrate despite its vivid presence in the mind. Theories of *learning*
have evolved wherever human communities have had sufficient leisure
and luxury to turn their attention away from the primary goals of sub-
sistence and survival towards the decidedly secondary goals of improving the minds of their children; but theories of *play* are both recent and
anomalous. Modern educational theory is often described as commenc-
ing with Locke's (1690) account of the child as a *tabula rasa* or 'blank
slate' to be inscribed with adult knowledge, an account that went
unchallenged until the publication of the Romantic proposals of
Rousseau (in *Emile*, 1762) and the subsequent pioneering efforts at
child-centred education initiated by Pestalozzi and Froebel (Nutbrown
et al. 2008). These early kindergartens were characterized, not by the
'free-flow play' advocated by late-twentieth-century educators, but by
carefully sequenced learning activities such as Froebel's 'occupations',
along with virtuous habits such as gardening and handicrafts (Anning
1997). Montessori's (1912) manual prescribing her 'scientific pedagogy'
was precise as to the types and sequencing of 'didactic material' which
should be presented to children, and the 'intellectual work' (not play)
which was to occupy their day.

The belief that 'well-planned play … is a key way in which young children learn' (QCA 2000: 25) not only arrived relatively late in the history
of theories of instruction, but has remained relatively 'local' to European
and English-speaking communities. Its appearance marked the conver-
gence of a number of emergent streams of thought: streams originating
in the child study movement and the growth of developmental psychology
as a discipline (Smith 2006); in the radical democratizing proposals of
Dewey (1916) and the experimental learning environment created by
Susan Isaacs (1929); in the ethological studies in the 1950s which prompted
the first experimental studies of the impact of play on the cognition of
human children (Sylva et al. 1976); and in the gradual dissemination of
the work of both Piaget (1951) and Vygotsky (1933). In England, once
the liberal-progressivism of the 1960s had taken hold (CACE 1967), the
orthodoxy that children 'learn through play' seemed unassailable, even
if actual practice rarely matched the rhetoric (Bennett et al. 1997). By the
early 2000s, belief in play as an instrument of early learning dominated
the pre-school curricula of European, American and Australasian nations,

and had begun to infiltrate the curricula of former colonies with very different cultural traditions (Hamza 2009).

These then are the kingdoms where, for a brief historical period, play has been king, and these are the early childhood domains where it has reigned. In other eras and in less privileged parts of the world such ideas have had little purchase, but the scientific knowledge which informs dominant discourses pays little attention to such places – a fact which, as educators, we should always keep in mind.

Learning as participation: a more inclusive stance?

This Western advocacy of 'learning through play' has been located by socio-cultural theorists (Rogoff et al. 1996) within a broader pendulum swing of ideas which is characterized by periodic shifts in preference from adult-led to child-led theories of instruction. The trajectory of this pendulum is bounded by the oppositional beliefs in learning as *transmission* (adult-led) and learning as *acquisition* (child-led). The adult-led mode is universally recognized as *pedagogy* – intentional actions to bring about learning – while the child-led mode will be generally recognized as *play* – voluntary, exploratory and spontaneous (Smith 2006), but may or may not be viewed as instructional.

The persistent tension between these opposed models can be resolved, Rogoff suggests, by defining learning differently: as the *transformation of participation in cultural activities*. Such a transformation sees a child's performance in culturally valued activities change over time from that of novice to that of expert, as a result of drawing on the affordances of the environment, under the guidance of more experienced individuals:

> Guided participation involves adults or children challenging, constraining and supporting children in the process of posing and solving problems – through material arrangements of children's activities and responsibilities as well as through interpersonal communication, with children observing and participating at a comfortable but slightly challenging level.
>
> (Rogoff 1990: 18)

Cognitive development, in other words, occurs in the course of 'children's everyday involvement in social life' (1990: 18), including their intent participation in all the activities which they see other children, and adults, performing. Such participation, Rogoff argues, depends for its effectiveness on the *intersubjectivity* or 'shared understanding' which exists between the expert and the novice (1990: 71). The activities may include 'play' (as in most Western childhoods) but they may equally include some form of 'work', or of didactic instruction. Research into this broader conception of learning was until recently associated with the non-formal learning activities of children in developing societies such as Kenya (Harkness 1980), Liberia (Lave and Wenger 1991) or Cameroon (Nsamenang and Lamb 1998) rather than with the learning of children in industrial nations. When the research gaze shifts to Western societies, and to institutions such as schools and pre-schools, a tension emerges: is the apprenticeship model described by Rogoff and others equally effective in developing school-related knowledge such as literacy, mathematics or science, or is it only applicable to learning skills such as fishing or weaving, childminding or goat-herding? Socio-cultural theory challenges us to attempt to answer that question through looking carefully at what children learn, and how they learn it, in environments such as schools and pre-schools, where different cultural activities prevail.

The following sections propose that a model of learning through participation in cultural activities can encompass a pedagogy of play, along with other pedagogical models, and thus can accommodate the diverse cultural contexts in which children learn. I begin with a brief clarification of the notion of culture, and hence of the range of 'cultural activities' which children may encounter.

Whose culture, whose activities?

Rather than attempt to explore the multiple meanings and implications of 'culture', it can be helpful to revert to the simple reminder, by the English cultural critic Raymond Williams, that 'Culture in all of its early uses was a noun of process: the tending of something, basically crops or animals' (1973: 87). By extension, as Michael Cole argues, it often describes the construction of an environment for growing up in: 'an artificial environment in which young organisms could be provided optimal conditions for growth' (Cole 1998: 15). Since families and communities, and the caregivers and educators charged with bringing up young children, hold implicit goals and values for the kinds of adults these children will become, and implicit theories of how to achieve these goals, the 'cultures' provided for young children are inevitably shaped towards these ends. Family and community cultures, like school and pre-school cultures, are fashioned to bring about the desired outcomes for children, although these outcomes will vary from one group to another. Different families may provide an environment which prioritizes play, or one which prioritizes work, as the appropriate activity for children; one which fosters deference and compliance, or assertiveness and challenge; conformity or non-conformity; independence or interdependence (Göncü et al. 2000). Thus, children's enculturation in their home communities will have taught them distinctive participation repertoires. They may have 'learned' to care for younger siblings and fold the washing; or to navigate a CD-ROM or build a complex Lego model from a diagram; or to recite and copy alphabets, or sing along with the ABC songs on *Sesame Street*.

Educators, similarly, build their environments and their practice on their conscious or unconscious beliefs about what is best for children: the knowledge and skills they should acquire, and the optimal ways to acquire them. The early learning environments beloved of Western educators, with their airy open spaces, clear bright colours, natural objects and invitations to play and have fun, communicate a coherent system of beliefs about young children's learning. Children 'need' (we tend to believe) sand and water, paints and crayons, blocks and climbing structures, and the 'artificial environment' we create is designed to meet those needs. These 'material arrangements of children's activities and responsibilities' (Rogoff 1990: 18) are the physical embodiment of our beliefs about learning, and are very often grounded in the importance of play for childhood.

In consequence, as children enter their first group care setting, or make the transition to a subsequent one, they encounter a plethora of new cultural activities and new ways of learning. They must, in Rogoff's terms, gradually transform their participation in these new activities in order to become an expert in the setting. Learning how to learn in a new setting is a major challenge for children, especially when the values, goals and cultural activities of the setting contrast starkly with those of the home (Brooker 2008). The status and function of play, for the different stakeholders in any setting – peers, parents, practitioners – are one factor which informs the range of cultural activities in which children must acquire expertise.

Practitioners, parents and the pedagogy of play

Practitioners who are committed to the idea of learning through play, and to the rights of young children to play unfettered, may feel constantly embattled and beleaguered. In England, despite the powerful mantra of learning-through-play (Bennett et al. 1997), early educators complain of top-down pressures from statutory subject-based curricula for school-aged children, and increasingly for pre-schoolers (Soler and Miller 2003), prompting ongoing struggles to incorporate traditional early childhood ideologies into the recommended pedagogy. Tensions lie along several axes: between free choice and compulsion for children; between adult-initiated and child-initiated activities; between structured and unstructured learning tasks; and between convergent and divergent forms of knowledge.

Ultimately, the 'struggle' described by Soler and Miller (2003) is not simply between different theories of learning but between different views of children: as immature, inexperienced and ignorant people whose learning depends on the tutoring of more mature, experienced and knowledgeable adults, or as competent individuals who are capable of making meaning from their experiences of the world, in collaboration with others and with the support of cultural tools. And since such views are themselves fundamentally *cultural,* in the sense that they have been constructed through experience from the beliefs of previous generations, and transmitted through early experiences in the family and community, these tensions have their roots within families and education systems, and are made visible when children pass from their home culture to that of the pre-school. As a result, practitioners often describe pressure from parents to 'sit them down and teach them' as the most pressing constraint on their practice; while at the same time, many parents feel disappointed that their educational aspirations for their children are unmet (Brooker 2002). Where are children in this debate, and what do they make of their experiences?

Learning through cultural activities at 2, 3 and 4

This section presents examples of children's early learning – their participation in cultural activities within different play-based contexts – in a range of English settings. They illustrate some of the ways that children learn through participation in the environments they experience before school, and in their first encounter with formal schooling; and the extent to which practitioners' understandings of this learning may be aligned with those of parents.

The episodes have been chosen to illustrate some of the complexity surrounding this issue. In the case of younger children, for instance, there may be a broad consensus between parents and practitioners on the goals for their development: most adults want children to develop at their own pace, to demonstrate well-being, and to display a positive sense of self. As children approach school age, however, there may be a growing concern for children to show they are acquiring academic knowledge and skills; a growing division between a focus on the 'basics' of literacy and numeracy, and a recognition of the value of broader life-skills; and a growing polarization in beliefs about the most effective ways for children to learn. The children and parents presented here exemplify some of these issues.

All three observations were undertaken in the course of studies of children's transitions (Brooker 2002, 2008). The first two snapshots occurred in the pre-school environment of a London children's centre offering early education in a free-play setting for children from 6 months to 5 years, as well as family and community support services. The third case study was located in the 'reception' classroom of a primary school in an English provincial town, in which 'play-based learning' was directed towards planned curriculum objectives. The parents and teachers of all three children were interviewed in the course of these studies, and their perspectives highlight the different ways that play and learning may be interpreted by adults from different backgrounds.

Davey appropriates the outdoor environment

Davey, aged 2 years, was observed in his fifth week in the toddler room of a children's centre. Until recently he had spent most of his time, in his dad's company, in a small flat with no access to the outdoors, so that the encounter with an open-plan environment full of strange adults and children presented him with many new learning challenges and a range of unfamiliar cultural activities – climbing and building, painting and modelling, music groups, malleable materials, and simply digging outdoors. The observation was as follows:

In the garden

He is pushing a very heavy wooden cart, making a real effort to push, then stop and re-direct the steering, then move forward again. He looks in to check the contents: two paint brushes; moves forward a bit further then removes the brushes from the truck and walks purposefully to the back of the garden to the shed, which he then 'paints' with the brushes. Turns round, beaming with confidence and self-importance, and addresses other children (apparently to tell them what he is doing), pointing to the shed wall. Moves away a few feet to 'paint' the low posts round the sand pit, and then walks away to the slide.

Stands at bottom of slide and 'paints' with brushes, using a damp patch on the slide surface to pick up a bit of moisture and spread it. 'Cleans' the brushes carefully with his fingers. Runs to the ladder on the slide and goes up carefully with a brush in each hand, so he can't hold on to the rails; gets on to the small platform at the top, sits there and then leans down to 'paint' the top part of the slide with his damp brush.

Decides to go back down the ladder but has even more difficulty getting on to the ladder and down it with a brush in each hand (uses his elbows to wedge himself against the rails). Returns to the ground, walks round and 'paints' the slide again from the bottom end; stops, to allow a girl to slide down; then starts again.

Davey's growing participation in the cultural activities offered by the nursery environment is clear. The garden contains many affordances which Davey is identifying for himself, through observation of other children or simple experiment: there are carts which can be pushed and used for transporting (or shared, or used for rides, as he was to discover); brushes which can be used for workmanlike 'painting' of surfaces (and small collections of rain-water which may be used in place of paint); structures for climbing and sliding which require careful negotiation and improvisation if they are combined with other purposes, such as 'painting'; and children whose attention can be engaged through tentative interaction. These resources, which are typical of a traditional 'free-flow' nursery environment, obviously make sense to Davey, and to his dad, who reflected that

> He teaches himself a lot of things I think because he's quite inquisitive and he tries to find out how things work and if he can't he'll go and ask someone … like the red tractor in the playground, I got told yesterday that he plays with that every day and at first he wasn't too sure how it went up and down but now he's doing it on his own!

Davey's play, in an observation like this, could be described as work-like and potentially gendered. His mode of exploration is an approved *cultural activity* in the nursery environment, and is actively promoted by his key worker:

> I know that Davey likes his outdoor space and he doesn't have it at home, he doesn't have access to it … so the first thing I do is go outside, let them be where they want to be – and he's got the things he likes – the sand, the trucks, the tractor.

At the same time, Davey is showing his awareness of the wishes of other children who are sharing his space and resources. For 2-year-olds in this urban setting, increasing appropriation of the cultural tools of the nursery (which are intended to support their developing physical, social and communicative competencies) addresses goals which are shared by everyone.

Larissa: regulating peer relationships

In the kindergarten section of the same children's centre, 3-year-old Larissa was another subject of the transitions study. Larissa and her friends were also regularly found playing out of doors, and the goals of their 'cultural activity' were those of their peer culture. This observation was made in Larissa's fourth week in kindergarten.

> Larissa prances across the open space, followed closely by Saskia, and at a distance by Millie, Eva and finally Cara. Larissa and Saskia sit on a bench and the next two join them while Cara hangs back. All except Cara now begin to skip and dance in a circle, apparently spontaneously, although they stop, confer and start up again more than once. At some point the activity becomes 'My Little Pony' as they toss imaginary manes ('Mine is pink' says Larissa).
>
> Following Larissa's lead, the four girls now sing 'Horsey, horsey, don't you stop' as they skip in a circle with knees raised, tossing their pony heads. But Cara intervenes, apparently making a bid for leadership: 'This is a butterfly song, right? Everybody, this is a butterfly song!'
>
> Larissa stops, stares briefly and loudly begins, 'Horsey, Horsey, don't you stop ...'; Saskia, Millie and Eva join in, with some giggling and sideways glances suggesting that they are aware of the way that power is being exercised. Cara makes one more 'butterfly' bid, which is ignored, and then falls off the scooter she is balancing on, and wails 'I want my mum'. This evokes no sympathy, as the girls respond vaguely 'she's over there' (outside the centre) while continuing to be ponies.
>
> Cara makes two further attempts ('This is not a horsey horsey, this is a butterfly song', and then 'this is a kangaroo song and this is how a kangaroo goes'). Each time Larissa looks directly at her and deliberately begins, 'Horsey, horsey ...' and the others copy her.

Larissa's key worker, Anessa, is aware of the power relationships in the peer group:

> I knew from the start she was quite a popular child, everybody wanted to be her friend and they'd fight over her, 'I want to be with you, I want to be with you', and she negotiates everything, and it's like she's the leader of the pack and everyone does what she says.

If Anessa is concerned by this, she doesn't say so, because her goal has been to build Larissa's confidence ('her confidence has only just come ... so I have had to make a conscious effort to pull that out of her'). Like the staff in this setting, Larissa's mother describes 'learning social skills' as a priority of early education, though she insists, surprisingly, that Larissa 'finds it frustrating being followed around ... she doesn't like it when people copy her'. Friendship is a key concern for Larissa in her mother's opinion:

> ... she knows who her friends are – and that's another thing that's going on in this age group with this group, 'You're not my friend', this business, and that can be a bit hurtful sometimes; if she's in or out affects her mood.

In this centre, parents talk daily to their child's key worker, and meet regularly to review a portfolio of documented activities, so that their goals for the children are discussed and shared. For the 3-year-olds, these shared goals include establishing a secure sense of identity, and making friends. To a superficial gaze, Larissa and her friends are 'learning' in the ways that the setting promotes, although a closer view prompts concerns as to *what* is actually being learned: the 'pleasure' of playing is here closely bound up with the exercise of power within the peer group. For now, however, Larissa's social learning – accomplished through participation in traditional, girl-group outdoor games – satisfies the expectations of her mother as well as her professional educators.

Khiernssa: 'Learning cultures' at home and school

Khiernssa was one of 16 4-year-old children whose home and school learning was observed during their first year in an English primary school, as part of a study of the culture and pedagogy experienced by children of diverse cultural backgrounds (Brooker 2002). As the youngest child of highly aspirational Bangladeshi parents, she had experienced a formal 'home' curriculum which included explicit tuition in school-like knowledge, and was also steeped in the cultural activities of her family and community.

With regard to the former, she received daily tutoring from her father and siblings and was learning to recite alphabets in Bengali, Arabic and English, as well as to count, add and subtract. The family's regular evening session, involving all three children, consisted of taking turns to read aloud from school story-books; copying out pages from these books; being tested on letters, words and spellings learned the previous day; and reciting Quranic verses. When I was present with my tape recorder, Khiernssa was encouraged to demonstrate her achievements by reciting numbers and letters into the microphone. In terms of family and community knowledge, Khiernssa was apprenticed to her father's traditional activities (growing vegetables on an allotment, tending pigeons and chickens in the back yard) as well as to the activities of the mosque and mosque school; and she was equally at home in the world of the

Bollywood films which she watched with her mother every day, joining in the songs. Within her own community context, she was an active and accomplished participant.

On entry to school – a colourful welcoming environment whose play-based pedagogy was rooted in an ethos of 'having fun', Khiernssa was assessed against the school entry profile, and by additional research instruments (Brooker 2002). On the former she appeared rather 'unready' for the learning activities that were on offer: she was indisposed to engage actively with toys, games and picture books, unwilling to get dirty or messy, and unresponsive to adult invitations to 'play' or 'choose'. On more formal assessments she achieved some high scores, identifying 23 out of 24 letters and sounds, for instance, the direct result of her home instruction. But her transformation in participation in the learning culture of the classroom was slow and reluctant. When interviewed at the end of her first term, she expressed her resistance to some important learning opportunities:

> *Researcher*: Can you think what you like best about school?
> *Khiernssa*:   Home corner! They got babies! – I like real babies,
>   I like Rufia's baby, I like Amadur's baby ...
> *Researcher*: Is there anything at school you really *don't* like?
> *Khiernssa*:   I don't like play water: they boys. And sand: they
>   boys.
>
> (see Brooker 2006)

This gender rule was applied comprehensively across the classroom, despite the fact that her neighbourhood friends were mostly male. Conversations with her mother confirmed that her views of learning were at one with her daughter's, and at odds with the preferred pedagogy of the classroom:

> She has to work harder, you have to stop her playing ... every day, play, 'what did you do?' – 'play', then after school – play; Monday, Tuesday, Wednesday – play ... she has to stop playing!

The setting offered many different opportunities for learning, both formal (instructional) and informal (adult-led or child-initiated), but most of these opportunities fell outside Khiernssa's cultural repertoire. She learned to 'play' by spending long days in the home corner with a couple of friends, nursing dollies and soft toys; and she leapt at the invitation to 'work' (in her family's terms) by writing letters or her name, and copying pictures from books. Her teachers' carefully planned strategies for experiential learning made little sense to her, as this observation of an adult-led 'science' activity demonstrates:

Learning about the effects of heat on food

Becky (the nursery nurse) calls together a group of five Bangladeshi children, including Khiernssa. All have some English but none is proficient. She allocates them to chairs round a table on which an electric toaster stands.

Becky: OK, then – are you all looking this way? What are we going to be doing?

Abu Bokkar: Toast [he has observed other groups undertaking this activity].

Becky: That's right! We're going to be … what have we got here? What's this?

All: Bread … bread …

Becky: Bread, and now are you all going to feel what it's like …?

She passes two slices of bread around the table; the children hold the slice when it reaches them, uncertainly; put their palm flat against the slice, imitating Becky; pass it on, hastily.

Becky: So what's it like? [silence] Is it cold? Is it a little bit soft, all soft …?

All: Bit soft [nodding].

Becky: So now what we're going to do is …

Abu Bokkar: Toast!

Becky: What we're going to, we're going to put it in here, in the toaster …

She inserts slices; switches on; looks around the room; checks clipboard with lists; the children look at each other, look around the room; start to pinch and poke each other; giggle; eventually the toast pops up.

Becky: So now … now what's it like?

[Holds toast slices in air prior to circulating.]

Abu Bokkar: Toast!

Becky: But what's it like? Is it going to be … is it going to be …

[Mimes touching toast and starting at the heat.]

Abu Bokkar: Toast!

Becky: But what's it …?

*Abdul
Rahman*:   HOT!

Becky: Well done, Abdul, you knew it was going to be ...
             [turns to other children] what's it going to be? Do
             you want to feel it?
All: Toast ... hot ...

Becky passes the slices round. The children cautiously touch
them. Shortly after this they are dismissed, and Becky makes
notes on her list to record their learning.

The children's potential for learning from this activity was evidently ham-
pered by their confusion as to how and why they were intended to participate, as well as by their inability to access the conceptual framework that
underpinned it, or the language in which this was presented. As a 'cultural
activity' it also appeared to mystify many of the English-speaking children
(for whom eating the toast would have made more sense). In Rogoff's terms,
the children's participation, in a literal sense, was undertaken without any
shared understanding of the task or its aims; without intersubjectivity.

The most challenging examples of the 'play pedagogy' in this setting
occurred when the staff made the greatest effort to be playful and 'child-
friendly': setting up an area as a 'monster pit' in which children were
intended to scare and excite each other, or a 'jungle' in which they could
roar and play with furry tiger toys; outings to a park or playground where
children were encouraged to swing high, spin fast and race down hills.
Khiernssa and her girlfriends viewed such activities with a mixture of fear
and disdain, yet they were at the heart of the setting's playful pedagogy,
a visible demonstration of a belief in childhood as a time for fun and
excitement, and children as motivated by novelty and challenge. The
classroom's learning activities at no point resembled those of Khiernssa's
home, and in consequence her parents' own instructional efforts
remained largely invisible and unacknowledged.

Learning cultures

Documenting children's learning through documenting their participation in cultural activities is an idea which proves highly problematic in
practice, because of the very different cultural activities, beliefs and values
which make up the complex worlds of children living in plural societies.
The activities found in children's home cultures change over time, and
vary with children's age as well as their gender and ethnicity; and over
time, children construct their own hybrid cultures, which incorporate the
values of their families, peers and school. But the critical moments, like
the start of school, when children encounter new and strange 'learning
cultures' are times when some children fail to understand the rules for
participation, or choose to participate in avoidant activities, using the
solidarity offered by their peer culture to resist the agenda offered by adults.

If children are to continue learning in all the cultural contexts they experience, and make connections between the ways they participate in each, the adults who construct these environments must allow some of their most deeply-held convictions to be challenged by other views: beliefs about childhood and the role and status of children; about goals and values for children's present and future lives; and about the nature of learning itself. Research on the pedagogy of play, since the 1970s, has moved from the laboratory into the classroom, and from the classroom into the family and community. We could now try, in Rogoff's terms, to 'provide bridges from known to new' (1990: 65), for the adults as well as children whose learning is at issue.

References

Anning, A. (1997) *The First Years at School*, 2nd edn. Buckingham: Open University Press.

Bennett, N., Wood, E. and Rogers, S. (1997) *Teaching through Play*. Buckingham: Open University Press.

Brooker, L. (2002) *Starting School: Young Children Learning Cultures*. Buckingham: Open University Press.

Brooker, L. (2006) From home to the home corner: observing children's identity-maintenance in early childhood settings, *Children & Society*, 20(2), April: 116–27.

Brooker, L. (2008) *Supporting Transitions in the Early Years*. Maidenhead: McGraw-Hill.

CACE (Central Advisory Council for Education) (1967) *Children and Their Primary Schools [The Plowden Report]*. London: HMSO.

Cole, M. (1998) Culture in development, in M. Woodhead, D. Faulkner and K. Littleton (eds) *Cultural Worlds of Early Childhood*. London: Routledge/The Open University.

Dewey, J. (1916) *Democracy and Education*. New York: Basic Books.

Göncü, A. and Gaskins, S. (2006) *Play and Development: Evolutionary, Sociocultural and Functional Perspectives*. Mahwah, NJ: Lawrence Erlbaum Associates.

Göncü, A., Mistry, J. and Mosier, C. (2000) Cultural variations in the play of toddlers, *International Journal of Behavioural Development*, 24(3): 321–9.

Hamza, S. (2009) *Contextualising Policy in Early Childhood Education*. Jos, Nigeria: University of Jos.

Harkness, S. (1980) The cultural context of child development, in C. Super and S. Harkness (eds) *New Directions for Child Development*, 8: 7–13.

Isaacs, S. (1929) *The Nursery Years*. London: Routledge & Kegan Paul.

Lave, J. and Wenger, E. (1991) *Situated Learning: Legitimate Peripheral Participation*. Cambridge: Cambridge University Press.

Locke, J. (1690) *An Essay Concerning Human Understanding*, reprinted 1841, London: Tegg.

Montessori, M. (1912) *The Montessori Method: Scientific Pedagogy.* London: Heinemann.

Nsamenang, B. and Lamb, M. (1998) Socialization of Nso children in the Bamenda Grassfields of Northwest Cameroon, in M. Woodhead, D. Faulkner, and K. Littleton (eds) *Cultural Worlds of Early Childhood.* London: Routledge/The Open University.

Nutbrown, C., Clough, P. and Selbie, P. (2008) *Early Childhood Education: History, Philosophy and Experience.* London: Sage.

Paley, V.G. (2004) *A Child's Work: The Importance of Fantasy Play.* Chicago: University of Chicago Press.

Piaget, J. (1951) *Play, Dreams and Imitation in Childhood.* London: Routledge & Kegan Paul.

Qualifications & Curriculum Authority (QCA) (2000) *Curriculum Guidance for the Foundation Stage.* London: QCA.

Rogoff, B. (1990) *Apprenticeship in Thinking: Cognitive Development in Social Context.* Oxford: Oxford University Press.

Rogoff, B., Matusov, E. and White, C. (1996) Models of teaching and learning: participation in a community of learners, in D. Olson and N. Torrance (eds) *The Handbook of Education and Human Development: New Models of Learning, Teaching and Schooling.* Oxford: Blackwell.

Rousseau, J-J. (1762) *Emile* (Book 2), reprinted 1974. London: Dent.

Rubin, K., Fein, G. and Vandenberg, B. (1983) Play, in E. Hetherington (ed.) *Manual of Child Psychology: Socialization, Personality and Social Development,* vol. 4. New York: John Wiley & Sons Ltd.

Smith, P. (1994) Play and the uses of play, in J. Moyles (ed.) *The Excellence of Play.* Buckingham: Open University Press.

Smith, P. (2006) Evolutionary foundations and functions of play: an overview, in A. Göncü and S. Gaskins (eds) *Play and Development: Evolutionary, Sociocultural and Functional Perspectives.* Mahwah, NJ: Lawrence Erlbaum Associates.

Soler, J. and Miller, L. (2003) The struggle for early childhood curricula: a comparison of the English Foundation Stage Curriculum, *Te Whaariki* and Reggio Emilia, *International Journal of Early Years Education,* 11(1): 57–67.

Sylva, K., Bruner, J. and Genova, P. (1976) The role of play in the problem-solving of children 3–5 years old, in J. Bruner, A. Jolly and K. Sylva (eds) *Play: Its Role in Development and Evolution.* Harmondsworth: Penguin.

Vygotsky, L. (1933) Play and its role in the mental development of the child, reprinted, in J. Bruner, A. Jolly and K. Sylva (eds) *Play: Its Role in Development and Evolution.* Harmondsworth: Penguin.

Williams, R. (1973) *Keywords.* London: Fontana.

4 Reflecting the child

Play memories and images of the child

Anette Sandberg and Tuula Vuorinen

Introduction: temporal and cultural positions on play

In recent decades there has been a change in the understanding of childhood and of children's role in society. James et al. (1998) point out difficulties concerning the concept of 'childhood' since the meaning of childhood differs between and within societies. It is therefore problematic to use the concept 'childhood' as it conceals the plurality and diversity that lie within the concept. They state further that there is neither a universal childhood nor a universal child. Earlier constructions of the child based upon psychological ideas of universal patterns of maturation have been challenged by a social and cultural perspective (Prout 2005), while categories such as gender, ethnicity and social belonging are now seen as equally important within child development. At the same time it is now recognized that, although childhood has been viewed as an isolated phenomenon, it actually exists in relation to adulthood. The concept 'child' is, in that sense, constructed in relation to the concept 'adult'. Prout (2005) links these changes within childhood research to an aspect of modernity. Recent changes in society have contributed not only to changing the conditions within which children are brought up, but also to bringing forward the diversity within childhood research. Childhood is seen as situated in time and place, since children are located in different environments in different times. Today childhood is also partly connected to institutions, such as pre-school and school, and other activities organized by adults.

In addition, children are viewed from a new perspective and seen as active and competent people. Children are attributed agency, and regarded as subjects who have both the right and opportunity to influence their own lives (Sheridan and Pramling-Samuelsson 2001; Dahlberg et al. 2002; Pramling-Samuelsson and Asplund-Carlsson 2003).

Säljö (2000) describes how the child enters a world that already exists and how the child learns to understand the world by communicating with people already taking part in its culture. The world is mediated to the child because it is already interpreted and conceptualized by others. Our way of thinking and our conceptions are therefore always shaped by the culture and by the intellectual, linguistic and psychological tools used in the culture. The language and the artifacts of any culture are the most important tools for children to acquire in developing their understanding of the world in everyday life. Learning is therefore based upon our ability to communicate and interact with others in order to make sense of, and understand, our social and cultural environment. Such communication and interaction are situated, as the way we talk and act differs between contexts.

The aim of this chapter is to describe and analyze play through a cultural-historical perspective. Cultural values are implicitly incorporated in play (Vygotsky [1930] 1990; Säljö 2000). How we understand play, and the values that we give play, differs over time, and between cultures. In this chapter, we are interested in examining play memories as a way of understanding play, and the values given to play, over time and within cultural communities. There are several starting points for this chapter. One is the importance of adults who now work with children, remembering how they played as children, because it is easier to understand children's contemporary play if one remembers earlier experiences. Another reason is the lack of previous research in this field. Research on adults' own experience of play is fairly limited (Sandberg 2003) yet it is essential that research also acknowledges adults and their view of play because it is adults who create the conditions of play for children, and adults are the model for children's play behaviour, as well as interacting with children in play. Another reason is that play is considered to have great significance for children's development and learning. Children need to play because play develops, for example, their imagination (see Vygotsky [1930] 1990; Vygotskij 1995). Fantasy creates activities which depend on the meaning of past experience, because this experience is the starting point for imagination. Creativity is also attributed great importance in today's society and in the future. Another argument is that play belongs to childhood and provides no value in the adult world (Sutton-Smith 1997). In both theory and practice, play is expressed as a pastime, but paradoxically play experiences are also considered important and vital. Sutton-Smith (1997) points out that there is an ambiguity in looking at play as something that belongs to childhood and not adulthood. When children play, it is understood as a means of development, but when adults are playing, it is viewed as a pastime. Play in adult life may be perceived as relaxation from work, but is not usually viewed as a process supporting development.

Childhood today is very different from earlier childhoods, and the prerequisites and conditions for children's play are undergoing constant changes. Linden's (1999) study shows, for example, that persons born in the beginning of the twentieth century had only a few, and often home-made, toys, and that individual play is described as most common among the participants. Kim's (1990) study, with parents of disabled children, showed, on the other hand, that relations to people, rather than toys, had created the most powerful play impressions among the participants. In other studies (Sandberg and Pramling-Samuelsson 2005; Vickerius and Sandberg 2006), the participants remember social play with friends or siblings more strongly than individual play.

This study adopts a cultural-historical perspective which not only highlights how knowledge and abilities are created and recreated in play, but also contributes to making visible the values and judgements which lie behind our views on play. The language used when, for example, describing memories of play, shows underlying attitudes towards children's play today. In the educational context, analysis of the experience of play gives teachers and students concepts and models which enable them to reflect on the phenomenon of play in a conscious way. This can form the basis for new understanding and knowledge. This argument led us to the following research questions: How do pre-school teachers, students majoring in education, and students of teacher education describe their memories of play in their early years? And, how do pre-school teachers, students majoring in education and students of teacher education experience children's contemporary play, in comparison to their own experiences and memories of play?

The project: generational differences in play memories

This study is a part of a larger project, 'Dimensions of childhood play', initiated by Mälardalen University, Sweden. Earlier studies (Sandberg 2003; Sandberg and Tammemäe Orr 2008) have also described play memories and environments surrounding play (Sandberg 2003; Vickerius and Sandberg 2006). Pre-school teachers' experiences of play have been described also, focusing on a gender perspective (Sandberg and Pramling-Samuelsson 2005).

There were 111 participants in this study, ranging in age from 22 years old to 63 years. This meant that the oldest participants lived their childhood in the 1940s, and the youngest participants lived their childhood in the 1980s. Thus, there was an age gap of 41 years separating the youngest participant from the oldest. Fifty-nine of the participants were pre-school teachers, while 52 of the participants were currently studying pedagogy or the teacher education programme. All of the participants were women.

This study is based partly on interviews of a retrospective character. Retrospective interviews have a number of methodological problems. Not only do people forget information over time, but they may also remember the past through ideas that they have acquired far later in life. Furthermore, adults have a tendency to idealize their childhood. Kristjánsson (1995, 2001) states that adults can never maintain an objective view of childhood, partly due to overestimating and 'misrepresenting' their memories, and partly due to their intellectual skills developing. One way to allow people to recall their childhood is to relate it to concrete events (especially important events) from their lives, since the memory will rarely fail in this case. However, thoughts and feelings are increasingly influenced by other factors over time.

In this investigation, the questions were semi-structured in their design, therefore enabling participants freedom to formulate their answers. This process was then followed by the step that Bryman (2002) describes as 'consideration coding' of data. This means that the transcripts were read through, but no notations were made other than deleting repetitions and irrelevant comments. The thoughts and findings that were evident in the reading were taken note of in the form of notes in the margin, while keywords and themes were marked. It could be seen that during this phase, patterns began to emerge in the participants' responses, such as 'play in the countryside', which was described mainly by the older participants.

Findings: generational differences in play and play memories

The results of this project show some similarities and differences in the following areas: (1) the favourite and the strongest play memory; (2) outdoor and indoor play; (3) toys; (4) participation in play; and (5) experienced differences and similarities in children's play today compared with the participants' own memories of play. Comparisons between statements from participants aged 35 years or older, and aged 34 years or younger, were made in order to analyze changes in play in relation to changes in society. The participants' memories of play were also compared with their views on contemporary play. The categorization, referred to as 'older' and 'younger' participants, in the following description of the result is used to show some significant differences related to age.

In their favourite play memory from their own pre-school years, the older participants include mainly individual play, and play with toys and natural materials. In contrast, the younger participants mostly refer to social play including with friends. The descriptions of the favourite play memory in the school years follows a similar pattern, as the younger women include peers in their memories of play more often than the older participants. Furthermore, the younger women refer to play during school breaks more often than the older group. Outdoor play was included to a greater extent among all the participants when describing a strong memory of play at the time when participants reached school age.

The participants' strongest play memory was described as 'forbidden' actions or 'accidents', such as getting hurt, or behaving badly towards friends. The older women further refer to farm environments to a greater extent than the younger ones who, when referring to their strongest play memory, often refer to pre-school environments. Role playing, with or without dolls, has a special place among participants, but the content of the play differs between the two age groups as the older ones include games involving farm work and ecclesiastical ceremonies in their memories while the younger participants refer to playing shops and hairdressers. For example, this older participant described her play:

> [My strongest memory of play is from] when we would play funeral. The oldest boy was the priest, the others would be the 'congregation' and I'd be dead. I'd be placed in a bowl made of zinc that we had on the lawn. I remember it as being terrifying and exciting. The priest would read aloud about judgment day and was terribly serious, they'd sing to me and I was both scared and thrilled.

Media-inspired games occur among both age groups as they recall how they used to play games based on a 'cowboy' theme. Among the younger participants, other themes emerge. Some are based on the writings of the Swedish children's author, Astrid Lindgren, and others mirror the range of television programmes shown in the 1970s and 1980s, such as *Ronia the Robber's Daughter.*

In the school years, outdoor play dominates both groups' descriptions of their strongest play memory. However, the younger participants include peers in this memory to a greater extent than the older ones. The younger group also, unlike the older group, refers to a competitive element in these memories. Adult participation in play is rarely mentioned, but a difference in fathers' and mothers' participation in play becomes visible, as fathers were described as participants in outdoor play and mothers in indoor activities.

The most common toy that participants remember from their pre-school years is the doll and it is the number one toy among older participants. Younger participants also mention other toys, like stuffed animals, My Little Pony and Playmobil. One difference between the age groups is the access to Barbie dolls. The older participants relate playing with Barbie dolls to play that occurred during the school years, while the younger participants remember playing with Barbie at an earlier age.

In the school years, outdoor toys like skipping ropes, balls and natural materials dominate among the older participants. The majority of these participants name these either as toys which were used by them in their play, or as their favourite toys. Among younger participants, outdoor toys are not mentioned to the same extent as in the older group. The Barbie doll, however, is mentioned more frequently among the younger participants than it is among the older ones. Several participants rated the Barbie doll as a favourite toy even in later years, but suggested it became more embarrassing to play with Barbie dolls the older they became. Several participants describe how playing with Barbie went underground as they became older: 'I stopped playing with Barbies when I was twelve and by then it was a bit of a secret, that you were playing with Barbies.'

When the participants were asked to compare children's play today with their own experiences of play, both younger and older participants often viewed children's current play from a deficit perspective. The participants expressed deficiencies mostly in children's ability to use their imagination and creativity in play, as well as in children's ability to initiate and maintain play. Participants who grew up in the 1940s, 1950s and early 1960s state that children no longer use their imagination in play. They often associate the lack of imagination with the increased range of toys, suggesting that toys that are ready-made and specifically made for a definite purpose seem to limit children's ability to see other uses for them. They explain: 'When I was a kid, imagination was very important in figuring out solutions, making up games, making accessories to the games you made up since there didn't exist a lot of "ready-made" toys.'

Participants feel that children today have lost some of their love for play and their ability to initiate play. Children are supposed to have 'trouble playing' and are not seen as initiating play to the same extent as earlier generations. They have to be 'activated' or 'started' in play. Participants state that the adults surrounding the children are to some extent responsible for these changes in children's play because they have not allowed children to play freely without distractions. Adults, mostly parents, are seen as interrupting, controlling or even replacing play with other activities. Various kinds of after-pre-school activities are seen as limiting the child's 'free' time for play at home. The lack of time for play in general is seen as an explanation for the difficulties the participants noted in children's play, as children are not given the opportunity to develop through play in the same way as the participants believe they did themselves as children.

Changes in the interplay between children, or in the relations children have with each other, are identified in the study, although respondents differ as to whether the number of participants in children's play has increased or decreased. Some, often older participants, feel that the number of participants in children's play has increased and state that 'young children more often play in larger groups'. Younger participants feel on the other hand, that both the number of participants and the age range in children's play have been reduced. They state, for example, that they would 'play with children of all ages', and that it was then 'a matter of course that all the children would play together after school'.

The increase in the range of media available to children is mentioned as a cause for children's lack of initiative, and children are described by participants as passive media consumers who are 'fed' different television shows and commercials. Participants further state that there is 'too much' indoor play, and that adults as well as the range of media and toys exert excessive control over children's play: 'There are vast amounts of television shows, movies, etc. with figures, different characters who form the game. They [the children] are influenced by the mass media, television, videos, movies, etc.'

The participants give different explanations for what they perceive to be changes in children's play habits. The participants in the older age group mention more overall changes in society referring to technology, economic change, urbanization and women's entry into the workforce. The younger participants refer mainly to more specific changes, as they seem to picture increased stress levels among children and parents, and also point out the impact that an extended range of media and toys may have on children's play habits. The outdoor environment is also mentioned as more dangerous than in earlier generations, for example, the participants talk about the increase in road traffic, and even the number of people living in the community who might be considered as potential threats to children.

Discussion: reflecting on play histories

When comparing younger and older participants' memories of play, factors such as increased affluence, women's entry into working life, urbanization, secularization, the increased range of media and the expansion of child-care institutions in Sweden were identified as elements of difference across the generations. The changes in society are partly reflected in the external conditions of play, but also in its content. It is mainly in the descriptions participants give of play in the pre-school years that the changes become discernible.

In this study, it becomes apparent that the participants from different age groups or generations experienced different environments and used different play artifacts. The impact of the welfare state in the twentieth century, and the shift to a society of consumption, are mirrored in the play memories of the participants. For example, children's access to the number and range of toys across the generations was notable. Older participants state that they had a very limited access to ready-made toys during their pre-school years. All participants remember having a doll, but for most of the older participants that was all they had. In other respects, they had to make do with natural materials and discarded household items. The younger participants, however, refer to a more generous and varied ownership of toys during their pre-school period. The increase in toy ownership among the younger participants concurs with developments identified in earlier research, which suggests that the number of toys owned by a child has increased from a few toys during the first half of the twentieth century, to potentially hundreds of toys towards the end of the century (Nelson and Nilsson 2002; Sandberg 2003; Nelson and Svensson 2004). Nelson and Svensson (2004) state that the children's increased ownership of toys can partly be seen as representative of prosperity, but that it can also represent the ideals which society develops. The child has, during recent years, begun to have a part of the family's resources and marketing has also started to target children more directly (Aird 2004).

Furthermore, in the study, the older participants connect play with Barbie dolls to school age, while the younger participants describe play with Barbie dolls as occurring already in pre-school age. Whether the Barbie doll's entry into the younger participants' pre-school play should be seen as an expression of the trend which Aird (2004) states is called KGOY, or 'Kids are Getting Older Younger' is, however, doubtful, as these differences may also illustrate the Barbie doll's market breakthrough period during the 1960s. The older participants thus did not have access to Barbie dolls in their pre-school years, since most of them would have reached school age when Barbie dolls appeared on the larger market.

It may not be remarkable that older participants often include individual play, and play with toys and natural materials, among their favourite play memories. It is perhaps more surprising that the younger participants, who actually had access to a wider range of toys, rarely mention play with toys as their favourite memory of play. Instead they refer to social play, including other children. These differences also appear in earlier research as the participants in Lindens' (1999) study mainly refer to individual play and the things in their environments, while participants in other studies mainly refer to social play with friends and siblings (Sandberg and Pramling-Samuelsson 2005; Vickerius and Sandberg 2006).

The changes in society are further made visible in the participants' statements concerning strong memories of play. The older participants remember including farm work and ecclesiastical ceremonies in their play while the younger participants refer to playing shops and hairdressers. These differences in children's play are highly influenced by phenomena taking place during their lifetimes.

As a result, the older participants in the study are able to see more differences between children's play now, and in the past, than are the younger participants, confirming that human beings are always a product of their time and environment. This finding mirrors Vygotsky's ([1930] 1990) argument that people are the products of their cultures and histories. As Davydov and Kerr describe:

> The development of human personality takes place during its upbringing and teaching, and has a specifically historical character, content and form; therefore in different historical eras, we see different types of individual psychological development.
>
> (1995: 15)

Most likely, these differences in interpretation around children's contemporary play reflect the fact that a longer period of time has passed between their comparisons. The oldest participants mostly grew up in the 1940s and 1950s, while the youngest grew up during the 1970s and 1980s, thus, they were exposed to different societal conditions.

The general opinion of the participants of this study is that a radical change in children's play has taken place in recent decades. Children's space for free play is described by participants as more limited, both in regard to time and space. Participants mainly view the increase in commercialism, the increased range of media, and adults' control and limitation of children's play as important markers of children's play today, compared to their own play memories. Children's play environments do seem to have diminished during the past two decades as play has become more controlled and supervised by adults, at the same time as different corporations try to gain market shares by colonizing children's world of play. Participants state that children do not have the same opportunities to develop through play as they themselves had when they were young. A lack of toys, a lack of media and the absence of adults in children's play may, according to participants' statements, be interpreted as important prerequisites for the development of children's creativity, imagination, power of initiative and social skills.

The children of today are mainly described from a perspective based on insufficiency, as they are seen as lacking certain desirable qualities in comparison to earlier generations. We believe it is troubling that children's contemporary play is seen this way, and especially troubling is that participants view children's abilities and possibilities when it comes to using their imagination and creativity as limited, as these are qualities which are highly valued in the knowledge society.

Children's media consumption is often cited as the reason behind children's reduced play time in the home, as video games and watching television are believed to take precedence over playing with friends. This conception is debatable from several perspectives as research (Nordlund 1996; Sandberg and Vuorinen, forthcoming) partly shows that children, as a rule, choose to do something else rather than watch TV if the opportunity exists, especially together with friends. Buckingham (2001) further states that it is impossible to generalize and base assumptions on the large group contained within the concept of 'child', as there are considerable variations within the group regarding, for example, age, gender and social belonging. Sandberg and Vuorinen (forthcoming) found that video games, and the like are mostly enjoyed by boys. Nordlund (1996) also sees differences in the media consumption by children, and states that it is difficult to generalize about the media habits of children. However, he feels that it is possible to assume that children are not made passive and lonely by media consumption, but that it is rather the children who already are passive and lonely who become media consumers. Buckingham (2001) shows how adult views of children are reflected in the perception of children and media. Children can be regarded as passive media consumers who are directly affected by the media, on the basis of a behaviourist vision of learning and development. Children can also be seen as active and critical viewers who reflect upon the media content. Buckingham further states that the debate about children and media violence has very little to do with media, but instead is rooted in moral or political convictions and in people's unsettling experiences of social change and the fear of the future.

Conclusion: play memories today

Just as there are numerous definitions of play (see, for example, Piaget 1962; Bateson 1973; Vygotsky 1978), so there are variations in the participants' memories of play. The wealth of varying definitions and memories of play gives play its value as a pedagogical tool in early childhood education. Sandberg (2003) previously defined play as development, experiences, activities and roles. While these definitions of play were not used in the project findings reported in this chapter, these dimensions of play, which include social and physical elements, as well as the concept of change over time, coincide with the aspects of play recalled by the participants. Participants describe play with different individuals in different physical environments, and play that contains something new and exciting. The dimensions are characterized by environments and activities as well as collaboration.

Data from this study have both theoretical and pedagogical importance. Concerning theory, they show the different ways in which participants related to the view on children and play. The cultural-historical perspective on play and children is foregrounded, and the cultural values are incorporated implicitly through children's play. The value of play is derived from the individual's knowledge of play, and thereby also the individual's definition of play. However, previous play experiences and cultural background are also deciding factors in how individuals perceive play. Awareness of this fact is important for pre-school provision, and for making it possible for children to have the space to utilize their full play potential. Concerning pedagogies, teachers in pre-school can use the memories revealed by this study to discuss children's play from their own experience, and to make visible and discuss the conceptions that exist about play now and then. Above all, it is important to discuss which view of the child is manifested in the notions of play, and how adults view the increased influence of the media and the commercialism which characterize play today. Certainly, children's play today, especially boys' play, tends to be in the crossfire of media decrees and adults' constraints. Thus, there are many reasons to look at the reality which children face today, and to consider which conditions the children encounter in regards to play, as well as in what way adults' play ideals are important when it comes to children's opportunities to process their impressions of everyday life.

References

Aird, E.G. (2004) Advertisings and marketing to children in the United States, in P.B. Bufall (ed.) *Rethinking Childhood*. New Jersey: Rutgers University Press.

Bateson, G. (1973) *Steps to an Ecology of Mind*. New York: Ballantine Books, Inc.

Bryman, A. (2002) *Samhällsvetenskapliga metoder* [Methods in Social Sciences]. Stockholm: Liber.

Buckingham, D. (2001) Electronic child abuse?, in M. Barker (ed.) *Ill Effects: The Media Violence Debate*. London: Routledge.

Dahlberg, G., Moss, P. and Pence, A. (2002) *Från kvalitet till meningsskapande* [From Quality to Forming of Meaning]. Stockholm: HLS Förlag.

Davydov, V. and Kerr, S. (1995) The influence of L.S. Vygotsky on education, theory, research and practice, *Educational Researcher*, 24(3): 12–21.

James, A., Jenks, C. and Prout, C. (1998) *Theorizing Childhood*. Cambridge: Polity Press; New York: Teachers College Press.

Kim, F. (1990) Play through my life. Unpublished manuscript.

Kristjánsson, B. (1995) Vardandets barndom – (be)varandets barnforskning, in L. Dahlgren and K. Hultqvist (eds) *Seendet och seendets vilkor: En bok om barns och ungas välfärd* [Seeing and the Condition of Seeings: A Book about Children and Youth Welfare]. Stockholm: HLS Förlag.

Kristjánsson, B. (2001) *Barndomen och den sociala moderniseringen. Om att växa upp i Norden på tröskeln till ett nytt millennium* [Childhood and the Social Modernization: To Grow Up in the Nordic Countries on the Threshold to a New Millennium] (Studies in Educational Sciences, 48). Stockholm: HLS Förlag.

Linden, A. (1999) *Lekminnen. En studie baserad på tecknade lekminnen och intervjuer med personer födda mellan 1917–1936* [Play Memories: A Study Based on Drawn Memories of Play with Persons Born Between 1917–1936]. Västerås: Mälaradalens Högskola, Inst. för Samhälls-och Beteendevetenskap.

Nelson, A. and Nilsson, M. (2002) *Det massiva barnrummet: teoretiska och empiriska studier av leksaker* [The Massive Child Room: Theoretical and Empirical Studies of Toys]. (Studia Psychologica et Paedagogica series. Series Altera). Malmö: Malmö Lärarhögskola.

Nelson, A. and Svensson, K. (2004) *Barn och leksaker* [Children and Toys]. Stockholm: Liber.

Nordlund, J. (1996) *Television och socialisation* [Television and socialization]. Lund: Studentlitteratur.

Piaget, J. (1962) *Play, Dreams and Imitation*. New York: W.W. Norton.

Pramling-Samuelsson, I. and Asplund-Carlsson, M. (2003) *Det lekande lärande barnet i en utvecklingspedagogisk teori* [The Playing Learning Child in a Developmental Pedagogical Theory]. Stockholm: Liber.

Prout, A. (2005) *The Future of Childhood: Towards the Interdisciplinary Study of Children*. London: Routledge Falmer Press.

Säljö, R. (2000) *Lärande i praktiken. Ett sociokulturellt perspektiv* [Learning in Praxis: A Sociocultural Perspective]. Stockholm: Prisma.

Sandberg, A. (2003) *Vuxnas lekvärld. En studie om vuxnas erfarenheter av lek.* [The Play World of Grown Ups: A Study of Adults' Play Experiences]. (Göteborg Studies in Educational Sciences 189). Göteborg: Acta Universitatis Gothoburgensis.

Sandberg, A. and Pramling-Samuelsson, I. (2005) An interview study of gender differences in preschool teachers' attitudes toward children's play, *Early Childhood Education Journal*, 32(5): 297–305.

Sandberg, A. and Tammemäe Orr, H. (2008) Drawings and conceptions of play by children ages 7–12, in P.G. Grotewell and Y.R. Burton (eds) *Early Childhood Education: Issues and Developments*. New York: Nova Science Publishers.

Sandberg, A. and Vuorinen, T. (forthcoming) Children's conceptions of play and learning from a gender perspective.

Sheridan, S. and Pramling-Samuelsson, I. (2001) Children's conceptions of participation and influence in preschool: a perspective of pedagogical quality, *Contemporary Issues in Early Childhood*, 2(2): 169–94.

Sutton-Smith, B. (1997) *The Ambiguity of Play*. London: Harvard University Press.

Vickerius, M. and Sandberg, A. (2006) The signification of play and the environment around play, *Early Child Development and Care*, 176(2): 207–16.

Vygotsky, L.S. ([1930] 1990) Imagination and creativity in childhood, *Soviet Psychology*, 28(1): 84–96.

Vygotsky, L.S. (1978) *Mind in Society: Development of Higher Psychological Processes*. Cambridge, MA: Harvard University Press.

Vygotskij, L.S. (1995) *Fantasi och kreativitet i barndomen* [Fantasy and Creativity]. Göteborg: Daidalos.

5 Conceptual and contextual intersubjectivity for affording concept formation in children's play

Marilyn Fleer

Introduction

> [T]he commitment to play in education settings has always been strong on ideology and rhetoric and weak, or at least problematic, in practice (Bennett et al. 1997). This in part reflects tensions between play as natural developmental activity, and play as intentional educational activity (Frost et al. 2005; Sutton-Smith 1997; Van Hoorn et al. 2002).
>
> (Wood 2008: 6)

Much of the research into the nature of play within the pre-school period has been defined in relation to some internal process (natural development) (see Vygotsky 1966; Gaskins 2007), or in relation to some external intentional activity (educational) (Sachs et al. 1984; Leseman et al. 2001; De Haan 2005; Hakkarainen 2006). In Western communities, Cartesian logic underpins how many professionals, researchers, curriculum writers and policy developers think about their work (Latour 2003). Few have theorized play in ways which treat the internal and the social world as inseparable (van Oers 1999).

Vygotsky (1966) put forward a dialectical view of play, where psychological functioning and external activity mutually constituted each other. Contrary to popular belief, he argued against an intellectualization of the concept of play, suggesting that the cognitive dimensions of play could not be separated out from the affective dimensions of play (Gaskins and Miller 2008; see also Levykh 2008 for a related discussion of emotions and ZPD). He also argued that development in play could not be removed from the relations between internal psychological functioning and external activity. This dialectical approach to play provides an important alternative reading of play (see also Bodrova 2008) that goes beyond the dualism of a natural developmental view or a purely intentional educational play pedagogy (Wood 2008).

In this chapter, empirical evidence from a study which investigated play and learning in relation to the reciprocity between everyday thinking and scientific thinking (or schooled academic concepts) during playful encounters in early childhood centres is presented, with a view to better understanding how concept formation for 4- and 5-year-old children is supported (or not) during play. Due to space constraints, it has not been possible to present a full discussion of all the related concepts of affect, motives and imitation, necessary for realizing a cultural-historical view of play (see Fleer, in press for this broader theoretical discussion). However, a brief discussion is given of Vygotsky's (1966, 1987) work on concept formation and play.

Concept formation

According to Vygotsky (1987), concept formation should be thought about at two levels – at an everyday level and a scientific or academic level. At the everyday level, concepts are learned as a result of interacting directly with the world – developing intuitive understandings of how to do things, such as mixing cooking ingredients into a bowl, and placing the contents into the oven to cook. These are important everyday concepts about how the world works (such as rules, expectations or social roles). At this level, children may not know the science behind their actions. For instance, it is unlikely that a 4-year-old child will have knowledge of the chemistry associated with applying heat to substances when cooking or the density of everyday cooking material. At the scientific or academic level, Vygotksy argued that concepts are introduced to children through some form of instruction. That is, concepts are explicitly examined or taught to children. However, when these concepts are introduced to children away from the child's everyday experiences, he argued that they are disembedded and hold little meaning for children.

Vygotsky (1987) suggested that everyday concepts and scientific concepts should be thought of as being dialectically related to each other, and that everyday contexts lay important foundations for learning scientific or school-based concepts. Developing everyday concepts in the context of children's everyday world is important for living, but it is also important for making sense of scientific ideas. Everyday experiences and the everyday concepts that are learned through these experiences lay the foundations for scientific learning; in the same way as scientific concepts learned at school pave the way for thinking differently about everyday concepts. However, these two processes must be contextually and conceptually related. Thinking consciously about scientific concepts while in an everyday context sets up an opportunity for transforming everyday practice. That is, children can act and think differently in everyday life when they have conceptual understanding.

Hedegaard and Chaiklin (2005) suggest that the most powerful learning programmes are those where the professional keeps in mind the everyday concepts and the scientific concepts when planning for learning, a procedure which they describe as the *double move* in teaching. The concept of a double move in pedagogical practice in play-based programmes is useful for thinking about how teachers advance *shared sustained thinking* (Siraj-Blatchford 2009). Through a double move, the teacher first of all determines the everyday practices and concepts that children build as their own personal knowledge. Teacher knowledge of children's everyday concepts and contexts is important because it is through this that they can connect conceptually with children, in order to frame learning experiences and conversations with children during play and to afford scientific concept formation. However, the concepts should not just be conscious to the teacher, but they should also be conscious to the child.

Consciousness of play activity

Consciousness of concepts as discussed by Vygotsky in relation to play is a very important idea. Vygotsky (1966: 7–8) argued that consciousness 'originally arises from action', while action is defined as someone being a participant in everyday life or as the child's imitation of everyday activities. Vygotsky (1966: 9) argued that 'What passes unnoticed by the child in real life becomes a rule of behaviour in play.' In other words, cultural rules and concepts enacted in real life without children explicitly being aware of them (such as interpsychological functioning) can be actively considered by children when they play (supporting intrapsychological functioning) (see Vygotsky 1997). In discussing a study by Scully, Vygotsky gives the example of two children who in real life are sisters, and who pretend to be sisters in their play. In order to play at being sisters they must follow the rules of how sisters interact together and through this they make conscious the concept of 'sisterhood'. Vygotsky (1966: 9) offers this as evidence that 'there is no such thing as play without rules and the child's particular attitude toward them' and that only 'actions which fit these rules are acceptable to the play situation'.

As Vygotsky (1966) further noted, children are not free to play in whatever way they wish. Everyday life determines and frames how play may occur. Shared understandings of these rules in play have been shown to be systematically communicated (see also Göncü 1997). For instance, long-standing research (Bretherton 1984) has shown how metacommunicative strategies ensure that play partners build shared intentions during play, and through this add to the evolving play scripts. Shared intentions enacted through play have also been identified by van Oers (2009) in the Netherlands. Particular forms of communication (originally theorized by Vygotsky) known as *predicates* demonstrate how through shared meaning, children use an abbreviated form of speaking because the rules for everyday life which are being played out are well understood between the play partners. However, unlike traditional developmental theories of play, which would suggest that play is internally driven, a cultural-historical perspective would show that the rules of everyday life and the child's experiences of everyday practice shape how play is enacted.

The concepts reviewed in this section about the nature of play, governed by rules, and generating conceptual consciousness through situated action, provide important directions for studying play. However, we know very little about what kinds of conditions generate the particular kinds of concepts in play that are valued in particular communities.

Study design

Research focus

The study sought to examine the reciprocity between everyday thinking and scientific thinking (or schooled academic concepts) during playful encounters in early childhood centres, with a view to better understanding how concept formation for 4- and 5-year-old children is supported during play. Although concept formation can relate to many cognate areas, in this study the focus of attention was on Western science concepts and play within a European heritage community.

A group of 24 pre-school children (14 boys and 10 girls, aged from 4 years 4 months to 5 years 5 months, and with a mean age of 4 years 11 months) participated in the study. All the children were from European heritage families. The staff were briefed on the aims of the research. The focus of attention for the play programme in the rural centre was *materials and their properties*, and data were gathered through a series of measures as described here.

Video recordings

All the children were video-taped over four school weeks during their free-play time (a total of 15 days). A total of ten pre-school sessions were video recorded, resulting in a total of 60 pages of field notes, 220 centre-based photos and eight hours of video data of the play activities of the children.

Family interviews

Five families were given disposable cameras and asked to take photographs of everyday experiences that the children engaged in at home and in the community which they thought related in some way to science (a total of 65 family-based photographs were taken). One member of each family was interviewed about the photographs to see if they saw any links between the home and centre contexts in relation to science. These interviews were video-taped and transcribed. Most interviews lasted 20 minutes.

Staff interviews

The staff were interviewed five times during additional field trips (each session lasting up to two hours) about the centre programme in relation to the science they were introducing to the children in the centre through play. The staff were also asked to view the family photographs and to comment on any connections between the home and the centre they knew about, planned for, or could see in the photographs.

Organization of the video-data and categories used for analysis

All the video-tapes were categorized into play segments. Play segments where the theme of the play appeared to begin were noted and where it ended was also noted. Endings tended to be where the play theme changed (such as water play or baby play). Play themes were recorded as occurring across space (e.g. different parts of the centre) and time (e.g. on subsequent days). Coding specifically focused on everyday concepts and scientific concepts being played out by children; pedagogical practices which afforded the connections between everyday concepts and scientific concepts; and teacher knowledge of science concepts (see methodological paper by Fleer 2008, for full details of coding schedule).

Findings: conceptual consciousness in play

One example is given to illustrate the major findings of this study in relation to the significance of play as a pedagogical tool for supporting children's learning and development in the pre-school years in European heritage communities.

Generating narratives from everyday life as a imaginary situation

A group of three girls (Jayde, Lana and Freya) are inside a wooden boat which is within the outdoor area of a rural pre-school located near a fishing port. The teacher and the assistant teacher have been running a pre-school programme involving coloured water, plastic containers, tubes, funnels and a series of bottles with pump action dispensers. Many of the children are in the outdoor area funnelling coloured water. The teacher has recorded in her programme that she is teaching science using materials which will facilitate 'potion play'. The assistant teacher is inside working with a group of children on an art activity and the teacher is moving equipment around the outdoor area to support the children's 'potion play'. The three girls now move outside of the boat and cluster around a bottle of red coloured water which has a pump action dispenser, several spoons and a soft toy (Humpty Dumpty). The group of three girls work together and generate a play script in which they dispense medicine to Humpty Dumpty who has fallen off the wall.

Jayde takes a lead in the play, initiating the play script about Humpty Dumpty by announcing, 'He [Humpty] fell off the wall again and this is a girl Humpty.' Five girls are now surrounding the soft toy. Lana responds by picking up Humpty, sitting the soft toy on the seat again saying 'Humpty fell off the wall again.' Freya moves closer and picks up a spoon, places it under the dispenser of the coloured water bottle and says, 'Wait, I'll spray it, I have to spray it.' She fills the spoon with red liquid from the bottle. Jayde says in response, 'Oh hi ah, Humpty Dumpty.' Another child joins the group saying, 'Hello, how are you today?' to no one in particular. All the children look up at her, and then turn back to the Humpty Dumpty lying on the seat. Freya passes the spoon to Jayde, saying, 'Here you go.' The children dispense a spoon of red liquid to Humpty. Another child moves forward and says, 'Ah, let me see.' She touches Humpty Dumpty's arm and says, 'Touch it here.' Jayde says, 'Yes, he's dead, he's dead, I knew he, he's dead.'

In this play scenario the group of children bring together the well-known narrative of 'Humpty Dumpty' and their everyday understandings of medicine. Their play script focuses on 'healing Humpty Dumpty who has fallen off the wall'. Potions for these children are not about materials and their properties to be gleaned through mixing (e.g. density of substances), but rather about medicine and caring for people in the community. This play example is not illustrative of the conceptual focus in science that the teacher had hoped for or had assumed would be generated.

In this particular centre, the teacher has a clear view of how learning should be framed for children. She believes that the materials she provides should suggest the plot of the play, and therefore generate the learning for children. In the interview, she stated:

There's children coming out and in [of play] ... when[ever] they want ... I really liked the independence ... I *did not set* up one thing ... the children did it all themselves ... and *I was really pleased* with *that because I just think people set things up too much for the children.*

(Interview with staff)

The teacher, through providing a range of materials, did seek to generate scientific learning through play. Through organizing the theme of 'potions' she provided opportunities for the children to mix substances so that they could learn about how materials behave and how they do or do not mix. This was her learning intention. Her pedagogical approach was to allow the materials to do 'the teaching' of the scientific concepts. This is not an unusual view of learning pedagogy in early childhood education. It is also not unusual in science education, as a discovery learning approach also seeks to allow children to focus on discovering the learning concepts through 'playing with the materials/equipment' (Karpov 2005). However, as Vygotsky has argued 'it is vital to discover exactly what this activity does for development, i.e., how the imaginary situation can assist in the child's development' (1966: 9). As the teacher hoped, the materials scattered around the pre-school did indeed 'suggest possibilities' for the children's play. The children generated an imaginary situation where the spoons and coloured water (potions) were used to medicate Humpty who of course kept 'falling off the wall' (as the rhyme suggests) and who required continual medical assistance. The plungers were suitable for dispensing medicine, and the coloured water in the bottles was ideal for representing medicine. The children's play did focus on the materials within the bottles, but it did not lead to thinking about mixing the substances.

The play that resulted allowed the children to follow the rules for 'giving and receiving medicine' as the children would have experienced it in their own lives. As Vygotsky argued 'there is no such thing as play without rules and the child's particular attitude toward them' (1966: 9). The children used the known narrative of 'Humpty Dumpty' to collectively build the play script. The addition of the line: 'Humpty fell off the wall again', allowed all the children to participate in administering medication. It signalled to all the players that the repetition of medicating Humpty was possible in this game. This additional action statement allowed the play to continue. However, the additional action statement sat within the predetermined play script which was an imitation of administering medicine in everyday life through the imaginary and known rhyme of 'Humpty Dumpty'. Clearly 'only actions which fit these rules are acceptable to the play situation' (Vygotsky 1966: 9).

In keeping with the teacher's philosophy, the materials alone provided the stimulus for the play. The children generated their own play scripts, and the teacher did not participate in the children's play. The imaginary situation that resulted allowed the children to explore relevant daily activities through play, as Vygotsky suggested (1966: 9): 'what passes unnoticed by the child in real life become a rule of behaviour in play.' Through administering medicine the children were coming to understand the actions performed by adults as they gave medication to their children. They were consciously exploring the rules of 'being compliant' as you receive your medication, and through this 'getting better' and being ready to 'fall off the wall again', so that the play could continue. The play activity clearly held, and generated, motives (Leontiev 1978) for the children. It is also a real example of the kind of imaginary play that stems from children's everyday lives, where taking medicine is usually unpleasant, but a necessary part of life with rules and expectations that could be imitated (Vygotsky 1997) by the children in their play. Vygotsky stated:

> I think that wherever there is an imaginary situation in play there are rules. Not rules which are formulated in advance and which change during the course of play, but rules stemming from the imaginary situation. Therefore to imagine that a child can behave in an imaginary situation without rules, i.e., as he behaves in a real situation, is simply impossible.
>
> (1966: 10)

The rules of the imaginary situation framed the play activity of the children. The narrative did not lend itself to consciously exploring the mixing of substances. That would have required an additional story line to be introduced (e.g. this medicine is not working, we need to make our own medicine). Because the teacher's philosophy was framed within a non-interventionist role, it is unlikely that this particular play activity would have moved towards the mixing of substances without new directions being provided. The narrative within the play framed what actions were possible by the children, and through following those particular rules of play, children's thinking was forged in particular directions.

Discussion

It was shown in the study reported in this chapter, that the children were furthering their everyday understandings of 'medicine and caring' and were not conceptually engaged with the concepts that the teacher had planned. This finding works against the belief that free play can be effectively used as a pedagogical tool in early childhood education for furthering concept formation. In essence, the concepts that the teacher had imagined would be considered by the children during their play with the materials she had provided, were *conceptually disembedded* from the practices and the imaginary situation being played out by the children. This is an important finding for early childhood educators interested in play as a pedagogical tool for furthering concept formation.

The findings of this study also suggest that for concept formation to occur in the way that the teacher had intended, a different pedagogical framing would be needed. In this study, had the teacher framed the introduction of the materials with a particular purpose (rather than letting the children work it out for themselves), the children would have been more focused on the intentions of the learning activity. The findings suggest that pedagogical framing needs to be both conceptual and contextual. If the teacher wished a particular kind of conceptual engagement to happen through the materials, then the pedagogical framing needed to occur *before* the children generated their own imaginary situation. This finding points to the need for a better theoretical view of play and a more finely grained model of play as a pedagogical tool for furthering children's concept formation.

Hedegaard's work is helpful for solving the theoretical problem that has arisen in this study. When drawing upon her concept of a double move, it becomes immediately evident that teachers who wish to use play as a pedagogical tool for concept formation need to determine both the children's everyday concepts and their contexts, and the scientific concepts that they wish to introduce. As Vygotsky showed, children's play can make visible their experiences of their world, and lend some insights into the everyday concepts they have acquired as they interact with others. What is important here is that the teacher should *read the children's play context* and through this generate *contextual intersubjectivity*. When a teacher has contextual intersubjectivity, s/he can more easily determine what might be a motivating activity (Leontiev 1978) to conceptually engage children in order to explore a particular scientific concept.

For instance, in the play vignette discussed earlier, the teacher could expand on the imaginary situation generated by the children, through introducing a new story line, such as, 'The medicine is not working on Humpty Dumpty, let's research what we need to do, and make our own.' Followed by, 'We have to know about mixing medicines (substances). What can we find out?' In this theorization, we note that the children and the teacher can enact new practices together through play because they have also achieved *conceptual intersubjectivity*. That is, the teacher and the children are both acting and thinking with the same imaginative act in mind or are participating and thinking within the same activity.

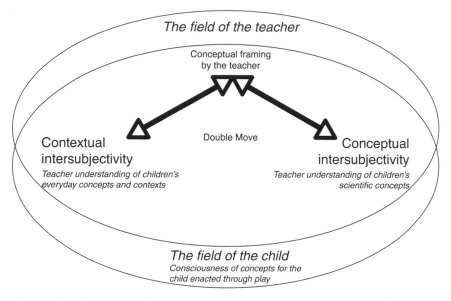

Figure 5.1 A model of teacher conceptual and contextual intersubjectivity in play.

When this occurs, it is possible for the teacher to move in and out of the imaginary situation.

This theorization is represented as a model and is shown in Figure 5.1. This model makes explicit the role of the teacher in play when new scientific concepts are being introduced by the teacher within children's play scripts (see Fleer, in press for a further elaboration of this model). This model has not been developed to explain other forms of development that result from valuable play experiences which are focused only on the children's play agenda.

Conclusion

For too long we have assumed that the leading activity in children is play (Kravtsov and Kravtsova 2009), and we have not clearly explicated what this means when we use 'play' as a 'pedagogical tool' for supporting conceptual learning. The study reported in this chapter points to the problems that arise when we do not have a sufficiently robust understanding of the conceptual development of children during play, or a theoretical model to explain conceptual development during play. It also demonstrates the significance of the dialectical relations between the mediating role of the teacher and the child's lived social world. Vygotsky's work on everyday concepts and scientific concepts (Vygotsky 1987), his writings on consciousness of concepts through play (Vygotsky 1966), and Hedegaard's concept of a double move, are useful for theorizing how concept formation occurs during play. These psychological concepts give greater insight into how play is generated and how it can be used as a pedagogical tool for supporting learning in the early years. With this new theoretical framing, it is possible to see the importance of conceptual and contextual intersubjectivity on the part of the teacher. The model of conceptual and contextual intersubjectivity allows teachers to more purposefully understand how play as a leading activity in European heritage communities leads to conceptual development in pre-school aged children.

Acknowledgements

Australian Research Council (Discovery) funding provided the resources for the study reported in this chapter. Dick Gunstone was the co-researcher named on the application. However, due to personal circumstances he was unable to contribute to the part of the study reported in this chapter. Importantly, it is acknowledged that Avis Ridgway made an enormous contribution to the project through acting as the main field officer for this study. Carol Fleer provided specialist expertise to the project through transcribing video and audiotapes. The time given by the pre-school staff, children and their families is also acknowledged.

References

Bodrova, E. (2008) Make-believe play versus academic skills: a Vygotskian approach to today's dilemma of early childhood education, *European Early Childhood Education Research Journal*, 16(3): 357–69.

Bretherton, I. (1984) *Symbolic Play: The Development of Social Understanding*. New York: Academic Press.

De Haan, D. (2005) Social pretend play: potentials and limitations of literacy development, *European Early Childhood Education Research Journal*, 13(1): 41–55.

Fleer, M. (2008) Interpreting research protocols: the institutional perspective, in M. Hedegaard and M. Fleer (eds) *Studying Children. A Cultural-Historical Approach*. Maidenhead: Open University Press, pp. 65–87.

Fleer, M. (in press) Concepts in play: a cultural-historical view of early learning and development. Cambridge University Press.

Gaskins, S. (2007) The cultural relativity of Vygotsky's theory of play, paper presented at the Invited Symposium on Play and Culture, International Society of Cultural Activity Research, July, Seville, Spain.

Gaskins, S. and Miller, P.J. (2008) The cultural roles of emotions in pretend play, paper presented at the International Society for Culture, and Activity Research, San Diego, USA, September.

Göncü, A. (1997) Development of intersubjectivity in social pretend play, in M. Woodhead, D. Faulkner and K. Littleton (eds) *Cultural Worlds of Early Childhood*, London: Routledge and Open University Press, pp. 117–32.

Hakkarainen, P. (2006) Learning and development in play, in J. Einarsdottir and J.T. Wagner (eds) *Nordic Childhoods and Early Education: Philosophy, Research, Policy, and Practice in Denmark, Finland, Iceland, Norway and Sweden*. Charlotte, NC: Information Age Publishing, pp. 183–222.

Hedegaard, M. and Chaiklin, S. (2005) *Radical-Local Teaching and Learning: A Cultural-Historical Approach*. Aarhus: Aarhus University Press.

Karpov, Y.V. (2005) *The Neo-Vygotskian Approach to Child Development*. New York: Cambridge University Press.

Kravtsov, G. and Kravtsova, E. (2009) Cultural-historical psychology in the practice of education, in M. Fleer, M. Hedegaard and J. Tudge (eds) *Childhood Studies and the Impact of Globalization: Policies and Practices at Global and Local Levels*. New York: Routledge, pp. 199–210.

Latour, B. (2003) Do you believe in reality? News from the trenches in the science wars, in R.C. Scharff and V. Dusek (eds) *Philosophy of Technology: The Technological Condition. An Anthology*. Oxford: Blackwell.

Leontiev, A.N. (1978) *Activity, Consciousness, and Personality*. Trans. M.J. Hall. Englewood Cliffs, NJ: Prentice-Hall.

Leseman, P.P.M., Rollenberg, L. and Rispens, J. (2001) Playing and working in kindergarten: cognitive co-construction in two educational situations, *Early Childhood Research Quarterly*, 16: 363–84.

Levykh, M.G. (2008) The affective establishment and maintenance of Vygotsky's zone of proximal development, *Educational Theory*, 58(10): 83–102.

Sachs, J., Goldman, J. and Chaille, C. (1984) Planning in pretend play: using language to coordinate narrative development, in A. Pellegrini and T. Yawkey (eds) *The Development of Oral and Written Language in Social Context*. Norwood, NJ: Ablex, pp. 119–28.

Siraj-Blatchford, I. (2009) Quality teaching in the early years, in A. Anning, J. Cullen and M. Fleer (eds) *Early Childhood Education. Society and Culture*. London: Sage, pp. 147–57.

van Oers, B. (1999) Teaching opportunities in play, in M. Hedegaard and J. Lompscher (eds) *Learning, Activity and Development.* Aarhus: Aarhus University Press, pp. 268–89.

van Oers, B. (2009) Developmental education: improving participation in cultural practice, in M. Fleer, M. Hedegaard and J. Tudge (eds) *Childhood Studies and the Impact of Globalization: Policies and Practices at Global and Local Levels.* New York: Routledge, pp. 213–29.

Vygotsky, L.S. (1966) Play and its role in the mental development of the child. *Voprosy psikhologii,* 12(6): 62–76.

Vygotsky, L.S. (1987) Thinking and speech, in L.S. Vygotsky, *The Collected Works of L.S. Vygotsky,* vol. 1, *Problems of General Psychology.* ed. R.W. Rieber and A.S. Carton, trans. N. Minick. New York: Plenum Press, pp. 39–285.

Vygotsky, L.S. (1997) The history of the development of higher mental functions, in L.S. Vygotsky, *The Collected Works of L.S. Vygotsky,* vol. 4, ed. R.W. Rieber, trans. M.H. Hall. New York: Plenum Press.

Wood, E. (2008) Contestation, transformation and re-conceptualisation in early childhood education, in E. Wood (ed.) *The Routledge Reader in Early Childhood Education.* New York: Routledge, pp. 1–18.

6　New maps for old terrain

Creating a postdevelopmental logic of gender and sexuality in the early years

Mindy Blaise

Introduction

Postdevelopmental scholarship has been instrumental in postcolonial and development studies, highlighting issues of power related to global development and rejecting modes of thinking and living produced by modern development (Harris 2008; Peet and Hartwick 2009). They have begun this work by mapping new alignments of power beyond the colonial period. In a similar way, I am aiming to 'map' the new alignments of power along gender and sexuality in the early years. In my work I have used the term postdevelopmentalism to capture a broad set of ideas and practices that aim to question developmental discourses in the field of early childhood education. I first used this term when encouraging teachers to imagine 'queer possibilities in the early childhood classroom' (Blaise 2005: 185). Postdevelopmental pedagogies that teachers might use for supporting such possibilities include challenging children's categorical and fixed thinking about gender and sexuality, supporting children's interpersonal skills, and unpacking discursive practices with children. Since then, I have explored how teachers might enact proactive rather than reactive pedagogies towards children's sex, gender and sexuality in the early childhood classroom (Blaise 2009a). Being proactive requires teachers to think differently about childhood and teaching/learning,[1] and to allow children opportunities to explore their own understandings of gender and sexuality. Failing to acknowledge children's skills at negotiating gender and sexuality discourses limits how well we can understand childhood, power and identities.

Taking a proactive stance in the field of early childhood education is not easy. Traditionally, early childhood teachers have drawn on ideas that often require them to focus on universals, progression, certainty and knowable outcomes (Cannella 1997; Dahlberg et al. 2007; Burman 2008). In addition, asking teachers to be proactive when the field is mostly reactive towards children's gender and sexuality (Tobin 1997) might be considered unrealistic. Expecting teachers to think in radically different ways about teaching/learning and childhood requires much more than idealistic and hopeful thinking. Instead, a different logic is needed for understanding gender and sexuality in the field of early childhood and for inventing pedagogies that go against the taming, predicting, and evaluating of teaching/learning and childhood (Dahlberg and Moss 2009).

This chapter expands postdevelopmentalism by providing several (re)readings of data generated from a year-long ethnographic case study of children's play (Blaise 2005) in order to map out a new logic for understanding gender and sexuality in the early childhood classroom. This will be done by first conducting a queer (re)reading of play by using Butler's theory of gender performativity ([1990] 1999, 1993, 2004) to illustrate how children construct and 'do' gender. Second, (re)readings of play using the Deleuzian/Guattarian concept of 'assemblages of desire' ([1984] 2004, [1987] 2004) will develop a different logic about young children's play and prompt an awareness of the degree to which gender and sexuality are a part of children's everyday life. This (re)analysis is part of my own postdevelopmental practice. Rather than assuming that the original 'findings' were complete and finished, I am curious to see how using Butler and Deleuzian/Guattarian concepts for (re)reading data might produce different and unexpected understandings of gender and sexuality in the early childhood classroom. In addition, it is one way to develop analytical tools useful for supporting the new logic required by a postdevelopmental framework. Inspired by the innovative microanalysis begun by Renold and Ringrose (2008), who have brought together Butler's work with that of Deleuze and Guattari, in order to analyze how the cracks and movements within the heterosexual matrix are already happening around us, this chapter attempts a similar task.

Rethinking reality

As others have argued (i.e. Colebrook 2002), some of Deleuze and Guattari's concepts are useful for encouraging a different way of thinking about reality. Rethinking reality means no longer focusing on the universals, progression, certainty and knowable outcomes of child development. In regards to children's gender and sexuality, this kind of logic means not concentrating on children developing into sexual beings, or determining if their play is based on gender norms. Instead, a Deleuzian/Guattarian-inspired reasoning works to create new values, desires or images of what it is to be and to think.

Regarding children's gender and sexuality, the logic of developmentalism is fundamentally static and does little to help us understand the complexities of children's gender identities. On the other hand, Butler ([1990] 1999, 1993, 2004) and Deleuze and Guattari ([1984] 2004, [1987] 2004) inspire us to think differently about gender and sexuality, by rethinking the relationship between sex, gender and sexuality and by exploring the productiveness of desire. The concepts and ideas put forward by these philosophers are useful for expanding the ideas of postdevelopmentalism. A postdevelopmental logic is a different style of thinking that comes with a different philosophical vocabulary (Colebrook 2005) that is unfamiliar within the field of early childhood education. This vocabulary includes terms and concepts such as *performativity, intensities, flows, connections, desire, lines of flight* and *becoming*, to name a few. Each of these concepts opens up a radically different way of thinking about teaching/learning and childhood. As Grosz (1994) and Colebrook (2002) remind us, entry into this Deleuzian/Guattarian framework is challenging and at times can be confronting, confusing, weird and counterintuitive. Although their logic allows for movements and connections of ideas and understandings in ways that at first might seem out of place in early childhood, this style of thinking has the potential to produce a different reality that can transform practice.

Rethinking reality urges teachers, researchers and others to wonder how children are collectively experimenting with gender. In order to do this, teachers will need to rethink their own realities, forcing them to tear apart the assumptions they have about childhood and teaching/learning. Working from this stance, teachers can become interested in the intensity and unpredictability of children's gender play, rather than being concerned or anxious. Instead of having a clear endpoint in mind about how children should be doing gender, a postdevelopmental logic encourages teachers to harness children's productivity and inventiveness in ways that allow for experimentation with doing 'girl' and doing 'boy'. One strategy that might be useful for rethinking reality, including reconfiguring the dichotomies and cause and effect relationships that ground Western thought, can be accomplished by rethinking how we understand gender (Grosz 1994).

Rethinking gender

Queer theory rejects the idea that gender is simply an expression of sex, or that gender and sex are biological or natural traits that reside inside us. Foucault (1978) argues that sexuality is neither a fact of life nor something that is natural. Instead, sexuality is considered a constructed category of experience, which has historical, social and cultural origins. By re-examining the relationships between sex, gender and sexuality, it becomes possible to question the belief that children are born with a fixed gender or sexual identity. Butler ([1990] 1999) contends that gender is the process through which different human cultures make sense of sexual identity. Her understanding of gender as performative is the idea that a gendered identity is produced only as it is enacted. At first, this conceptualization of gender performativity might seem similar to a gender socialization perspective where girls and boys are learning (and doing) certain gendered practices. Gender performativity rethinks the sex–gender–sexuality relationship in two important ways. First, it rejects the assumption that sex is seen as prior to gender or the common-sense logic that believes there must be a time when the sexed subject is un-gendered. Second, it contests the idea that there is a 'doer behind the deed' (Butler [1990] 1999: 34) because gender identity is produced through specific bodily practices, gestures, actions and declarations. Gender identity is an *effect* of doing gender, rather than a cause. For Butler, gender is not a noun, but a verb, because it is always doing. Butler also believe that '[g]ender is the repeated stylization of the body, a set of repeated acts within a highly rigid regulatory frame that congeal over time to produce the appearance of substance of a natural sort of being' ([1990] 1999: 45). Following Butler's logic, by acting out or performing gender, children are making sense of and producing what it means to be 'girl' and/or 'boy'.

Queer theory is concerned with heterosexual discourses and how they influence the social construction of gender (Warner 1993). When gender is viewed as a social activity, performed in normative ways, it becomes impossible to understand gender except through what Butler calls the 'heterosexual matrix' ([1990] 1999: 6). This matrix should be thought of as a specific and regulatory structure that produces femininity, masculinity and heterosexuality as intelligible. From this perspective, the concept of femaleness or maleness becomes meaningless in the absence of heterosexuality. Heterosexuality, as an institutionalized set of power relations, is enforced through rewards for appropriate gendered behaviours and you run the risk of being marginalized if you choose to deviate from conventional ways of being either a 'girl' or a 'boy'. This understanding of gender assumes that heterosexuality functions to produce regulatory notions of femininity and masculinity. Particular forms of femininity are produced in relation to particular, and highly valued, forms of masculinity. These critiques of heterosexism are not attacks on specific heterosexual practices, but rather on the discourses of heterosexuality and how they have become embedded in our thoughts and everyday actions (Rich 1980; Butler [1990] 1999; Sedgwick 1990). Finally, queer theory discloses how heterosexual practices have been normalized and thus have become instruments of power, positioning heterosexual relationships as the most valued and acceptable form of sexuality.

There is a growing body of early childhood research that utilizes queer theory for understanding the significance of heteronormativity in children's play (i.e. Boldt 1997; Blaise 2005, 2009a; Taylor and Richardson 2005; DePalma and Atkinson 2007, 2009; Robinson and Davies 2007). In particular, these studies have used Butler's conceptualization of gender performativity ([1990] 1999, 1993, 2004) and how hegemonic gender practices are produced through the heterosexual matrix ([1990] 1999), to understand the ways in which children are engaging with heterosexual gender norms for the purpose of constituting gender in early childhood. The year-long ethnographic case study I conducted with 5- and 6-year-olds (Blaise 2005) intentionally applied feminist poststructuralism and queer theory to understand children's play. 'Findings' showed that children do know about gender and (hetero)sexuality and were drawing from gender discourses in order to produce and regulate femininities and masculinities in their kindergarten classroom.

Gender-bending

Gender-bending is a term I and others have used to describe children's non-normative gender behaviours and play (Boldt 1997; Blaise 2005). Drawing from my previous qualitative case study of young children's gender and sexuality (Blaise 2005), I write about a girl named Madison who was a gender-bender because she would often pretend to be either a teenage 'boy' or a 'boy' puppy. Video data and observational field notes document these forms of play. In addition, small-group audio-recorded discussions capture Madison and her girl friends talking about their reasons for playing and doing 'boy', as well as why some of the girls refuse to take part in gender-bending (Blaise 2005).

The following vignette is part of a longer video transcript that includes two girls, Madison and Anne, playing at the dramatic play centre with a boy named Liam. The total time spent playing was 30 minutes. Madison spends most of this time using large blocks to build herself a bedroom, including a large raised bed.

    Madison: (Enters through the doorway she has built, on her knees, with markers [textas], masking tape and construction paper.) Mom, stop messing up my bed! That's my bed. That I built. It's sleep time.

    Anne: (Slowly pulls a long necklace and bracelet out of a jewellery box, holding the necklace high up in the air. She begins swinging the necklace back and forth.) I bought this ... for a present for y::o::u (in a sing-song voice).

Madison: Yuck! (Grabbing the jewellery out of Anne's hand, throwing the bracelet into the kitchen area) I'm not a girl. I am **not** a girl! These are girl things and I don't wear them. (Turns and walks out of the dramatic play area. She returns in a few minutes, after Anne leaves her bedroom.) Oh, I need to make my bed. (Takes a scarf and drapes it over her bed. Folds another scarf into a pillow.)

This exchange between Madison and Anne shows how young children are exploring gendered power relationships within the heterosexual matrix, but with a slight twist. That is, while Madison plays 'boy', she experiences power in relation to Anne who is playing the mother, which is usually the most powerful role. Using the jewellery as a way of engaging with Madison is a strategy that might have interested other girls in the classroom, but not Madison. Instead of being tantalized by the jewellery, Madison dismisses these accessories and their associated femininity when she loudly exclaims that she is '... not a girl!' and throws the bracelets into the kitchen area, saying they are 'yuck'. 'Doing' or playing this kind of girl is not an option that Madison chooses and her actions can be read as marginalizing particular forms of hyper-femininity that many girls in her class value and find pleasurable. Although Madison might be experiencing power in her play as a 'boy', in this particular vignette, Anne does not. This is an intriguing moment because it contradicts the literature highlighting the power that some girls find when accessing the storylines of 'mother' through their play (i.e. Walkerdine 1990; MacNaughton 1995). In this case, Anne is not experiencing power as the mother. As 'mommy', Anne is momentarily powerless and unable to imagine how to repair the tearing of the heterosexual matrix that Madison's gender-bending causes. On the one hand, Madison's gender-bending can be seen as an example of how she is challenging the heterosexual matrix, showing the permeability of the matrix (Butler 2006). Although Madison's gender-bending might be a moment when the heterosexual matrix is ruptured, the identities of both Madison (as a boy) and Anne (as a mother) are still governed by the matrix. At first glance, one could argue that the coherence of what it means to be a girl is challenged when Madison gender-bends, yet another reading questions whether her play is disrupting the gender binaries of 'femininity' and 'masculinity' at all, because she and Anne are both enacting normative gender roles.

   Although Butler's theories of performativity and the heterosexual matrix are useful for understanding how gender is constructed through heteronormativity, they do not provide us with the conceptual tools for making sense of how children might be resisting the matrix. In order to do so a different logic is necessary for understanding reality. Renold and Ringrose (2008) raise important questions about resistance, agency and the heterosexual matrix in their qualitative work with tweens and teenage girls. They turn to Deleuze and Guattari ([1984] 2004, [1987] 2004) for the purpose of mapping girls' resistance to the heterosexual matrix. Inspired by Renold and Ringrose's (2008) work, I am able to see the usefulness of utilizing both Butler and Deleuze and Guattari for developing a postdevelopmental logic. This encourages a different way of thinking about reality and how children become 'girl' and 'boy', without relying on simple cause and effect explanations.

Deleuzian/Guattarian concepts

Gilles Deleuze (1925–95) and Félix Guattari (1930–92) are part of a generation of French poststructuralist thinkers, such as Michel Foucault and Jacques Derrida, whose ideas have been used to rethink subjectivity, knowledge and power. As poststructuralists they were responding to the impossibility of founding knowledge either on experience or on systematic structures. Deleuze and Guattari did not see the impossibility of organizing life around closed structures as problematic. Instead, they saw this as an opportunity to experiment with, invent and create different ways of knowing (Colebrook 2002). Deleuze and Guatarri's intellectual project is an invitation to the field of early childhood to think differently about teaching/learning and childhood.[2]

In recent years this challenge has been taken up by utilizing some Deleuzian/Guattarian concepts (i.e. Dahlberg and Moss 2005; MacNaughton 2005; Mozere 2006; Blaise 2009b; Olsson 2009) to elucidate alternative ways of perceiving teaching/learning and childhood. For example, MacNaughton (2005) worked with a group of early childhood professionals by using the concept of a 'rhizome' to develop a rhizomatic perspective for transforming practice. She argues that a rhizomatic logic provides a more complex understanding of gender and gender stereotypes that do not rely on a simple cause and effect relation. Olsson (2009) conducted a two-year project in Norway, with a group of pre-school teachers who were interested in reconceptualizing their practice. She employs several Deleuzian/Guattarian concepts, including 'assemblages of desire' with pre-school teachers as they attempt to regain movement and experimentation in their practice. Olsson's study is significant because it shows how she and pre-school teachers worked at a practical level with the concept of 'assemblages of desire' to rethink the relation between the individual and society.

In order to craft a postdevelopmental logic that is useful for understanding gender and sexuality beyond a simple cause and effect relationship, the rest of this chapter takes off at different points from those of Olsson (2009) and Renold and Ringrose (2008). The following (re)readings do not aim to provide a 'how to' guide for using postdevelopmental logic – this would go against the spirit of Deleuze and Guattari's work. Instead, it engages with the Deleuzian/Guattarian concept of 'assemblages of desire' to explore different ways one might understand children's gender, sexuality and social reality by 'turn[ing] desire on its head' (Olsson 2009: 141).

Assemblages of desire

'Desire' is one of the central concepts developed by Deleuze and Guattari and can be found across a number of themes in their writing (Ross 2005). Just as their work understood the body as productive and capable, so too is desire seen as active and productive (Grosz 1994). This is a radical departure from the ways in which desire is usually understood. From a psychoanalytic perspective, desire is based on the Oedipus complex and is seen through the concept of 'lacking'. That is, the traditional logic of desire is based on wanting to acquire something that we yearn for or do not have (Deleuze and Guattari [1984] 2004). This logic of lack also presents desire as a fantasy, rather than the production of the real. For Deleuze and Guattari, 'If desire produces, its product is real. If desire is productive, it can only be productive in the real world and can produce only reality' ([1984] 2004: 28).

When desire is thought of as productive, rather than the cause of fantasizing, needing or yearning something, it can be repositioned as an effect (Deleuze and Guattari [1984] 2004). In other words, by presenting desire as a production of reality, lack and need are repositioned not as a cause, but merely as an effect. By turning the cause and effect relationship around, a new and different logic of desire is created. When desire is understood as real and productive, it functions to make new links and connections (between people, ideas, objects, etc.) in ways that we might never have considered. Desire, now viewed as a series of practices, is capable of bringing things, ideas and people together, as well as separating them in order to make new realities. This bringing together and pulling apart plays a significant role in creating new relationships, which then produce new realities.

As a series of practices, desire is neither singular nor holistic. Instead, desire is always assembled, connected to language and bodies, and always comes as 'assemblages of desire'. Assemblages of desire are seen as a series of flows, movements or intensities. It is a concept that allows for parts (individuals) and wholes (societies) to exist as assemblages. As Olsson states, 'You act and live in assemblages, and starting out from *unconscious* desires that you cannot control, you construct assemblages through and with other people' (2009: 177). They are fragments that are able to link together or be pulled apart, over and over again (Deleuze and Guattari [1987] 2004). Assemblages of desire might be an assortment of children's play, or singular moments of play happening across time and space. Assemblages can be influenced by an array of circumstances and actions such as the climate the teacher creates in the classroom, attitudes of class-mates, the weather, the availability of materials, etc. Assemblages of desire are a different way of understanding social reality. In this case, they give texture and dimensionality to the ways in which children are producing gender in the early childhood classroom.

Working within a Deleuzian/Guattarian-inspired postdevelopmental logic, assemblages do not follow a linear or hierarchical order. Instead, they are uncertain, unpredictable and open-ended. Understood as assemblages, it is impossible to predict the outcomes of Madison's play. Instead, the focus is turned towards appreciating what is taking place between Madison and others and how they are caught up in assembled desires. Noticing these in-between movements and flows, rather than the outcomes of play, makes it possible to notice the connections between children and between children and ideas, thus producing reality.

Another way in which assemblages of desire reconfigure cause and effect relationships is that they are not hierarchical. For example, Madi-son's current play would not be considered more advanced or developed than how she played two or four years earlier. This style of thinking challenges linearity, progression and certainty. Instead, assemblages are the *provisional* linkages of elements, fragments and flows. These linkages are unrelated in status and substance. From this stance, assemblages all have the same ontological status (human, nonhuman, animate, inanimate). Children are not positioned as inferior to adults (or animals, objects, emotions, etc.) and play has 'equal' status to other activities. As such, this logic encourages us to radically rethink relationships. Gender-bending is neither better nor worse than any other kind of play. As an assemblage, it is just one of many other assemblages without a set order, and should not cause alarm. Since there is no hierarchy of being or predetermined order to the collection of assemblages, there is also no plan to conform to something 'better'. The logic of assemblages of desire is of endless experimentations, intensities, flows, alignments and realignments. In other words, Madison is not trying to be a particular kind of 'girl' or 'boy' because she is failing in how she currently does 'girl'. Rather, she is inventing and experimenting with others and producing ways to do gender that we might not be able to recognize. Although my reading of Madison's play through the heterosexual matrix was useful for seeing the significance of heteronormativity, defining her play as gender-bending might be limiting, preventing me from seeing the in-betweens or connections and how everyone is caught up in a variety of assemblages of desire.

'But I hate being a girl'

It is centre time, the time of the day when children are able to choose an area of the classroom to play. I have been sitting at the snack table talking with four other children, including a girl named Penny. Madison has been playing at the dramatic play centre, comes to the snack table, sits down and joins our conversation.

Mindy: Madison, what do you like to play when you go to the dramatic play centre?

Madison: Well, I like to play house ... and I pretend that I'm the brother ... the **older** brother.

Mindy: But you're a girl?

Madison: But I hate being a girl.

Mindy: Why?

Madison: Because I just hate being ...

Penny: (Interrupting) But girl is **much** more prettier.

Madison: I just hate being prettier.

Here, Madison publicly announces her desires, proclaiming that she hates being a girl, especially a 'prettier' girl. Through the logic of lack, Madison's claims might be read as a yearning to be something better and different than the girl she is, so she does this by seeing herself as 'the older brother'. A postdevelopmental logic turns this lack around by seeing Madison's desire to do 'boy' as a productive force. In other words, playing 'boy' produces another way of doing gender. While this kind of gender performativity might be unthinkable for some children in the classroom (such as Penny), as an assemblage of desire it could open up new possibilities and connections with others. Madison's repeated statements of hating to be a girl can also be understood as 'intensities', another Deleuzian/Guattarian expression. That is, Madison's passion and energy for doing gender differently bring forth gender-bending. As an assemblage of desire, we are unable to predict the kind of gender Madison's play might produce, but we can reasonably assume that she is deliberately and intensely experimenting with gender.

Boy puppies

Madison did not perform masculinity exclusively as a teenage boy. Video data shows that she also enjoyed being a boy puppy.

> Katy, Kelly, Madison and Theresa are playing in the dramatic play area. Katy is the mother, Kelly and Theresa are sisters, and Madison is a puppy. Katy and Kelly are at the pet shop buying a puppy. Madison is down on the floor on her hands and knees. She is panting like a dog.

> | | |
> |---|---|
> | *Kelly*: | (Petting Madison) I want to buy this little doggy … Mommy, mother … Look at the puppy. |
> | *Katy*: | (Bending down and begins petting Madison) A show puppy! |
> | *Madison*: | Looking up) No, I'm just a little boy puppy. |
> | *Katy*: | (Interrupting) **No** (looking down at Madison) pretend you're a show champion. Do you know what a show champion is? It's a really fun dog, they play a lot … |
> | *Madison*: | (Interrupting) **No**, (looking up at Katy … standing up and facing Katy) I want to be a puppy Dalmatian, a **boy** puppy Dalmatian (gets back down on her hands and knees, starts barking, panting, licking and places both of her hands underneath her chin as if she has paws). |

> For the next 5 minutes, Madison, as a boy puppy, spends her time barking and rescuing Katy and Kelly from their burning house.

Madison's choice to play a boy puppy is an expression of desire and produces yet another reality. Pretending to be the dog is a familiar role in the dramatic play centre. However, it is a role that traditionally does not have a lot of power as it is usually given to a boy and controlled by the girl playing mother. Madison's 'Lassie' version of power is a different way to be a rescuer, without having to resort to being the 'macho' male hero. As a puppy, Madison still gets to experience power as she rescues others, but she is not marginalizing them. As compared to the ways in which Madison played being a teenage boy, this boy puppy play is different. Since romance is not involved in the relationships that Madison has with others while pretending to be a puppy, her play undercuts the heterosexual matrix. Even as a boy puppy, Madison gets to be happy as she barks, licks and is warmly loved. As a series of practices, Madison's boy puppy play allows her to experiment and invent with others new ways of doing gender. Madison's boy puppy play can be thought of as a series of align-ments or realignments with gender, as she is making connections with others while rescuing Katy and Kelly from the fire. This assemblage is pulling apart the heterosexual matrix and creating opportunities or space for doing gender differently.

My desires

It is impossible to deny my desires as a researcher in this study. (Re)visit-ing fieldnotes that I generated during the project allows me to see how these desires were evident during data collection. For instance, fieldnotes show that I made 12 written comments about Madison's gender play. Some of these include:

> Did she really say, 'I'm not a girl! I'm a boy?'
> This is juicy data!
> I **have** to talk to Madison about her play. Why is she pretending to be a boy?
> I wonder who else is a gender-bender? How might I find out?

These written comments show that I had an investment in particular kinds of gender performances that some children performed. I have vivid memories of the excitement I felt when realizing that Madison was pre-tending to be a boy and I was interested in finding out more about this kind of play. This interest, combined with the written comments I made throughout the study make me wonder about my desires and how they can be (re)read as part of an assemblage of desire implicated in Madison's desires. Working from a logic of lack, my research desires would be con-sidered problematic because they show the ways in which I am not an objective researcher. Instead, I am privileging Madison's gender-bending rather than considering all children's play as significant data. My interest in finding out who else is doing this kind of play might be read as an attempt to determine a set of qualities that predict which children are more likely to gender-bend. In addition, my desire to find out why she is pretending to be a boy shows how I am caught up in wanting to 'know' or to unearth a rational explanation for this kind of play.

A postdevelopmental logic (re)reads my research desires as producing new connections with Madison and others who are experimenting with gender. It situates me within the social reality of the classroom and rec-ognizes that individual children do not own the process of producing gender. Instead, gender production is taking place between people, emo-tions, ideas, objects and discourses in the classroom. From this reasoning, my presence in the classroom allows or encourages new assemblages of desire. Research desires can be (re)read as part of a research methodology that puts into motion new relationships between researchers and participants. Referring to the ways in which Deleuze and Guattari ([1984] 2004) see desire as productive, research relationships can be seen as producing reality through the assemblages they create.

Mapping gender and sexuality

Although I have only presented a few assemblages of desire, they highlight how the field of early childhood might engage with a Deleuzian/Guattarian-inspired postdevelopmental logic for understanding gender and sexuality that is not based on the idea of lack. The concept of assemblages of desire, when combined with Butler's ([1990] 1999, 1993, 2004) theory of gender performativity, is useful for understanding how children and adults are collectively producing gender. When seen as assemblages of desire, a more nuanced and textual way for understanding gender becomes possible. Just like Olsson (2009), I have also found assemblages of desire a productive idea. Therefore, mapping assemblages of desire is a useful strategy for recognizing that gender and sexuality are already a part of the social reality of children's lives. These mappings allow us to consider how the processes of gender and sexuality work through the multiple encounters children have in their play with ideas, discourses, objects, emotions and others. While these assemblages can never be complete, they begin a process of mapping gender and sexuality in the early childhood classroom, showing the productive role of desire. For instance, they show how Madison embodied gender and how others engaged with this. These assemblages also show how children are collectively experimenting with gender and sexuality discourses, highlighting how the materials of the dramatic play area are used to produce new gender realities.

Mapping gender and sexuality through assemblages of desires still demands a different logic because assemblages do not present themselves in a linear or hierarchical sequence. Making sense of these assemblages is not about containing children's play in order to determine how or why they are 'doing' gender. Instead, mappings encourage the field to see gender and sexuality as fluid, intense, uncertain and endlessly experimental. Rather than predicting, controlling, moderating, supervising or evaluating children's gender and sexuality, a Deleuzian/Guattarian-inspired logic encourages teachers to focus on desire as the driving force of gender and sexuality and to anticipate play that is full of experimentations, intensities and movements. In doing so, the field will need to invent unique pedagogies that acknowledge gender and sexuality as an ongoing production that children are already a part of. Mappings might be one strategy for helping the field to see the 'old terrain' of the early years in new, exciting and hopeful ways, encouraging teachers and researchers to *work with* children's desires as they invent a range of ways of doing 'girl' and/or 'boy'.

Acknowledgements

I would like to thank Mary Lou Rasmussen and Jessica Ringrose for their support as I engage with unfamiliar ideas and attempt to make them relevant for the early years.

Notes

1. I am deliberately using teaching/learning as a postdevelopmental concept for disrupting the notion that teaching and learning are separate and distinct acts. Teaching/learning recognizes the significance of the complex relationship that exists between teaching and learning.
2. For a thorough discussion regarding the background of Deleuze and Guattari and an overview of their philosophical ideas and intellectual project, see Olsson (2009).

References

Blaise, M. (2005) *Playing it Straight!: Uncovering Gender Discourses in the Early Childhood Classroom*. London: Routledge.

Blaise, M. (2009a) What a girl wants, what a girl needs: responding to sex, gender, and sexuality in the early childhood classroom, *Journal of Research in Childhood Education*, 23(4): 450–60.

Blaise, M. (2009b) Revolutionising practice by doing early childhood politically: the Revolutionary Planning Group, in S. Edwards and J. Nuttall (eds) *Professional Learning in Early Childhood Settings*. Rotterdam: Sense Publishers, pp. 27–47.

Boldt, G. (1997) Sexist and heterosexist responses to gender bending in an elementary classroom, in J. Tobin (ed.) *Making a Place for Pleasure in Early Childhood Education*. New Haven, CT: Yale University Press, pp. 188–213.

Burman, E. (2008) *Deconstructing Developmental Psychology*, 2nd edn. New York: Routledge.

Butler, J. ([1990] 1999) *Gender Trouble: Feminism and the Subversion of Identity*, 2nd edn. New York: Routledge.

Butler, J. (1993) *Bodies that Matter: On the Discursive Limits of 'Sex'*. New York: Routledge.

Butler, J. (2004) *Undoing Gender.* London: Routledge.

Butler, J. (2006) Response, *British Journal of Sociology of Education,* 27(4): 529–34.

Cannella, G.S. (1997) *Deconstructing Early Childhood Education: Social Justice and Revolution.* New York: Peter Lang Publishing.

Colebrook, C. (2002) *Gilles Deleuze.* London: Routledge.

Colebrook, C. (2005) Introduction, in A. Parr (ed.) *The Deleuze Dictionary.* Edinburgh: Edinburgh University Press, pp. 1–6.

Dahlberg, G. and Moss, P. (2005) *Ethics and Politics in Early Childhood.* London: Routledge.

Dahlberg, G. and Moss, P. (2009) Foreword, in L.M. Olsson, *Movement and Experimentation in Young Children's Learning: Deleuze and Guattari in Early Childhood Education.* New York: Routledge, pp. xiii–xxvii.

Dahlberg, G., Moss, P. and Pence, A. (2007) *Beyond Quality in Early Childhood Education and Care: Languages of Evaluation.* London: Routledge.

Deleuze, G. and Guattari, F. ([1984] 2004) *Anti-Oedipus: Capitalism and Schizophrenia,* trans. R. Hurley, M. Seem and H.R. Lane. London: Continuum.

Deleuze, G. and Guattari, F. ([1987] 2004) *A Thousand Plateaus: Capitalism and Schizophrenia,* trans. B. Massumi. London: Continuum.

DePalma, R. and Atkinson, E. (2007) Exploring gender identity: queering heteronormativity, *International Journal of Equity and Innovation in Early Childhood (Special Queer Issue),* 5(2): 64–82.

DePalma, R. and Atkinson, E. (eds) (2009) *Interrogating Heteronormativity in Primary Schools: The Work of the No Outsiders Project.* Stoke-on-Trent: Trentham Books Limited.

Foucault, M. (1978) *The History of Sexuality: An Introduction* (vol. 1). New York: Pantheon Books.

Grosz, E. (1994) *Volatile Bodies: Toward a Corporeal Feminism.* Bloomington, IN: Indiana University Press.

Harris, L.M. (2008) Modernizing the nation: postcolonialism, postdevelopmentalism, and ambivalent spaces of difference in southeastern Turkey, *Geoforum,* 39(5): 1698–701.

MacNaughton, G. (1995) *The Power of Mum!: Power and Gender at Play.* Watson: Australia Early Childhood Association.

MacNaughton, G. (2005) *Doing Foucault in Early Childhood Studies: Applying Poststructural Ideas.* London: Routledge.

Mozere, L. (2006) What's the trouble with identity? Practices and theories from France, *Contemporary Issues in Early Childhood,* 7(2): 109–18.

Olsson, L.M. (2009) *Movement and Experimentation in Young Children's Learning: Deleuze and Guattari.* Hoboken, NJ: Routledge.

Peet, R. and Hartwick, E. (2009) *Theories of Development: Contentions, Arguments, Alternatives,* 2nd edn. New York: Guildford Publishers.

Renold, E. and Ringrose, J. (2008) Regulation and rupture: mapping tween and teenage girls' resistance to the heterosexual matrix, *Feminist Theory*, 9(3): 313–38.

Rich, A. (1980) Compulsory heterosexuality and the lesbian existence, *Signs: Journal of Women in Culture and Society*, 5: 631–60.

Robinson, K. and Davies, C. (2007) Tomboys and sissy girls: young girls' negotiations of femininity and masculinity, *International Journal of Equity and Innovation in Early Childhood*, 5(2): 17–31.

Ross, A. (2005) Desire, in A. Parr (ed.) *The Deleuze Dictionary.* Edinburgh: Edinburgh University Press, pp. 63–5.

Sedgwick, E.K. (1990) *Epistemology of the Closet.* Berkeley, CA: University of California Press.

Taylor, A. and Richardson, C. (2005) Queering home corner, *Contemporary Issues in Early Childhood,* 6(2): 163–73.

Tobin, J. (ed.) (1997) *Making a Place for Pleasure: The Missing Discourse of Desire in Early Childhood.* New Haven, CT: Yale University Press.

Walkerdine, V. (1990) *Schoolgirl Fictions.* London: Verso.

Warner, M. (ed.) (1993) *Fear of a Queer Planet: Queer Politics and Social Theory.* Minneapolis, MN: University of Minnesota Press.

7 Co-constructing knowledge

Children, teachers and families engaging in a science-rich curriculum

Barbara Jordan

Introduction

Play is a socio-cultural-historical construct. Vygotskian and neo-Vygotskian socio-cultural-historical theories have made major contributions to our thinking about children's play and the supporting roles of adults in this play. The term 'socio-cultural-historical theory' reflects understandings of the cultural and socially constructed nature of learning encompassed in 'social constructivism, cultural-historical, activity theory, cultural-historical activity theory (CHAT) as well as aspects of postmodernism/post-structuralism that have highlighted the shared discourses and practices in early childhood education' (Anning et al. 2009: 1). A baby born anywhere in the world learns his or her family's ways of thinking, of being and doing – and playing. Vygotsky (1978) envisaged this learning being mediated by the specific tools of the child's culture; physical tools include the environment, housing, furniture, equipment and ways of sleeping, eating and playing, all emanating from and contributing to the family culture. Psychological tools are the spoken language, systems of notation, symbols, and works of art, written language, schemata, diagrams, maps and drawings. Shared and collective tool use in their play is a major way in which children come to be socialized into their society, to learn to use signs and concepts for themselves, and to pass this learning on to the next generation.

Adults, as the more experienced tool-users and meaning-makers, contribute to learning through their relationships with children, through provision of play opportunities and through interactions that interpret our cultural heritage in support of children's particular funds of knowledge. Many of our cultural tools required for understanding the world are located within subject domain bodies of knowledge, such as the sciences, the arts and commerce, with adults having key roles in mediating relevant aspects of these bodies of knowledge during children's play. Meanwhile the domain knowledge that frequently guides early childhood teachers in their planning and assessment resides in what I am calling in this chapter the curriculum domain.

The curriculum domain

New Zealand's national curriculum document, *Te Whāriki* (Ministry of Education 1996: 30) states that

> Assessing or observing children should take place in the same contexts as meaningful activities and relationships that have provided the focus for the holistic curriculum ... assessment of children should encompass all dimensions of children's learning and development and should see the child as a whole.

This commitment is expressed in the principles of empowerment, holistic development, family and community and relationships. The strands integrate these principles and these have also been expressed as learning dispositions: belonging (taking an interest); well-being (being involved); exploration (persisting with difficulty); communication (expressing an idea or a feeling); and contribution (taking responsibility). Learning stories that increasingly document children's learning in New Zealand early childhood settings (Carr 2001) are generally constructed around these 'dispositions-in-action' (Ministry of Education 2004: Book 7: 10). Thus, principles and strands of *Te Whāriki* and the development of dispositions for learning have for many teachers become the domain areas of knowledge, the cultural tools that provide the framework for supporting teachers' documentation of children's learning. While *Te Whāriki* does not preclude teachers from co-constructing subject domain processes and contents with children (Smorti 2005), there is no expectation within the holistic strands that they do so.

Where children are separated from the rest of society in institutions catering specifically for them, the equipment and routines provided, which are themselves cultural and historical developments, play a major role in what and how children learn (Rogoff 2003). Early childhood settings are such institutions, and as such, they have considerable responsibility for how children are prepared for their roles in society. Effective programmes of play for learning in early childhood settings respond to children's 'funds of knowledge' (González et al. 2005) through selecting activities of the real world of children's homes and communities, providing links between the various facets of children's lives. The ways in which adults interact with children, and the activities and learning that they privilege over others, especially through the learning stories that are told and re-told in centres, at home and in each child's communities, have a strong influence on what children learn and come to value.

Holistic learning of cultural tools

Play is an essential medium through which children learn who they are as individuals and how they are expected to interact with others, in the various settings in which they engage (Vygotsky 1978: 102). All activities, interactions and understandings that contribute to children's behaviours that are appropriate and acceptable in their everyday settings, with people, places and objects, can be viewed as cultural tools. Children learn these tools, first of all in their families, then in their wider communities and in their early childhood settings. Teachers play key roles not only in supporting the early childhood setting's continually evolving use of cultural tools but also in a very concrete way, by influencing the culture of children's homes through their assessment practices.

Kei tua o te pae (Ministry of Education 2004, 2005, 2007), a set of booklets developed as early exemplars of the implementation of *Te Whāriki's* principles, expresses the phases a teacher needs to engage in when working with children as 'noticing, recognizing and responding'. How each teacher responds to what s/he notices and recognizes when children play, will depend on the culture of the centre and on the teacher's own understandings and experiences, on her or his beliefs about teaching and learning, and knowledge of children and their families. Teachers' responses to what they notice children engaged with also depend on their learning more about those interests in which children themselves could already be well informed, so that they and the children will be able to co-engage in developing ever greater complexity and breadth of understandings about the topic area.

Children's portfolios of learning have become valuable tools for documenting learning through the extension of identified play interests. Teachers can only notice, respond to and document the understandings which children demonstrate as they play, if they themselves share these understandings. In the intellectual realm, teachers can model, co-construct and fully extend children's thinking in their areas of interest only when they themselves have, or are prepared to research and develop, relevant conceptual understandings. Teachers require understandings of the processes, or ways of working, as well as of the content or conceptual knowledge of the disciplines, through which they can best support children in acquiring the cultural tools for success in each domain of learning through play.

Early childhood curriculum documents and teachers' own experiences in the sector tend to reinforce teachers in making high demands of children in their personal and social domains, and children's progress in these areas is carefully documented in their learning portfolios, often in terms of their dispositions (Nuttall 2005). Teachers in the sector generally exhibit excellent skills in developing and supporting relationships with children, in fostering their self-identities and communications with each other and with families (Cullen and Jordan 2004; Jordan and Cullen 2004). These are vital skills for teachers working with children, 'for nothing and no-one exists outside of relationships' (Dahlberg et al. 2007: 58). However, it is in the context of their relationships that adults have access to children's thinking providing opportunities for intellectual as well as personal and social teaching to occur.

Kei tua o te pae recommends that, having noticed children's particular interests, strengths and funds of knowledge (González et al. 2005), the next phase 'in the assessment and learning cycle' is to recognize the potential for extending understandings, and then to respond, by providing appropriate experiences and shared activities. Documenting the activities of children, teachers and families as learning stories has been found to be an effective means of supporting the continuity of learning across the settings of home and centre, and of engaging families in revisiting experiences with children (Carr 2005).

However, in part because early childhood teachers have been so influenced by developmental psychology and the consequent child-centredness of early childhood programming, they tend to 'tread softly' in the conceptual domains of traditional subject areas such as science, health, mathematics, art and literacy (Hedges and Cullen 2005). A commitment to providing a holistic, integrated curriculum, as expressed in the curriculum domain of national curriculum documents, should not be at the expense of also addressing the complex understandings that are inherent in these domains of subject knowledge. Unfortunately, in the absence for many teachers of sufficient knowledge, or interest in learning more, children are exposed to their teachers' reinforcement of lower level concepts such as colour, counting and shape, even when such reinforcement is inappropriate or unnecessary. As Nuttall's (2007: 35) research report demonstrated, 'students already know, on average, about 50% of what a teacher intends his or her students to learn'. Learning is about building on current knowledge within the complexities of activity and interaction with others; a continual focus on single concepts does not advance understandings.

Learning through science

There are two major aspects of science, expressed in *The New Zealand Curriculum* (Ministry of Education 2007) for schools, in two sets of strands; first, the process, or the skills, values and attitudes strand, called 'the

Table 7.1 Sample outcomes for *Te Whāriki* and *New Zealand Curriculum*

Te Whāriki Learning Outcomes: *Sample from strand 'exploration'*	*New Zealand Curriculum Learning Outcomes:* *Sample from Levels 1 and 2*
They develop working theories for making sense of the natural, physical and material worlds	Explore and act on issues and questions that link their science learning to their daily living
The attitude of not knowing and being uncertain are part of the process of being a good learner	Appreciate that scientists ask questions about our world that lead to investigations and that open-mindedness is important because there may be more than one explanation
The knowledge that trying things out, exploration and curiosity are important and valued ways of learning	Students will extend their experiences and personal explanations of the natural world through exploration, play, asking questions and discussing simple models

nature of science' (p. 28) and second, the four major contexts through which scientific knowledge has developed and continues to develop – the living world; the planet earth and beyond; the physical world and the material world. Since *Te Whāriki's* learning outcomes are also expressed in terms of knowledge, skills and attitudes, the description of the 'nature of science' corresponds well to the learning outcomes of the *Te Whāriki* strand of 'exploration' (Table 7.1).

The learning outcomes of *Te Whāriki* provide guidance for teachers in supporting children's evolving dispositions towards 'doing' science. What is missing in *Te Whāriki* is a correspondence or even reference to the science context strands of the *New Zealand Curriculum*; the repository of rich understandings which children can begin to access through their everyday play. An example from the strand 'Physical World' demonstrates the greater specificity of content that provides school teachers with some guidance of possible topics of investigation: 'Students will explore everyday examples of physical phenomena, such as movement, forces, electricity and magnetism, light, sound waves and heat' (Achievement and objectives by level, charts: Levels One and Two, Science). The potential for teachers to include the language and understandings of these topics must be present every day in every early childhood setting, as children move through their lives in the real world. However, in the absence of guidance about these phenomena in their mandated curriculum document, early childhood teachers may easily overlook this potential.

Understanding that *Te Whāriki* was published in 1996, it might be expected that the exemplars that have been more recently published

(Ministry of Education 2004, 2005, 2007) would provide some guide-lines in accessing subject discipline context knowledge in order to extend children's intellectual realms. The assessment exemplars of *Kei tua o te pae* (Ministry of Education 2004, 2005, 2007) provide docu-mented evidence of collaborative planning between teachers, of the empowerment of children in holistic learning environments, of family involvement in centres' programmes and of continuity of learning across the home and centre settings. Collectively, the 20 booklets address the four principles and the five strands of *Te Whāriki*, with a focus on 'assessment as a powerful force for learning'. They are 'designed as a professional development resource to enable learning communities to discuss assessment issues in general' and to make 'visible learning that is valued' (Book 1: 2). One randomly selected learning story from *Kei tua o te pae* will now be examined to identify the learning that is privileged throughout this approach to assessment in relation to teachers' own understandings and sharing of domain knowledge within children's holistic learning through play.

Analysis of an exemplar Learning Story

Kei tua o te pae includes documentation of a child called Aminiasi setting himself the goal of constructing and flying a kite (Book 2: 8–13). This is an example of a teacher comprehensively documenting a child's personal and social learning while missing the ready potential for also addressing the intellectual (science) learning that will be continually revisited each time Aminiasi and his peers and adults read this learning story. An analy-sis of the documented story indicates the learning that is reinforced and the teacher's foci in supporting this. The teacher-author of this story demonstrated her science process knowledge in relation to kite-making and kite-flying in the following ways:

- She tuned in to and valued the child's interest and provided opportunity for ongoing investigation.
- She provided positive reinforcement; supporting the child's skills in construction. She reassured Aminiasi that he was capable of making a kite 'you can (do it)'.
- She supported his disposition of persistence and his plans to make his next kite 'a butterfly kite'. Re-told his story from the printed version.
- She co-constructed the kite with Aminiasi, researching kite-making in books, sharing the excitement of the printing of Aminiasi's story and reading it together.

- She supported problem-solving in continually mending the broken tail.
- She read the documented story and responded to the photographs.

The teacher documented a few low-level concepts (science content), identifying that Aminiasi:

- explored shapes and suitable materials for the kite;
- named 'triangles' as the kite's shape (though not diamond, or that 'kite' is the name of both the object and the shape);
- named the colour of the tail 'yellow'.

In documenting Aminiasi's kite-making experiences, his teacher has accessed the curriculum domain knowledge of *Te Whāriki*. However, there is no reference to the physical movement and forces: how the kite flies, the support of the air and the pull of gravity, or the origin of wind. In planning for further extension, the teacher talks about encouraging the drawing of plans, collecting resources and trialling the final product, all valid processes of science. However, language such as push, pull, trajectory and force could easily have been included in the discussions, especially in thinking about 'what next'. A teacher with some science understanding might have considered investigations of floating and sinking, or of planes and helicopters in flight, with some reference to aerodynamics. The documented learning story and the plans for extension fulfil many of *Te Whāriki*'s expectations, for example, that children are being provided opportunities to develop: 'the ability to make decisions, choose their own materials, and set their own problems' (exploration, goal one, Ministry of Education 1996: 84); 'spatial understandings, including awareness of how two- and three-dimensional objects can be joined together and moved in space and ways in which spatial information can be represented, such as in maps, diagrams, photographs, and drawings' (exploration, goal four, Ministry of Education 1996: 90). The latter goal in particular should require the teacher to conduct her own research in the topic of children's interests, such as in kites and how they fly. The child is *experiencing* some of 'how things move and can be moved, for example by blowing, pushing, pulling, rolling, swinging and sinking'. At the same time, the activity meets the requirement that 'children have access to technology to help explore movement' (p. 91). However, the level of *exploration* of these concepts is low, because of the reliance on experience to support the learning with very little input from the teacher's own understandings. Nor are Aminiasi's own content understandings documented in any way.

No teacher can be expected to have all the content knowledge required to appropriately extend every child's spontaneous interest through accessing a number of subject knowledge disciplines, and certainly not in one session or one learning story. But every teacher can be expected to find out the relevant language and the concepts and processes that children require to make sense of their world. These are foundational tools of our culture. In the kite story the teacher saw it was important to reinforce Aminiasi's concepts of colour and shape; this is out of context of the action in comparison with the forces of floating and flying, especially for a 4-year-old. Unless there was a compelling reason to simplify Aminiasi's learning, this exemplar shows a teacher who is only able to co-construct or plan to extend the knowledge and understandings which she herself possesses in her tool-kit.

A science-rich learning story

In a teaching team that values subject domain knowledge alongside *Te Whāriki*'s holistic and empowering principles, the teachers will integrate their own understandings into children's play programmes. At First Years Preschool, a rural community centre in central New Zealand, the programme for over-2s is led by a supervisor with a passion for science. Lisa's leadership has inspired her team in the development of an equipment- and experience-rich environment that values children's rural funds of knowledge and extends their understandings as they and their families extend their teachers' funds of knowledge. Figure 7.1 presents a learning story 'Learning about rotors' that documents First Years Preschool teachers' co-construction of understandings with children; it provides evidence of learning in all three realms (the personal, the interpersonal and the intellectual) through an exploratory activity that remains true to a holistic, integrated curriculum based on children's play interests and funds of knowledge from their homes. Table 7.1 follows Figure 7.1 and outlines the learning dispositions and curriculum content.

The teacher-author of this story demonstrated her science process knowledge in relation to model helicopter construction and flying in similar ways to the author of the *Kei tua o te pae* story:

- She tuned in to and valued the children's interest and understandings about helicopters and rotors, providing opportunity for ongoing investigation.
- She provided positive reinforcement; supporting the child's skills in construction and in taking his own photographs.

In documenting the two boys' play, the author of this story also challenged the boys' usage of some key conceptual concepts:

Learning about rotors

Today Jaden and William built these creations from the K'nex resource. They were very proud and wanted a photo taken. We talked about what they'd built; Jaden said it was a propeller for a helicopter. I wondered out loud whether this was the right word – I said I thought that perhaps helicopters have rotors.

We found a book about aircraft in the resource room, and together we investigated the difference between propellers and rotors. Jaden was so interested that he wanted to take a photo of the page! William was also very interested in helicopters; he said "I'll have a look" (at the book). William said "Dad has Bell helicopters flying at our place, because the hills are too high for the trucks to get up" and he told us we "need a tail rotor so the helicopter can go forward and not just spin around and go up".

Jaden, you used the book as a plan, and used the two-dimensional image to make your three-dimensional rotor. I can tell you know the rotor blades make the helicopter go up because of the way you were moving the blades and the whole construction up and down at the same time.

Then when William talked about **needing a tail rotor as well, he modelled going up with the main rotor and forward with the tail rotor.**

Gosh Jaden you are so clever. I loved how you involved me in your learning and together with William and with Lisa (Head Teacher) we found out more about helicopters and planes and we will continue to do this. Several weeks later you still remembered that helicopters do not have propellers even though you did not remember the word "rotor".

Love from Julie xxx

Jaden and William each constructing their helicopters, using their previous learning stories and the text book as references; Julie is in the background co-constructing thinking with them.

Figure 7.1 Learning story: Analysis of learning about rotors.

- She challenged and extended the terminology of propellers versus rotors in aircraft.
- She shared the language of one- or two-dimensional constructions.
- She documented the children's physical demonstrations of understanding concepts of helicopters lifting off the ground.

Julie's support of Jaden's authentic play experience demonstrates her strong content knowledge in all three realms of learning. Of particular note is that Julie and Lisa both contributed to the children's intellectual understandings from their own knowledge bases about the differences between a propeller and a rotor. The boys' conceptual understandings to date have been noted and the teachers now need to take stock of their own understandings about helicopters and collaborate to think about activities they could provide that would potentially extend the children's thinking. The teachers' own research will be likely to lead them to considering such concepts as the aerodynamics of flight and stream-lining, air and air pressure, Bernoulli's principle (Hosking 1990: 17); moving and fixed wings, and sailing boats and windmills. A collaborative teacher brainstorm about possible activities of construction, art, dance, music or text designed to engage children's interests, might include: models of lifting objects through moving air (blowing); making darts, kites, parachutes, yachts, balloons, gliders, jets, planes and helicopters; experiencing the flight of sycamore, maple and dandelion seeds, and the very different physical structures and flights of insects, birds and bats. With multiple options in mind, the teachers will be continually aware of the children's developing interests; while William might engage fully with extending his thinking about helicopters and flight, Jaden could as readily proceed on a tangent and become interested in growing sycamore seeds, or in different forms of transport. Teachers with new understandings that they are keen to share with children need to take care at this point that they do not take over the children's investigations; there is a fine line between scaffolding and co-construction of understandings (Jordan 2009). In this centre, 'Learning about rotors' was an early learning story in this type of evolving sequence. Further stories were written, documenting the children's ongoing development in breadth and complexity of understandings, in all domains of learning, accessing the tools of both curriculum domains and subject knowledge domains.

Conclusion

Children's learning through play is the result of complex interactions and reciprocity between an early childhood setting's team philosophies of learning and their teaching practices in the context of their centre (Rogoff 1998). Teachers' understandings of their roles as leaders are exemplified in their interactions with each other and with children and their families. Not all teachers in early childhood settings will have a background of interest and strengths in science. However, whole team collaboration can inspire teachers to support each other in learning more about the science in which children are currently interested, in order to extend children's understandings and their techniques as young scientists. Co-constructive interactions between adults and children that are supportive of children's interests build on the understandings that all participants bring to their learning. Adults need to continually develop their knowledge in order to share some of this with children at the appropriate time, in appropriate ways and at levels at which the children are ready to engage.

The documentation of children's learning as learning stories that become pages in each child's learning portfolio enables the cultural tools, in all domain areas, both curriculum (dispositions) and subject (sciences, arts) to be revisited and reinforced over time. As children share their stories with each other, with teachers and with their families, these stories reaffirm the understandings and the knowledge bases of the teachers who wrote them. Given that each story is the result of teachers' selections from a large set of possible activities in the child's time at the centre, the contents of each story hold the potential to influence future play activities, choices and learning. It is important that under-5-year-old children learn the foundational understandings of which they are capable, and it is incumbent on early childhood teaching teams to continually 'up-skill' themselves in the domain understandings and processes of the sciences, where many teachers lack confidence.

A socio-cultural-historical model of programming provides the foundation for teachers, children and families to co-construct play in a manner that values children's and teachers' understandings and supports important cultural learning that will ensure children are well prepared for learning for life. Both curriculum and subject domain knowledge can be made available in interactions that extend learning for children and for their teachers. Such programmes are founded on: teachers accepting their responsibilities as decision-making leaders of children's learning, researching topics of children's interests to be themselves more knowledgeable in the subject domains; the provision of authentic learning opportunities that support children's own understandings as well as the continuity of learning between home and the centre; and the encouragement of children's inquiry through strong relationships between teachers, children and families. Play is thus positioned as a tool for supporting the authentic learning in which every child is engaged as a co-constructor in and of her or his own culture.

References

Anning, A., Cullen, J. and Fleer, M. (2009) *Early Childhood Education: Society and Culture*, 2nd edn. Los Angeles: Sage, pp. 39–52.

Carr, M. (2001) *Assessment in Early Childhood Settings*. London: Paul Chapman.

Carr, M. (2005) The leading edge of learning: recognising children's self-making narratives, *European Early Childhood Education Research Journal*, 13(2): 41–50.

Cullen, J. and Jordan, B. (2004) Our elusive dream: towards an early years (birth to eight) curriculum approach, paper presented at NZARE conference, Wellington, 24 November.

Dahlberg, G., Moss, P. and Pence, A. (2007) *Beyond Quality in Early Childhood Education and Care: Languages of Evaluation*, 2nd edn. London: Routledge.

González, N., Moll, L. and Amanti, C. (eds) (2005) *Funds of Knowledge: Theorizing Practices in Households, Communities, and Classrooms*. Mahwah, NJ: Lawrence Erlbaum Associates.

Hedges, H. and Cullen, C. (2005) Subject knowledge in early childhood curriculum and pedagogy: beliefs and practices, *Contemporary Issues in Early Childhood*, 6(1): 66–79.

Hosking, W. (1990) *Flights of Imagination: An Introduction to Aerodynamics*. Washington, DC: National Science Teachers Association.

Jordan, B. (2009) Scaffolding learning and co-constructing understandings, in A. Anning, J. Cullen, and M. Fleer (eds) *Early Childhood Education: Society and Culture*, 2nd edn. Los Angeles: Sage, pp. 39–52.

Jordan, B. and Cullen, J. (2004) Associate teachers' perceptions of early years (0–8) teacher education students, paper presented at TEFANZ conference, Auckland, July.

Ministry of Education (1996) *Te Whāriki Early Childhood Curriculum*: *He Whāriki Mātauranga mō ngā Mokopuna o Aotearoa*. Wellington: Learning Media Ltd.

Ministry of Education (2004, 2005, 2007) *Kei tua o te pae. Assessment for Learning: Early Childhood Exemplars*. Wellington: Learning Media Ltd.

Nuttall, G. (2007) *The Hidden Lives of Learners*. Wellington: NZCER.

Nuttall, J. (2005) Looking back, looking forward: three decades of early childhood curriculum in Aotearoa New Zealand, *Curriculum Matters*, 1: 12–27.

Rogoff, B. (1998) Cognition as a collaborative process, in W. Damon (chief ed.), D. Kuhn and R.S. Siegler (vol. eds.) *Handbook of Child Psychology*, vol. 2: *Cognition, Perceptions and Language*, 5th edn. New York: John Wiley & Sons Ltd, pp. 679–744.

Rogoff, B. (2003) *The Cultural Nature of Human Development*. Oxford: Oxford University Press.

Smorti, S. (2005) Why don't we teach science? *Early Education*, 38(2): 13–20.

Vygotsky, L. (1978) *Mind in Society: The Development of Higher Psychological Processes*. Cambridge, MA: Harvard University Press.

8 Postdevelopmentalism and professional learning

Implications for understanding the relationship between play and pedagogy

Andrea Nolan and Anna Kilderry

Introduction

Early childhood education has traditionally devised and implemented play-based programmes which have aimed at extending each child's development in the social, emotional, language, cognitive and physical areas. By providing a learning environment in which the developmental needs of children can be met, play has for many years been seen by the early childhood sector as the most natural and appropriate learning medium (Wood 2009). In Australia, this perspective on play is articulated in policy terms in a discussion paper from the Council of Australian Governments (COAG) Productivity Agenda Working Group for Education, Skills, Training and Early Childhood Development (COAG 2008), which describes play as 'integral to the delivery of early learning programs for children from birth and in all care environments' (p. 16), providing 'a platform for children and teachers to participate in meaningful learning' (p. 40).

This type of developmental orientation has been evident both within the field and at a policy level and is arguably 'part of the taken-for-granted practices in Australia' (Farquhar and Fleer 2007: 28) which have informed pedagogy, practice and policy for many years. In recent years, however, alternatives to such thinking have emerged, along with a questioning of the particular beliefs informing developmentalism. These alternative approaches have emerged from a range of theoretical perspectives including the cultural-historical (Edwards 2003; Fleer 2005), the postmodern (Dahlberg et al. 2007), the poststructuralist (Gibbons 2007) and the feminist (MacNaughton 2006), and have moved the field towards perspectives which can be broadly termed 'postdevelopmental'. The pedagogical landscape of early childhood education has been changing, in consequence, from a focus on individual children and their domains of development to a consideration of the social and cultural basis of learning (Fleer 2005). Within the parameters of postdevelopmentalism, researchers and practitioners have begun to question the normative assumptions which developmental theories have traditionally promoted about children's development, learning and play.

In this chapter we consider some of the insights provided by postdevelopmental theorizing, and how these may inform early childhood practice, and reflect on what postdevelopmental play and pedagogy might look like. As professional teacher-educators, we are interested in examining the implications of such alternative insights for professional learning, since we suggest that these newly emerging perspectives will place new demands on early childhood educators and their understanding of play and practice. We begin with an overview of traditional developmental perspectives on play in early childhood education and care, leading into an examination of the critiques associated with this perspective. Situated within the Australian context, this chapter draws on our own experiences of working with undergraduate early childhood teachers.

Developmentalism and play

Child development has traditionally been concerned with the developmental stages of children, including their biological, social, emotional and cognitive growth, and is generally used to guide educators in their knowledge about how children develop (Raban et al. 2005). There has been a strong reliance on child development theory to inform early childhood practice (Spodek and Saracho 1991).

While the body of 'child development' knowledge within early childhood education has not been derived from one set of beliefs, it is evident that Piaget's conceptualizations have been central to the field's theories about both play and pedagogy (Walsh 2005). Piaget's genetic epistemology expressed his intention to theorize the origins of knowledge (Piaget 1959). However, within the field of early childhood education his main contributions have been interpreted as focusing on the active nature of children's learning. The ages and stages of cognitive development which were derived as a theoretical explanation for the genetic epistemology were positioned in the field as particular sequences in development and learning towards which teachers could work (Stott and Bowman 1996). In practice, Piaget's developmental theory was translated into a pedagogy which focused on individual children and their independent learning, in contrast to the more contemporary orientation which focuses on 'the context of modelled, shared or independent activities within a community of learners' (Farquhar and Fleer 2007: 33). There is evidence that, when teachers work from a developmental perspective the learning outcomes associated with particular activities are not made explicit to children, and the position of the educator, as MacNaughton (2003: 42) points out, is restricted to a 'relatively non-directive role in a child's learning'. Adults' role within this theoretical orientation was to 'create the right environment for learning but then allow the child to problem solve and to learn through their own active discovery' (MacNaughton 2003: 44). Since the focus was on the developmental progression of each child, teachers' main responsibility was to make sure that children progressed through stages of development. Educators established what children 'needed' to know through their observations of the children, and viewed play as the vehicle through which children would learn what they needed to know. Cues for curriculum development were therefore taken from the child's interests, abilities and needs, which were deemed relevant to the child's level of functioning (Seefeldt 1990).

This approach to teaching and learning saw play emerge as a marker of an appropriate early childhood educational environment, and positioned play as the principal method for acquiring skills and knowledge. According to this view, the child was a self-directed learner, working within a resource-rich environment (Raban et al. 2005), and adults had a limited role in terms of their conceptual or inter-subjective engagement with the child (Jordan 2009), instead investing effort into preparing the environment. This style of pedagogy involves the teacher in matching curricular content to the child's developmental level, and introducing more complex materials and concepts only when the child was deemed to have the cognitive ability to master them (Elkind 1989).

Child development as an informant for practice is not the issue being debated here. Rather, it is the particular dominance which developmental theories seem to have held in shaping a range of policy initiatives and practices associated with early childhood education. Grieshaber and Cannella (2001) have cautioned that this should not mean rejecting developmental theories outright, as it is important to recognize that a range of perspectives support diversity in the sector.

Pedagogy in early childhood education

The actual definition of the term 'pedagogy' varies across early childhood education and care contexts throughout the world. Some European interpretations of pedagogy include more than the skills associated with teaching and learning, and embrace holistic ways of working with people in which learning, care and upbringing are viewed as interconnected facets of life (Moss 2006). Within an Italian context, for instance, early childhood pedagogy is a theory of education, as well as a practical science, encompassing both the philosophical and political (Mantovani 2007). This outlook places educational relationships at the centre of pedagogy, where values guide the participation within a particular local context (Mantovani 2007). In the Australian context, approaches to pedagogy vary from setting to setting according to an educator's personal teaching and learning style, their educational, philosophical and epistemological beliefs, the curriculum policies they are guided by, and the philosophical orientation of their settings (Kilderry 2007).

Pedagogically, there is a strong link between the views educators hold about children and childhood, and the way in which play is seen and valued in early years settings (Fleer and Raban 2007). Educators' approach to children's play and learning derives from their own judgement and knowledge of the players and the learning situation, and on what they have been taught in their early childhood teacher education programmes (Nolan 2000). They create learning environments that reflect their perceptions of what play should look like (Gibbons 2007), so that their concept of 'pedagogy' becomes inextricably linked with how they perceive play. These interpretations are also mediated by the expectations of the particular management structures teachers are operating under (Nuttall et al. 2009), so that the curricula and pedagogy enacted in early childhood settings are related to traditional ideas about early childhood curriculum. This chapter draws on a broad Australasian orientation towards pedagogy which conveys the educators' approach to curriculum, learning and teaching.

Professional learning

Professional learning is a relatively new term applied to early childhood education, and is offered as an alternative to the term 'professional development' (Edwards and Nuttall 2009). One of the positive features of this shift in terminology is that professional learning implies that the educator has the ability to be an active learner in their context, rather than a passive consumer of policies and newly emerging theoretical ideas (Edwards and Nuttall 2009). It is known that changes in pedagogical practice are more likely to occur when the learning process undertaken by teachers is active and reflective, rather than entirely passive (Ministry of Education 2003), and research indicates that the most successful professional learning programmes are those that provide regular opportunities for participants to share perspectives and seek solutions to common problems in an atmosphere of collegiality and professional respect (Campbell 2003).

Understanding their own personal beliefs and values relating to teaching and learning enables educators to situate their practice in relation to theoretical orientations, and therefore supports the development of professional identities. Professional learning experiences that encourage teachers to think about the past are found to result in higher levels of reflection, which helps to raise teacher learning to a 'meta-level of appreciation' (Leshem and Trafford 2006: 23). A further important aspect of professional learning is the extent to which teachers are prepared to examine the 'myths' on which their practice may be based. Fresh perspectives can be achieved when teachers are provided with opportunities to engage actively in professional learning in ways that stimulate a deeper understanding of their own beliefs and experiences (Nolan 2008), and when opportunities to learn about alternative perspectives on play and pedagogy allow teachers to develop multiple perspectives and approaches to inform their work.

Towards postdevelopmental perspectives on play and pedagogy

Early childhood education and care have experienced the legitimation of values and practices that are derived from a developmental discourse, but these values and practices have recently been subject to challenge and critique. One such critique argues that a reliance on developmental theories restricts the knowledge base of the field, and thus limits opportunities for conceptualizing play and pedagogy in alternative ways (Dalhberg et al. 2007). This criticism draws attention to the way that developmental perspectives can be used to 'normalize' children in terms of particular developmental outcomes. For example, a view of development as occurring in linear stages allows the significance of children's social, cultural, economic and gendered experiences for their development to be ignored (Soto and Swadener 2002). Arguments such as these highlight the influence of social and cultural constructions of childhood, and the potentially negative effects of applying 'universal models and normalizing discourses about childhood and "best practice" (Soto and Swadener 2002: 42) to early childhood provision. The shift from, for instance, a developmental to a cultural-historical or poststructuralist perspective, permits individual differences in development to be viewed, not as deviations from the norm but rather as ways to understand the appropriateness of individual children's play to the context in which it has occurred.

The traditional, non-interventionist, approach to play, where children engage in self-directed activity within an environment which provides for their perceived individual needs in terms of their ages or stages of development has been criticized for a number of years (Fleer 2005). The pedagogy of open-ended play has also been critiqued as a culturally biased social invention rather than a universal 'truth' about children's development (Lee and Tseng 2008). There are also problems in assuming that conceptual learning is associated with children's play (Fleer and Raban 2007).

Play and pedagogy in a postdevelopmental context

Current early childhood literature (for example, Anning et al. 2009) reveals the recently expanded professional knowledge base for understanding play and pedagogy, which has resulted in a shift away from a universal understanding of development. These approaches permit educators to be more responsive to children's lifeworlds than was previously possible (Cope and Kalantzis 2000), and to employ a pedagogical focus which includes the care, education, socialization and citizenship dimensions of children's lifelong learning journeys.

Postdevelopmental orientations are inspired by theories and practices located outside child development theory, and suggest that play, and the pedagogical use of play, are not governed by individual children's 'needs'. Instead children are viewed as competent, socially active learners who are able to co-construct their learning intentions, learning strategies and learning outcomes in culturally meaningful ways with peers and adults (Jordan 2009). This shift in perspective has implications for pedagogy because it suggests a movement away from the notion of the 'teacher knowing best', to an approach in which children are considered to hold agency in relation to their learning.

The postdevelopmental context in early childhood education is a site of possibilities. It opens up a conceptual space for new ways of thinking about practice and stretches familiar theoretical boundaries. For example, from their utopian viewpoint, Dahlberg and Moss (2005) offer a very different theoretical platform for early childhood education. They have achieved this by troubling the familiar dominant discourses commonly found within early childhood education, and replacing these with a series of possibilities. Dahlberg and Moss have deliberately placed ethics and the politics of practice at the core of their theorizing, generating a new dialogue, vision and direction in which to move forward the practice of early childhood education. They suggest that:

> Confronted by what we argue is a highly instrumental and impoverished discourse about preschools, which privileges technical practice in the interest of achieving predetermined outcomes, we

have tried to imagine a different possibility: the preschool first and foremost as a public space for ethical and democratic political practice, where education takes the form of a pedagogy of listening related to the ethics of an encounter, and a lively minor politics confronts dominant discourse and injustice.

(2005: 178)

Certain common characteristics inform postdevelopmental perspectives. These include, for example, the processes of reconceptualizing, re-envisioning, deconstructing, resisting, disrupting and reframing taken-for-granted ideas and practices about children, childhood, development, learning and play. These processes result in the creation of new discourses and theories, which with time and opportunity for appropriate professional learning experiences can help to generate changes in practice. Our reading of the way in which postdevelopmental theory has evolved within the early childhood literature suggests to us five common characteristics which may be considered features of a postdevelopmental pedagogy. These are presented in Table 8.1.

Postdevelopmental approaches have significant implications for professional learning in early childhood education and care. First, they move on from the traditional foundations of developmental theory which has been used to guide early childhood practice for decades, and has been central to conceptualizing the pedagogy of play. Second, postdevelopmentalism creates a context in which new theoretical ideas can be explored and examined in practice. For example, in recent years the notion of childhood has been reconceptualized, early childhood pedagogy has been rethought and the whole concept of quality critiqued, and traditional approaches to the education of early childhood teachers have been challenged. Within the Australian context, the literature is characterized by discussions centred on postdevelopmental innovations, and early childhood teachers are involved in rethinking their practice (Raban et al. 2005).

Professional learning and postdevelopmentalism: an Australian perspective

From our own experience we have seen how postdevelopmental perspectives can shed new light on many of the assumptions about children's play that were once derived from developmentalism, and how these perspectives can open up spaces for discussing and developing new ways of thinking about play and pedagogy. We endeavoured to use postdevelopmental perspectives as articulated through the five characteristics of postdevelopmental pedagogy in our own teaching. In doing so, we

Table 8.1 Five characteristics of postdevelopmental pedagogy

Repositioning	Educators move from the position of planning for young children in developmental terms. This involves moving away from viewing children as developing in stages, and decentres learning from children's alleged developmental needs. The process of repositioning helps to shift developmentalism from its position of theoretical and practical supremacy in early childhood pedagogy.
Reframing	The educator takes an alternative (postmodern, cultural-historical, critical, feminist poststructuralist or postcolonial) view of children's development and learning. This reframing allows educators to see development, learning and play through a range of theoretical lenses other than that traditionally offered by developmentalism.
Engaging learners	Postdevelopmental pedagogical practices engage learners and teachers alike, by recognizing the diverse ways in which children and adults learn. The relationship between the educator, the child/ren, the community and the social and political situation becomes gradually more responsive and reciprocal.
Empowering	Using postdevelopmental perspectives encourages educators to view children as capable participants in their learning. Children are viewed as holding rights to share their ideas, express their views and to have their opinions about their care and education listened to. This involves thinking about children's right to access fair, just and equitable care and education.
Critically reflecting	Using postdevelopmental perspectives, educators critically reflect on their practice, and commit to devising equitable and ethical ways of working with young children. Critical reflection involves thinking about traditional assumptions in early childhood education, such as the role of play in early learning, and its effect on expectations of children's developmental progress.

have learned more about how postdevelopmental perspectives can be used in the professional preparation of early childhood teachers during initial teacher education.

For example, in one early childhood teacher education undergraduate degree course we deliberately problematized the curricular content so that the historical role of developmental theories in early childhood pedagogy could be examined by the pre-service teachers (Nolan and Kilderry 2001). Pre-service teachers were immersed in contemporary debates and theories originating from postdevelopmental perspectives. Our aim was to support the pre-service teachers to increase their awareness and understanding of how a world-view about development can work to create particular ways of perceiving children. We wanted to explore with the pre-service teachers how one world-view can shape the ways that children's play and learning are seen and acted upon in educational settings. We used the five characteristics of postdevelopmental pedagogy, including critical reflection, to open discussions with the pre-service teachers about their attitudes and values towards early childhood teaching. We supported them in using the five characteristics of postdevelopmental pedagogy to analyze and theorize the way they understood and constructed the relationship between play and pedagogy. We deliberately introduced multiple perspectives to contrast with the ideas they had been offered during their earlier (Technical and Further Education) training. We presented the students with situated knowledge, which involved locating theories in the historical contexts from which they originated, and then asked them to reflect on their own understandings of these theories, and their particular relevance to the communities and children they would work with. This technique helped them to understand the complex relationship between the origins of a theoretical position, and its current interpretation.

This technique provided a basis for the five characteristics of postdevelopmental pedagogy, as it helped the students to see theory as explanations for development emerging from particular times in history, rather than as universal and unchangeable 'facts' about children's development. The work of Stott and Bowman (1996) was important in helping the pre-service teachers to understand the way in which theory can be used as an aid for pedagogical reflection, rather than a straitjacket for thinking about how to teach. Our own teaching became characterized by elements of the five characteristics of postdevelopmental pedagogy, in that we were repositioning and reframing our own perspectives on childhood, and on how teachers can work with children. We worked to engage and empower our learners, using critical reflection as the basis for these pedagogies. At the time we described our approach as follows:

> We have deliberately challenged them [student teachers] to reconstruct the knowledge base they bring with them to this course to expand definitions of what constitutes good teaching and to accept that this knowledge base is continually changing. We have problematised the dominance of developmental psychology in the early childhood field, and immersed the students in recent research to provide currency. We have worked in this way to help the early childhood student teachers to increase

their awareness and understanding of how they have been trapped into upholding the dominant discursive regime.

(Nolan and Kilderry 2001: 3)

We recorded discussions with the pre-service teachers which highlight the ways that their experience of postdevelopmental pedagogies enabled them to think in new ways about central elements of early childhood education, such as pedagogy and play:

> Many of us work on the theory that children learn when they are ready. We follow the idea that children will develop through a series of stages, one after the other, which then gives them the skills required to 'learn' desired behaviours. It is this age appropriateness or developmentally appropriate practice that many of us find ourselves locked into.
>
> (Student A)

> As always, everything I hear, learn and discuss in class causes me to reflect on my own teaching practice. I examine what I currently do, compared to what I could be doing and look at why/ why not I do what I do.
>
> (Student B)

> A lot of the program planning ideas, curriculum ideas I have previously used I have now questioned, and I am searching for a better way.
>
> (Student C)

> One of the best aspects of this course is that I am able to think about my own practice and beliefs. I am challenged, not just handed a prescription to follow. I have been asked to think about what is appropriate to me and my situation. I now understand that there is no 'right way', just other possibilities.
>
> (Student D)

> What I have found is that nothing is permanent.
>
> (Student E)

Embracing the idea that their knowledge and practice would probably always be in a state of construction was a challenge for some of these pre-service teachers. However, our discussions suggested that many of them were beginning to absorb this notion, and developing their own pedagogical thinking so that it was framed in relation to the five characteristics of postdevelopmental pedagogy.

We learned from this experience that the process of critical thinking can encourage a consideration of divergent paradigms, in ways that can transform practice in a field of education currently characterized by a great deal of postdevelopmental debate and theorization. Our experience suggests to us that the movement towards postdevelopmental perspectives in early childhood education will have ramifications for teachers seeking to work in these ways. We believe that early childhood educators will need to be prepared to rethink their practices, and to explore the origins of the attitudes that have sustained these practices over the course of their careers. We believe that it will be important for teachers to have opportunities to chart how their attitudes and practices are linked to the construction and perpetuation of traditional notions of 'best practice' in relation to particular theoretical perspectives.

Conclusion

In this chapter we have sought to examine the way postdevelopmental perspectives are evolving in early years education, and working to reconfigure traditional conceptions of the play and pedagogy relationship. The practical implications of some of these challenges have been framed in terms of the 'five characteristics of postdevelopmental pedagogy'. We have also considered contemporary perspectives on professional learning, which challenge the traditional concept of 'professional development', and have attempted to bring these two areas of change together, discussing how professional learning and postdevelopmentalism can be used to bring about changes in practice. We believe that there is potential in the field to realize many world-views about children's learning and development in ways that will allow educators and researchers to acknowledge the multiplicity and complexity that comprise many of the social situations in which families and children live and work.

References

Anning, A., Cullen, J. and Fleer, M. (2009) Research contexts across cultures, in A. Anning, J. Cullen and M. Fleer (eds) *Early Childhood Education: Society and Culture*, 2nd edn. London: Sage, pp. 1–24.

Campbell, A. (2003) Teachers' research and professional development in England: some questions, issues and concerns, *Asia-Pacific Journal of Teacher Education*, 37(1): 1469–2945.

Cope, B. and Kalantzis, M. (2000) *Multiliteracies: Literacy, Learning and the Design of Social Futures*. Melbourne: Macmillan.

Council of Australian Governments (COAG) Productivity Agenda Working Group – Education, Skills, Training and Early Childhood Development (2008) A national quality framework for early childhood education and care: a discussion paper. Canberra: COAG.

Dahlberg, G. and Moss, P. (2005) *Ethics and Politics in Early Childhood Education*. Abingdon: Routledge-Falmer.

Dahlberg, G., Moss, P. and Pence, A. (2007) *Beyond Quality in Early Childhood Education and Care: Languages of Evaluation*, 2nd edn. Abingdon: Routledge.

Edwards, S. (2003) New directions: charting the paths of the role of sociocultural theory in early childhood education and curriculum, *Contemporary Issues in Early Childhood*, 4(3): 251–66.

Edwards, S. and Nuttall, J. (2009) Introduction: professional learning in early childhood settings, in S. Edwards and J. Nuttall (eds) *Professional Learning in Early Childhood Settings*. Rotterdam: Sense Publications, pp. 1–8.

Elkind, D. (1989) Developmentally appropriate practice: philosophical and practical implications, *Phi Delta Kappan*, Oct.: 113–17.

Farquhar, S. and Fleer, M. (2007) Developmental colonisation of early childhood education in Aotearoa/New Zealand and Australia, in L. Keesing-Styles and H. Hedges (eds) *Theorising Early Childhood Practice: Emerging Dialogues*. New South Wales: Pademelon Press, pp. 27–49.

Fleer, M. (2005) Developmental fossils – unearthing the artefacts of early childhood education: the reification of 'child development', *Australian Journal of Early Childhood*, 30(2): 207.

Fleer, M. and Raban, B. (2007) Constructing cultural-historical tools for supporting young children's concept formation in early literacy and numeracy, *Early Years: An International Journal of Research and Development*, 27(2): 103–18.

Gibbons, A. (2007) The politics of processes and products in education: an early childhood meta-narrative in crisis? *Educational Philosophy and Theory*, 39(3): 300–11.

Grieshaber, S. and Cannella, G.S. (2001) From identity to identities: increasing possibilities in early childhood education, in S. Grieshaber and G.S. Cannella (eds) *Embracing Identities in Early Childhood Education*. New York: Teachers College Press, pp. 3–22.

Jordan, B. (2009) Scaffolding learning and co-constructing understandings, in A. Anning, J. Cullen and M. Fleer (eds) *Early Childhood Education: Society and Culture*, 2nd edn. London: Sage, pp. 39–53.

Kilderry, A. (2007) Pedagogies in early childhood education, in R. New and M. Cochran (eds) *Early Childhood Education: An International Encyclopaedia*, vol. 4. Westport, CT: Praeger, pp. 883–7.

Lee, I.F. and Tseng, C.L. (2008) Cultural conflicts of the child-centred approach to early childhood education in Taiwan, *Early Years*, 28(2): 183–96.

Leshem, S. and Trafford, V. (2006) Stories as mirrors: reflective practice in teaching and learning, *Reflective Practice*, 7(1): 9–27.

MacNaughton, G. (2003) *Shaping Early Childhood: Learners, Curriculum and Contexts*. Maidenhead: Open University Press.

MacNaughton, G. (2006) Constructing gender in early years education, in C. Skelton, B. Francis and L. Smulyan (eds) *Sage Handbook: Gender and Education*. London: Sage, pp. 127–38.

Mantovani, S. (2007) Pedagogy, in R. New and M. Cochran (eds) *Early Childhood Education: An International Encylopedia*, vol. 4. Westport, CT: Praeger, pp. 1115–18.

Ministry of Education (2003) *Best Evidence Synthesis: Characteristics of Professional Development Linked to Enhanced Pedagogy and Children's Learning in Early Childhood Settings*. Wellington: Ministry of Education.

Moss, P. (2006) Structures, understandings and discourses: possibilities for re-envisioning the early childhood worker, *Contemporary Issues in Early Childhood*, 7(1): 30–41.

Nolan, A. (2000) The state of play in early childhood teacher training in Victoria. Unpublished PhD thesis, Deakin University.

Nolan, A. (2008) Encouraging the reflection process in undergraduate teachers using guided reflection, *Australian Journal of Early Childhood*, 33(1): 31–6.

Nolan, A. and Kilderry, A. (2001) Trapped by training: early childhood teacher preparation in changing times, paper presented at the 'Making Connections: Teaching, Learning and Research', 9th Annual Research Conference & Teaching and Learning Forum, Faculty of Human Development, Victoria University, Australia, 1–2 November.

Nuttall, J., Coxon, L. and Read, S. (2009) Structure, agency and artefacts: mediating professional learning in early childhood education, in S. Edwards and J. Nuttall (eds) *Professional Learning in Early Childhood Settings*. Rotterdam: Sense Publications, pp. 97–115.

Piaget, J. (1959) *The Language and Thought of the Child*, 3rd edn. London: Routledge & Kegan Paul.

Raban, B., Waniganayake, M., Nolan, A., Brown, R., Deans, J. and Ure, C. (2005) Empowering practitioners to critically examine their current practice, *Australian Research in Early Childhood Education*, 2(2): 1–16.

Seefeldt, C. (1990) Cognitive and appropriate: the kindergarten curriculum, *Early Childhood Development and Care*, 61: 19–25.

Soto, L. and Swadener, B. (2002) Toward liberatory early childhood theory, research and praxis: decolonializing a field, *Contemporary Issues in Early Childhood*, 3(1): 38–66.

Spodek, B. and Saracho, O. (1991) The relationship between theories of child development and the early childhood curriculum, *Early Childhood Development and Care*, 152: 1–15.

Stott, F. and Bowman, B. (1996) Deconstructing 'child development knowledge' and 'teacher preparation', *Early Childhood Research Quarterly*, 11: 169–84.

Walsh, D.J. (2005) Developmental theory and early childhood education: necessary but not sufficient, in N. J. Yelland (ed.) *Critical Issues in Early Childhood Education*. Maidenhead: Open University Press, pp. 40–8.

Wood, L. (2009) Developing a pedagogy of play, in A. Anning, J. Cullen and M. Fleer (eds) *Early Childhood Education: Society and Culture*, 2nd edn. London: Sage, pp. 27–39.

9   Who gets to play?

Peer groups, power and play in early childhood settings

Annica Löfdahl

Introduction

This chapter focuses on children's perspectives on play and their shared knowledge of its social dimension. Play is supposed to be the principal activity in Swedish pre-schools, and is seen as important in children's development. Through play, children are supposed to develop their identity, curiosity and also their ability to learn. A curriculum goal to strive towards stresses children's developing understanding and acceptance of our society's shared democratic values. In other words, both the content of play, and the way it is carried out in pre-school activities, seem to be of great importance when we try to understand children's peer cultures and the way children organize their social activities and relationships.

Theoretical grounds

My research on children and children's play seeks to identify and describe how children in pre-school settings construct shared knowledge about their regular social life together, and how this knowledge comes to be used, developed and changed over time. One important point of departure is to relate research questions to the pre-school, and thereby recognize that the pre-school is an institutionalized, but also institutionalizing setting which creates specific structural possibilities and constraints. In relation to these structural circumstances it is of great importance to focus on children's agency.

Together with colleagues in my research group (Löfdahl and Hägglund 2006, 2007; Löfdahl et al. 2008), I have developed the theoretical concept *children's social knowledge domains* as an elaborated and integrated theoretical perspective where childhood is regarded as a social construction and children are regarded as social actors with agency who are able to influence their everyday life. The term 'children's social knowledge domains' is used to represent common systems of norms and values that are tied to certain situations, rules, places or phenomena in the pre-school setting. The concept acts as a framework for integrated analyses of *interpreted reproduction* in children's peer cultures (Corsaro 2005a), *children's geographies* (Holloway and Valentine 2000) and concepts and models from the *sociology of childhood* (James et al. 1998; Mayall 2002; James and James 2004). Social knowledge domains hold information about children's positions, their places and values and attitudes in settings, and permit a consideration of the dialectics between structure and agency.

In the next section a more elaborated description of theories of children, childhood and peer cultures will be outlined, followed by a discussion of how they can provide an alternative to traditional theories in understanding children's development and socialization.

Children and childhood

Contemporary theories of children and childhood are often referred to as 'the new social studies of childhood'. To understand what is *new* we must compare these theories to previous knowledge of children and especially to traditional developmental psychology. Briefly, within this tradition, theories tried to explain children's behaviour in relation to future goals. Children were seen as passive receivers of the surrounding environment, and *socialization* was understood as the process whereby children assimilated norms, values and knowledge from adults in order to become participating citizens in the society (Burman 2008). Based on these theories, a specific knowledge about children and childhood was constructed, which proposed particular values which were used to judge children in accordance with its theoretical descriptions. Unfortunately, children were often judged as 'incorrect', when the theory did not correspond with the social reality, and pedagogical methods were developed to 'correct' their development in line with the theoretical requirements. From this perspective, childhood was seen as less important in and of itself, and was positioned more as a preparatory phase for adulthood. Childhood sociology and 'the new social studies of childhood' represent an alternative perspective from which children are viewed as beings in their own right, and childhood is understood as a participatory phase in life (James et al. 1998; Dahlberg et al. 1999; Mayall 2002).

In recent decades, theoretical concepts have developed within childhood studies that make it possible to describe, analyze and interpret children as competent social actors. In accordance with this tradition my research aims to study children and childhood on their own premises. The concept of the 'competent child' (Brembeck et al. 2004) derives from a view of children's agency which affirms that children are co-constructers in their own development and participants in societal processes, and thus are able to influence and change structures in their environment. When studying children's activities in pre-school from this perspective I have been interested in taking structural circumstances into consideration, in order to analyze how children make use of their agency, and how teachers' ideas of structuring the setting meet with children's agency. In this context, it is more fruitful to regard agency as varying according to the situation, rather than seeing it as something fixed and useful in every situation. If, like Hutchby and Moran-Ellis (1998), we regard children's competencies as situated in concrete social contexts, we must also consider both the possibilities and the constraints of these contexts. According to Lee (2001), agency is related to dependence rather than independence, as everyone, children and adults, depends on others to be able to act. This reasoning, rather than taking children's agency for granted, raises questions about how agency is constructed in pre-school peer groups. Children are not sole agents; rather, they construct and use their agency in interdependence with others in their peer cultures. For that reason we need to understand the relation between agency and peer cultures.

Peer culture

Later I will outline William Corsaro's (1985, 2005a, 2005b) theories about peer culture as an analytical tool which helps to make children's actions and shared activities in pre-school intelligible. When children spend long periods of time together, they develop their own *peer cultures*, a concept widely used within contemporary childhood research to describe children's perspective and interpretations of the surrounding culture, and the ways that they tackle issues important to their own lives and development. In Corsaro's (2005b: 110) definition, peer culture is 'a stable set of activities or routines, artefacts, values and concerns that children produce and share in interaction with peers'. It means that the processes by which norms, attitudes and values are expressed in children's play and activities are likely to be similar within a group of children in the same pre-school, while potentially varying across time and culture. Being a pre-school child means being part of a specific peer culture, and possessing knowledge about one's own and one's peers' status positions. For example, who one has the right to socialize with, which of the children decides the play, and how group members will behave towards each other. Peer cultures are built out of actions and interactions between children, and their content may be understood as *how* and *what* is negotiated *where*.

Within peer cultures children tackle the task of interpreting and understanding the surrounding culture, including the actions, norms and values they encounter in the behaviours of adults and other children. They interpret and reconstruct the surrounding culture, in order to make it intelligible and manageable in their own activities through a process which Corsaro calls *interpretive reproduction*. I adopt this concept as a way of expressing children's active participation in continuous ongoing processes, where culturally mediated knowledge, norms and values must continually be made intelligible again. In this way we might regard interpretive reproduction as a more dynamic form of *socialization*, as a mutual relation between the growing child and its surroundings. This contrasts with the traditional understanding of socialization in which a passive child is assumed to internalize the norms and values of adult society.

An interesting characteristic of children's peer cultures is the process of *secondary adjustments* (originally from Goffman's *Asylums*, 1961), which refers to the collective actions undertaken by children as a means of avoiding adults' rules in pre-school. Corsaro describes 'primary adjustment' as the subordinates doing what they have been told to, that is, obeying and adjusting. In the next step the adjustments become 'secondary', which means that children appear to have adjusted, although really they are undertaking a collective form of resistance which typically develops in institutions like the pre-school. Examples of secondary adjustments can be seen in play with negative social actions, such as ignoring and excluding other children from play, in spite of general institutional and adult-initiated rules which say that 'anyone can join'.

In general, interpretive reproduction and secondary adjustments are concepts that refer primarily to children's relations to adults and society, rather than to the possibility that the theory might also deal with resistance towards those of the same age, such as children within the same peer culture. My research indicates, however, that it is possible to talk about a *third adjustment,* as we have shown that the systems of social knowledge within the peer culture will also be subject to resistance, as children develop strategies for resisting their own rules and norms. The notion of children's collective action being intended to adjust and interpret the meaning in shared experiences of adult culture will also mean that they develop and communicate a shared system of social knowledge. These systems include experiences from their own ongoing social constructions of their peer culture, in which certain values and positioning are constructed towards other children in the peer group.

Peer cultures are not the only theoretical concepts to describe children's shared ideas of social characteristics. Theories from children's geographies also support the image of children as social actors who participate in their own development. These theoretical approaches in recent years have been used together, informing and enhancing each other (Holloway and Valentine 2000; Christensen and O'Brien 2003; Gustafson 2009). In the same way as they construct peer cultures, children are understood to construct the meaning of their physical spaces. In managing relations embedded in material practices and spaces/places, children are also seen to be co-constructing each other. As stressed by Cele (2006), place-interactive methods offer opportunities to gather concrete and reliable information about children's multi-faceted relations to their local environment. My research indicates that children's experiences of diversity, such as gender, age and ethnicity are often embedded in pre-school settings, give meaning to the setting, and as such contribute to the children's shared social knowledge.

Peer culture, childhood theories and child development

How can we make use of these theories in order to understand child development and socialization? How do they help us to move forward from the theories of traditional developmental psychology? Previous theories of child development presupposed a linear development where individual children passed through certain stages during the preparatory phase of childhood in order to become socially competent adults. As these stages were seen as more or less general to all children in all cultures, the context, the social and cultural environment and children's collective actions were viewed as relatively unimportant.

Instead of seeing children's individual development as isolated from its context, Corsaro's (2005b) theory of interpretive reproduction offers an alternative view, one which considers collective reproduction to be central to children's development. Corsaro uses a cobweb metaphor to catch the productive/reproductive aspects of development, describing child development as taking place in different social institutions (family, economy, culture, education, religion, politics, working life, etc.) between cultural information flows. Children participate in, and pass through, several such institutions during their childhoods. Rather than being viewed as linear, development is regarded as spiralling from the cobweb's centre towards larger and wider fields, from infancy to adulthood. Continuing to use this metaphor, the cobweb is a collective construction in which children's experiences from childhood constitute important parts of their life histories. Hence, individual development is embedded in the context, and so studies of both children's experiences and their childhood contexts are needed to understand both child development and societal change.

Theoretical concepts from childhood sociology can be helpful in seeking to understand children in the 'here-and-now'. Once again we must learn to regard the context as important and to understand both what is specific and what is general. If we regard children as co-constructors of societal changes, we recognize that they participate in constructing their own childhoods, which forces us to reconsider and revise our own theoretical concepts. The new social studies of childhood require us to construct a theory of development which recognizes a more dialogic and interactive process, as the following episodes illustrate.

Children's agency – examples from a Swedish pre-school

The empirical data reported in this chapter come from ethnographic studies conducted between 2000 and 2007 in Swedish pre-school settings. Children aged 3 to 5 years were observed during their activities and play, and data were collected by means of interviews, formal and informal talks, video recordings and field notes. Teachers, parents and children all gave their informed consent to participation. The Swedish pre-school is play-based, and organized in different rooms for play and aesthetic activities. Opening hours are usually from 6.00am to 6.00pm; the staff consists of three full-time teachers working with groups of 18–20 children who may spend up to ten hours per day in the pre-school depending on their parents' working hours.

Social difference and social order

My experiences from several ethnographic studies of children in pre-school reveal that, in the teacher's absence, children can behave very unkindly to each other. My first example illustrates how children negotiate the rules of 'being with' other children.

The teachers are busy with kitchen work, clearing the tables after breakfast. Some girls, among them Linda (4), Anna (4) and Malin (5), are in the art room drawing. Linda is new and also one of the youngest in the group. She asks Malin and Anna if she can join, but they don't want her to join them:

Anna: You always say that, always!
Malin: Yes, always and everywhere where we are, she asks hundreds of times, doesn't she, Anna?
Anna: You cannot be with us, Linda, we will be too many.

Malin: She follows us, and after a while she asks again. (to
            Linda) We don't want you to ask that again.
Anna: (to Linda) And you are not allowed to be with us, I say!
Malin: You cannot be a human being and ... you can't be
            anything if you are with us. Anna decides.
Anna: Yes, I decide that all children ...
Malin: She decides that you cannot be with.
Anna: Yes, because Malin is my best friend and I decide that
            you cannot be with!

It seems like Anna and Malin are competing to outdo each other in their
unkindness to Linda. By referring to a previous situation where Linda has
asked them to join, they decide not to let her join, and find reasons to
justify their rejections. It is easy to imagine Linda's situation and as an
adult observing one really wants to change the situation and let Linda be
with the girls. But what is actually going on; and would it be possible to
change this situation? On the one hand, we can identify an explicit
agreement about not letting Linda join; on the other hand, we can identify tacit agreement among all the other children round the table as no
protests are heard from them during this exchange. In this situation,
Anna and Malin have the power to define what counts, and to contribute
to the children's shared knowledge about the rules associated with 'being
with' (other children).

It is quite common for characteristics based on difference, such as age
and gender, to influence children's opportunities to participate in play.
Special rules and conditions are set up, as several studies from our
research group show. These include for example, assigning younger children the role of being dead, not yet born, or seriously ill, which reduce
or even exclude them from 'real' participation in the play (Löfdahl 2006;
Löfdahl and Hägglund 2007; Skånfors et al. 2009). Age is always present
in Swedish pre-school settings, for instance, through discussion about
birthdays, and is evident in age-specific rules for activities, spaces and
material, such as picnic events for the 5-year-olds, jigsaw puzzles for the
3-year-olds and special crayons for toddlers, etc.

In the following example, Chris (4) is playing with Sandra (4) and
Paula (3). Sandra and Paula are acting in a way that irritates Chris which
makes her activate age in the continuing negotiation.

Chris: Well, then I'll ask Emma, she can really be angry, she is
            five years and I am four years.
Sandra: And I'm already four years.
Paula: And I'm so many years (showing three fingers).
Chris: And I've already ... four ... two days, no three ...

Sandra:	I've also had my third birthday.
Chris:	I've done like the adults!
Paula:	I'm so many years (now showing four fingers).
Chris:	Four? You too?
Sandra:	(to Paula) Have you had your fourth birthday?

Chris and Sandra find out that she might have had a fourth birthday, but only once!

This example shows the importance of age for establishing and maintaining the social order. Sometimes it was not enough to refer to one's own age, and reference to older friends was needed to support one's position in the negotiations. We might understand the meaning of age as something that has to be interpreted and made intelligible by the children. The research findings show that age functions as a resource for activating what one wants, for example, to get rid of toddlers in play, or to obtain access to physical and social spaces. However, age is rarely activated to express friendship; rather it is used to mark out power and social positioning. Being older and talking about one's age works as a structural marker, frequently used in negotiations around accessing and deciding the content of play.

In a study of a multicultural pre-school settings (Löfdahl et al., unpublished), our analyses challenged assumptions in the Swedish curriculum regarding the pre-school as a cultural meeting place which influences children's understanding of diversity in a positive manner. Rather, we found that the social meaning of cultural diversity, similar to the construct of 'age', is actually integrated into children's shared constructions of social belonging and power. Aspects of diversity appear for example, when one girl is separated from the group during a home-language lesson – an apparently positive activity, though it ends up with her failing to join the group once the lesson is finished. Diversity also becomes visible during circle time, for example, in activities which require familiarity with aspects of Swedish nature, such as squirrels. This activity was intended to allow all children to participate and learn about a seemingly neutral theme. However, failing to act like a Swedish squirrel became a reason for children to exclude, rather than include, others in their play. From an institutional perspective, diversity deals with *defusing* differences when stressing equal conditions – peers, places and props for everyone, and simultaneously *maintaining* differences, for instance, by providing individual home language tuition. From the children's perspective, this seemed to be a paradox when understanding and managing cultural diversity and its social value. As our results show, it is far from certain that cultural diversity is a positive social resource in the peer group.

Physical and social spaces

Children develop specific knowledge which is linked with specific places and activities in pre-school, and construct meanings about these places and activities that do not always correspond to the meanings intended by adults in the institution. When analyzing the children's use of the 'art studio' I found that the room held meanings other than those intended by the teachers. The art studio was strategically placed in the setting, and from here children could keep a strict watch over who arrived or left, and what was going on in the other rooms. The art studio worked as a 'neutral' room where no one had the right to decide about access, but where negotiations concerning activities and places in the setting were continuously in progress. It meant that the children 'appeared' in the art studio when they arrived in the morning, between different activities, when play situations went wrong or concluded, or when they wanted to observe and control their peers.

For the children, art activities in this room took second place to the primary activities of discussing positioning and participation in play, although judging the art work of peers was an important part of such status positioning. The children looked at, and praised, each other's drawings as a way to establish contact, and to initiate, develop or strengthen a shared activity. They would also point out their own drawings as excellent, in order to position themselves in relation to others. However, the contrary worked as well when children were critical of the artistic abilities of others in order to diminish their status. In the following example, the two girls Malin (5) and Ella (4) sit alone in the art studio drawing with coloured pencils.

> Malin makes complaints about Ella's inability to discern the colours properly.
> Malin turns to me (as I sit next to them, observing) then to Ella, commenting in a scornful way.

> *Malin*:   She says black, she says, but it is blue! You are wrong Ella!
>   Ella leaves the room.

Through this and similar episodes, new constructions of the room's function emerged that influenced the possible and permitted play activities, in an example of how children used their common agency in a sort of 'social occupation' of the pre-school setting. They took possession of one area, and gave it a function quite different from what was originally intended. It is not independence, but *interdependence* with each other that allowed the children in the group to change both the physical and social structures in the pre-school. These changes were of importance to children's meaning-making, their development and their contribution to their own childhoods.

Peer cultures and teachers' work

When we want to understand what is happening in children's peer culture it is important to throw light upon the teachers' work and intentions with regard to activities. Parallel to the children's work with peer cultures are the teachers' efforts to develop a pedagogical environment that creates positive opportunities for learning and development. I will give a brief example from our data of one pedagogical theme which was introduced by the teachers in the beginning of the school year, followed by some examples of how the pedagogical theme was re-interpreted by the children.

One of the more or less invisible structures in the pre-school setting is the manner in which teachers and children strive to ensure that children are 'nice', 'kind' and pleasant to each other. In order to demonstrate the importance of these qualities, they activate the theme of 'Bamse'. Bamse is a famous figure in a Swedish children's book. He is a bear who has got several friends, even if some of them are less friendly, such as the wolf. Bamse and his friends are core figures in the theme. The figures visit the pre-school, and inspire the children to think and wonder about how to behave in order to fulfil the norm of being 'nice, pleasant and helpful'. How then do children respond to this content?

In my analyses I have defined children's different ways of relating, communicating and behaving to each other as discourses. During a short period in connection to the first visit of Bamse, I could identify discourses of comfort and being pleasant, where the children both requested and reminded each other how they should talk and behave, as in the following example:

> Sandra (4) and Anna (4) are talking to each other during a drawing situation when they start to quarrel about something. Both accuse each other of being ugly when Sandra says: 'You are not allowed to say ugly!!'

After a month or so, I observed how this 'nice and pleasant' discourse diminished. As long as the friendship theme was brought to their attention by the teachers, the children responded by making it intelligible in their everyday situations. After some time, this discourse was less articulated, and might be presumed to be a normalized social structure in the peer culture: the idea of 'being nice' was still present, but children no longer needed to be reminded of it. In this way we can view both children and teachers, through their agency, to be part of the shared understanding of the theme. However, observing their discourse over a longer period reveals that the children constructed an opposite discourse which permitted them to act unkindly towards each other. I interpret this change as the children being very well aware of how to behave according to the 'appropriate' standard. However, it is this awareness that they use to construct dissensions in the group. In relation to the children's agency, the teachers' pedagogical intentions and agency about 'being nice' are less powerful than using the rule about 'being nice' to create social dynamics which benefit one's position in the social situation. The following example, from the doll corner, illustrates a less-nice discourse among Ella (3), Paula (3) and Anna (4), in which they use all the bad language they know in order to become the most powerful participant in the play situation.

Ella:	Get out!
Paula:	No!
Ella:	(to Anna) Throw her out Anna, throw her out!
Anna:	I'm stronger than Pippi Longstocking!
Ella:	Me too. (Anna sticks her tongue out at Paula). My dad says ... I can be with ... if you are nice I can be with you.
Paula:	My dad says that you are not allowed to be with [me]!
Anna:	... and my dad says that you are stupid. If you want, I can call on my big brother and he can tell you, devil-shit!
Ella:	No, not to me!
Paula:	Not to me either.
Anna:	Devil-shit on you! Poo-poo!

Anna spits at Ella and Paula while leaving the doll corner.

There is no logic in who says bad things to whom in this situation, although all the girls are aware that their choice of language is not permitted. The teacher's efforts to teach about how to be friends have simultaneously shown the children how to act in the opposite way – to create hostility rather than friendship. The example illustrates how the children are testing this new knowledge about friendships. One way to understand this is to relate it to the process by which everyday actions eventually become banal: to be 'nice and pleasant' may even become tiresome for the children. It might be that the more we put the 'natural' thematic content into children's activities, the less they will reflect upon it. This is paradoxical, as the pedagogical intentions were to reflect on friendship in order for it to become a 'natural' part of the children's daily lives in the setting.

Conclusion and questions for further discussion

Results from my studies show how children, within and through their peer cultures, construct the conditions for participation in play and other activities in pre-school settings. Conclusions drawn from this synthesis of results are that social differences matter when children construct social order in their peer group – it makes a difference who you are, and what social and cultural knowledge you bring to a play situation. Not everyone gets to play!

When taking children's agency into account, it is clear that children are actively contributing to both stability and change in the structural circumstances that surround them. Aspects of power are built in to the physical milieu through children's shared meaning-making about spaces and places in pre-school. Constructing new social functions for the pre-school spaces and places contributes to the acceptance of certain play content, which is more suitable for some children than for others. These processes of making daily life in the pre-school intelligible and manageable require children to maintain the conditions for social control. Being a pre-school child and spending years together with other children in a pre-school setting mean something special. Opportunities to play and learn are also opportunities to learn about social structures, power relations, excluding and including activities. The teachers in pre-school have good pedagogical intentions when arranging their activities, but their pedagogical input is sometimes used by the children in a way opposite to that intended, in the interests of creating and maintaining their own social positioning.

The overall results show that children's social knowledge domains contain aspects of exclusionary activities, power relations and empathic values. These aspects sometimes differ from the anticipated pedagogical outcomes associated with using play as a means to promote children's social development. These results suggest the need for increased awareness among teachers about children's peer cultures and children's ability to construct their own meanings around pre-school activities. More awareness is also needed about the dialectics between children's agency, and the structural conditions in the setting. Finally, additional thought should also be given to children's own roles in arranging pedagogical activities in pre-school to accommodate their own manipulations of the social situation.

These conclusions suggest the following key questions as potential issues for further research and pedagogical consideration:

- What kind of impact will the children's constructions of 'social' knowledge have on their understanding of the social value of differences (age, gender, ethnicity), compared to the systems of norms and values that the teachers and other adults represent?
- What does it mean when children are engaged in actions of social segregation or exclusion at the same time as teachers are formulating rules such as 'anyone can join'?
- Do children rely on the expectation that adults are there, in the background, to care for those who are excluded? Does the absence of teachers influence the ease with which children are able to construct excluding social positions and structures?

References

Brembeck, H., Johansson, B. and Kampmann, J. (eds) (2004) *Beyond the Competent Child*. Frederiksberg: Roskilde University Press.

Burman, E. (2008) *Deconstructing Developmental Psychology*, 2nd edn. London: Routledge.

Cele, S. (2006) Communicating place: methods for understanding children's experience of place, Thesis, Stockholm University.

Christensen, P. and O'Brien, M. (eds) (2003) *Children in the City: Home, Neighbourhood and Community*. London: Routledge.

Corsaro, W. (1985) *Friendship and Peer Culture in the Early Years*. Norwood, NJ: Ablex Publishing Corporation.

Corsaro, W. (2005a) Collective action and agency in young children's peer cultures, in J. Qvortrup (ed.) *Studies in Modern Childhood: Society, Agency, Culture*. New York: Palgrave Macmillan.

Corsaro, W. (2005b) *The Sociology of Childhood*, 2nd edn. Thousand Oaks, CA: Pine Forge Press.

Dahlberg, G., Moss, P. and Pence, A. (1999) *Beyond Quality in Early Childhood Education and Care: A Postmodern Perspective*. London: Falmer Press.

Goffman, E. (1961) *Asylums: Essays on the Social Situation of Mental Patients and Other Inmates*. New York: Penguin Books.

Gustafson, K. (2009) Us and them – children's identity work and social geography in a Swedish school yard, *Ethnography and Education*, 4(1): 1–16.

Holloway, S. and Valentine, G. (2000) *Children's Geographies: Playing, Living, Learning*. London: Routledge.

Hutchby, I. and Moran-Ellis, J. (1998) Situating children's social competence, in I. Hutchby and J. Moran-Ellis (eds) *Children and Social Competence: Arenas of Action*. London: Falmer Press.

James, A. and James, A.L. (2004) *Constructing Childhood Theory, Policy and Social Practice*. New York: Palgrave Macmillan.

James, A., Jenks, C. and Prout, A. (1998) *Theorizing Childhood*: Cambridge: Polity Press.

Lee, N. (2001) *Childhood and Society: Growing Up in an Age of Uncertainty*. Maidenhead: Open University Press.

Löfdahl, A. (2006) Grounds for values and attitudes: children's play and peer-culture in pre-school, *Journal of Early Childhood Research*, 4(1): 77–88.

Löfdahl, A. and Hägglund, S. (2006) Power and participation: social representations among children in pre-school, *Social Psychology of Education*, 9(2): 179–94.

Löfdahl, A. and Hägglund, S. (2007) Spaces of participation in pre-school: arenas for establishing power orders? *Children and Society*, 21: 328–38.

Löfdahl, A., Hägglund, S. and Skånfors, L. (2008) Förskolebarns sociala kunskapsdomäner – ett sätt att tillsammans förstå, hantera och ordna den sociala vardagen [Children's social knowledge domains], in *Resultatdialog, 2008: Forskning inom utbildningsvetenskap*. Stockholm: Vetenskapsrådet, pp. 53–7.

Löfdahl, A., Hägglund, S. and Skånfors, L. Diversity in preschool: defusing and maintaining differences, unpublished.

Mayall, B. (2002) *Towards a Sociology for Childhood*. Buckingham: Open University Press.

Skånfors, L., Löfdahl, A. and Hägglund, S. (2009) Hidden spaces and places in the preschool: withdrawal strategies in preschool children's peer cultures, *Journal of Early Childhood Research*, 7(1): 94–109.

10 Framing play for learning

Professional reflections on the role of open-ended play in early childhood education

Susan Edwards, Amy Cutter-Mackenzie and Elizabeth Hunt

Introduction

Quality early childhood educational experiences have been characterized for many years by the belief that open-ended play supports children's learning and knowledge acquisition. Process over product has been emphasized as an important component of learning, suggesting that the act of participation in play is more important than what the play itself generates. This orientation has generated an acceptance of 'free play' in early childhood education based on the belief that during play children 'explore concepts at their own pace' (White et al. 2007: 99). This particular perspective has been scrutinized from a poststructuralist orientation, and used to describe open-ended, freely chosen play as means of ascribing particular forms of childhood, play and knowledge construction to children (Ailwood 2003; Gibbons 2007; Taguchi 2007). Concepts traditionally informing the theory and practice of early learning from the modernist-derived, developmental-constructivist paradigm have been critiqued, with contemporary theorization embracing a multitude of perspectives, including the 'new' sociology of childhood, feminism and postmodernism as means of reconfiguring traditional teaching practices in early childhood education (Soto and Swadener 2002; Edwards 2008). At the same time, cultural-historical theory has been used by researchers to re-theorize conceptions of development and play in early learning (see, for example, Fleer 2010). While this perspective has been used to examine the social and cultural construction of knowledge in early childhood education, it also references the cultural construction of play and reinforces the idea that play is a culturally defined activity (Gaskins et al. 2006). In combination, these many different perspectives have been used to question the assumption that open-ended play provides the most appropriate learning experiences for young children.

An important aspect of this re-theorization has been the extent to which teachers are able to engage with the relationship between the pedagogy of open-ended play, and the type of conceptual learning children experience when provided with these opportunities. This issue was considered during a research project which examined the extent to which pre-school children were able to identify the concepts teachers believed were embedded in the open-ended learning experiences they provided for their students within their classrooms (Cutter-Mackenzie et al. 2009). During this project, two teachers were invited to design play experiences for children, which were video-recorded. The children were invited to watch these recordings, and to comment on their play and learning. The discussions with the children were also video-recorded and later shown to the teachers, who responded to the children's perceptions of their play. While the original research focused on examining the relationship between the children's and teachers' perceptions of the play-based activity, this chapter focuses instead on the responses Elizabeth, one of the participating teachers, made in relation to the emerging data.

Elizabeth's responses to the data form the basis of this chapter because her pedagogical framing and interpretation of the relationship between her teaching and the children's learning fed directly into the intended project methodology. This meant that a modified project methodology was implemented based on Elizabeth's reflexive approach to practice within the context of the unfolding project. Elizabeth engaged in systematic and critical inquiry about her own teaching which led to a collaborative research endeavour allowing all three authors of this chapter to begin the process of making 'judgements against [the] theoretical underpinnings and norms of personal/professional practice' (Goodfellow 2005: 48). Elizabeth's attempts to examine how open-ended play worked to inform her teaching and learning provide an avenue for reflecting on how play has come to operate as a particular pedagogical form in early childhood education and care.

The intended and modified methodologies

Data collection for the project was based on the implementation of a specific play experience designed by Elizabeth. Elizabeth is an experienced teacher, having worked in the field for over 20 years. At the time of this project she was working in a kindergarten offering a sessional programme for children aged 4–5 years. Elizabeth was employed under a cluster management model by the local municipality. A key aspect of the

Table 10.1   Intended four-stage methodology

Stage 1	Elizabeth designs play experience (make this dirty water clean using the materials provided on the table, see Figure 10.1).
	Elizabeth records play experience in her usual programming notes.
	Elizabeth indicates what she believes are the concepts embedded in the play experiences in her research journal (filtration).
Stage 2	Children participate in the play experience designed by Elizabeth (video-recorded).
Stage 3	Children view footage of themselves participating in Elizabeth's play experience (video-recorded).
Stage 4	Elizabeth watches footage of the children viewing and responding to footage of themselves participating in her play experience.

management model was a commitment to open-ended play-based learning and the use of an emergent curriculum. The kindergarten was located in a middle-class, largely European-heritage community. For the purpose of this project, Elizabeth was asked to design a play experience that contained conceptual knowledge related to environmental education. This was because the focus of the original project was on determining the concepts children and teachers believed were embedded in the play experiences. Previous work by the researchers had suggested that environmental education concepts were strongly related to children's and teachers' daily lives and provided an appropriate context for examining conceptual learning (Cutter-Mackenzie and Edwards 2006). Elizabeth was then asked to identify the core concepts she believed were embedded in the experience she had designed. Initially, a four-stage methodology for understanding what Elizabeth believed were the concepts embedded in her play experience, and what the children believed they learned through participation in the play experiences, was used as the basis for the intended methodology (Table 10.1).

According to the intended methodology, the project would examine whether or not a discrepancy existed between what Elizabeth believed were the concepts embedded in her play experiences, and what the children believed they had learned from participating in the experience. The intended methodology was initially implemented up to Stage 2. However, after this early stage, Elizabeth began to change the methodology as she responded to the emerging data and reflected on the relationship between her teaching and the children's learning. Here Elizabeth inserted two further 'sub-stages' into Stage 2 before the project progressed to Stages 3 and 4 as intended. The purpose of these sub-stages was for Elizabeth to examine how changes in her teaching approach using play might relate to what and how the children were learning. Table 10.2 outlines the modified methodology.

Table 10.2 Modified methodology (shaded areas represent modification)

Stage 1	Elizabeth designs play experience (make this dirty water clean using the materials provided on the table, see Figure 10.1). Elizabeth records play experience in her usual programming notes. Elizabeth indicates what she believes are the concepts embedded in the play experiences in her research journal (filtration).
Stage 2A	Group A children participate in open-ended play experience designed by Elizabeth in which they are asked to make dirty water clean (video-recorded).
Stage 2B	Group A children (with an extra child included) participate in dirty water experience again. Prior to participation Elizabeth demonstrates the use of a filter (video-recorded).
Stage 2C	Group B children (new group of children) participate in dirty water experience. Elizabeth demonstrates how to make a filter and uses specific terminology, such as 'filtration' (video-recorded).
Stage 3	Group A and B children view footage of themselves participating in Elizabeth's play experiences (video-recorded).
Stage 4	Elizabeth watches footage of the children viewing and responding to footage of themselves participating in her play experiences.

The chapter now turns to an examination of Elizabeth's professional reflection on the role of play in early learning, and in doing so, considers the rationale for the modified methodology.

Reflecting on play-based learning: modifying the methodology

During the data collection phase of the project Elizabeth reflected on the findings emerging from the project. These reflections were recorded in Elizabeth's research journal and formed the basis of her beliefs (or suppositions) regarding the children's learning. As the project unfolded, Elizabeth's questioning of her prior beliefs regarding the way in which children learn promoted further modifications to the intended methodology. The following sections of this chapter detail the children's responses to the different forms of play-based activity implemented by Elizabeth and include reference to Elizabeth's professional reflections on the role of play-based learning in early childhood education.

Stage 2A: Have you worked it out yet?

Video footage from Stage 2A of the project showed three children, Clayton, Toby and Thomas, engaged in Elizabeth's planned activity. The

Figure 10.1 The materials provided for the filtering experience.

instruction given to the children was 'I want you to try and make clean water. You have lots of things here. So I am going to leave you to see if you can make that dirty water clean. You might want to pour some into another container. See how you go.' During this time the children were observed pouring the dirty water into a large trough. The materials (cotton wool, sand, gravel, plastic bottles with the bottoms removed) provided by Elizabeth for filtering the water were dumped into the dirty water, swirled and tossed about. Midway through the play Elizabeth returned to the children and engaged in some generalized discussion:

Elizabeth: How is it going, you three? Have you worked it out yet?
Children: No.

Elizabeth: Have you used those things [materials] over there?
Children: Yes.
Elizabeth: Have you used one of those [bottle funnels]?
Children: No.
Elizabeth: Maybe you could try one?

Elizabeth left the scene and the boys were observed attempting to pour water through the funnels. Since the funnels were not lined with any of the filtering materials, the water poured through and remained dirty. Clayton commented, 'We are making the water dirtier.' Twenty-three minutes after the activity had started, the children left the experience without having realized Elizabeth's instruction to make clean water.

Elizabeth recorded her reaction to the experience in her journal. Here, she mentioned her intention to modify the intended methodology, noting that she was interested in discussing the concept of filtration with the children. The need for some direct teaching and modelling as a means of supporting the children in the acquisition of conceptual knowledge was evident:

> What an interesting session that was. The three boys were certainly into the play element of the activity – Thomas, Toby and Clayton got straight into what was asked – to try and make the water clean. There was a lot of discussion, playing. Minimal instruction was given, as one of the aims of this research is to see how much 'instruction' is needed to help a child reach a scientific concept. For the children to get more knowledge/learning – there certainly needs to be more direct teaching and modelling. Next time I will have some discussion about the need to filter water. Have some materials ready. Talk about what we have learned about filtration – water goes through several processes. Have a sample ready – let the children use the sample – make their own – try other arrangements [with the filtering materials] to see which works better if the order is altered.

During informal conversation with the researchers, Elizabeth suggested the children had 'not learned anything' and indicated that she would like to try and demonstrate a model filtration system with the same group of children (Thomas, Toby and Clayton) prior to leaving them to play by themselves. Elizabeth was interested in determining the extent to which her intervention would impact the children's ability to complete the activity and to acquire some conceptual knowledge associated with the process of filtration. This was recorded in her journal:

[I have] decided to show an example. Have a look at the water and the particles in it. Talk about large ones and small ones, even microscopic ones we can't actually see! Talk about the example, gravel/pebbles/sand/cotton wool. How the water will seep/soak down through the layers and trap the particles. Let them try different variations to see what works best. For example, sand at the top or after the cotton wool? Follow up with a book on the filtering and cleaning of water. I have decided to follow up with the same group of children, but have added Nathan.

In this example, Elizabeth's deliberate decision to focus on supporting the children's acquisition of the scientific concepts influenced the extent to which she herself used both scientific and conceptual language when describing her modifications to the methodology. For example, Elizabeth described the learning experience prior to implementation in her journal as 'helping children to understand we need clean water to use'. The concepts associated with the intended experience were simply listed as 'to clean, purify and filter the water'. Elizabeth's belief that the children had 'not learned anything' from the open-ended experience sharpened her desire to focus the children's attention on the concepts embedded in the activity. This desire appeared to refine the focus for Elizabeth herself, and meant that her description of the modified methodology now included reference to key conceptual ideas such as 'particles', 'seep', 'soak', 'layers', 'trap' and 'filtering'. A deliberate focus on the learning associated with the activity appeared to centre Elizabeth's own understanding of the scientific knowledge to be gained through the play, rather than the activity associated with the play.

This finding suggests an important relationship between the pedagogical framing of the play and the actualization of play for learning. Elizabeth described this outcome herself, and was able to relate it to the preferred open-ended approach promoted by her employer. Here, Elizabeth suggested that the implementation of an emergent curriculum and a focus on the role of open-ended play in learning had led her to become what she considered 'to be quite lazy, because you can just leave the open-ended things out for them, and yes, they like to play with them, but it really doesn't get some of them moving – they can just be there [conceptually] and not move along'. In this example, Elizabeth described the pedagogy of play as being responsible for the learning, rather than herself as the teacher. When working from within an open-ended pedagogy, it seemed enough to describe the activity (such as 'helping children understand we need clean water'). However, when direct teaching/ modelling was *planned for* as part of the activity, the scientific concepts were brought to consciousness (Fleer 2009) for Elizabeth when she had to describe how the teaching would actually occur (such as 'talk about the particles').

Stage 2B: Is anything coming out yet?

Video data from Stage 2B of the project shows Elizabeth standing around a trough with four boys, Clayton, Toby, Thomas and Nathan. Materials identical to those provided during Stage 2A were placed on a nearby table. Elizabeth enacted her pedagogical decision to provide the children with some direct teaching/modelling and began by asking them what they tried to do last time. The children revealed that there were unable to make the water clean. The video then goes on to show Elizabeth generating discussion regarding the contents of the dirty water followed by a demonstration of her pre-made filter and its differing layers. Elizabeth poured the dirty water into the filter and then asked the children what was happening:

Thomas:	It is getting all the sand out.
Toby:	It's melting. It's spreading into wet sand.
Elizabeth:	It is, isn't it? The water is seeping down. It is making the sand wet. Is anything coming out yet?
All:	No.
Toby:	The water turns it into wet sand and it stays.
Elizabeth:	Let's see, what is happening to all the pieces of tan-bark?
Thomas:	It is all gone.
Clayton:	Mine is getting clean (pouring dirty water through his hands).
Elizabeth:	You are using your hands to filter the water. I wonder if you can try and feel the bottom of this? And see if you can feel the cotton wool? Is that feeling damp? Oh look! Have a look! What is happening?
Thomas:	Water is coming out.
Elizabeth:	Toby, look! What colour is the water?
Toby:	It is dripping.
Thomas:	White! White!
Elizabeth:	It is dripping.
Clayton:	Clean.

Following Elizabeth's demonstration, she then invited the children to make their own filters. Two of the children (Thomas and Nathan) picked up bottles, stuffed cotton wool in the bottom of each one and poured dirty water through. Elizabeth left the activity while the boys discussed the need to squash the cotton wool into the funnels. The children's conversation demonstrated their success in cleaning the water:

Thomas: Oh look, mine is coming out! Look, boys!
Toby: Is it cleaner?
Thomas: Yep.
Toby: Mine is coming out cleaner. Yeah!
Clayton: Mine is coming out cleaner!
Thomas: It is turning the cotton wool into dirty wool. Yeah, it is getting all the dirty water out.
Clayton: Clean! Mine is clean!
Toby: Clean!

Clayton ran inside with his dripping funnel to show Elizabeth the clean water. Elizabeth and Clayton returned to the activity, and Elizabeth asked the children to consider different ways of layering the materials within the filters.

Elizabeth's response to this implementation of the activity was recorded in her journal. While focusing on the sense of achievement exhibited by the children, Elizabeth also considered the extent to which the children's previous open-ended experience may have contributed to their ability to complete the activity when provided with some direct teaching. This consideration was based on Elizabeth's observations of one of the children, Nathan, who had not participated in Stage 2A of the project. Elizabeth noted that Nathan appeared to be engaged in exploratory play with the materials, as well as trying to create a filter whereas the other boys moved straight into creating filters:

Well, the eyes really lit up. When I showed the boys the sample we talked about what was in the dirty water – tanbark, dirt in large clumps and small particles. Talked about the need to filter out the rubbish. Talked about what was in the sample, sand, gravel, pebbles, cotton wool. Poured some water in – watch. Noticed the sand getting damp! Quite excited when they saw the clean water drip out. They certainly got into trying their own filtering systems. Nathan tried without cotton wool – discussed the need to stop gravel and sand pouring straight through – Clayton's eyes nearly fell out of his head. They were very excited when they made their own clean filtered water – tried different ways. Clayton raced in with his sample, clean water pouring out of his filter – very excited. Question: if they were given the scientific goal or sample first would they play first or work on the experiment? Nathan was doing both because the other boys were right into the experiment having already had a play session. I am interested in a repeat showing of the sample first with a new group – this could provide interesting results. In other words should the children be given the materials to play first/experiment themselves, or should they get the direct teaching first to help them reach the concept?

Here Elizabeth posed a sophisticated pedagogical question that related strongly to her previous reflection on the role of open-ended learning in children's play. Elizabeth's earlier reaction to the children's open-ended play led to the decision to provide some direct teaching/modelling. However, her observation of Nathan raised the question of whether or not the children actually needed the open-ended experience first to realize the knowledge she deliberately focused on in Stage 2B. This suggested a further refinement of Elizabeth's interpretation of the role of play in early learning. Following the Stage 2A experience, Elizabeth's thinking and planning demonstrated an increased understanding of the type of scientific knowledge that would be gained through the children's play. This awareness was now paired with a question regarding the extent to which open-ended play could be used as a tool for preparing children for the later, more focused play. Rather than valuing the 'process' of open-ended play, Elizabeth deliberately linked open-ended play to an outcome when she questioned the extent to which it could be used as a preparatory stage for later conceptually focused play. These ideas were explored in Elizabeth's journal when she reflected on her personally held beliefs about early learning and the particular approach to pedagogy promoted by her employer:

> Having been in a situation where play-based learning has been encouraged to the point where the children choose everything, I have felt quite frustrated by this approach. I have always felt that we kindergarten teachers need to have that element in our programme. I feel this research project is really knocking this type of programming on the head, especially if we want the children to reach their potential, to reach a higher level of understanding or learning. However, after our second videoing session we are now faced with the question – should the children have free play with the materials first then be shown the materials for higher learning, or is it better to give them the information for the higher learning and then let them explore that knowledge through play? What have we got ourselves into?

Elizabeth's first modification to the intended methodology had generated a second question regarding the relationship between play and learning. This led Elizabeth to propose a further modification to the intended methodology. Elizabeth decided to investigate the type of learning evidenced in a group of children who were provided with the modelled example of the filter, without any previous opportunities for free play with the filtering materials.

Stage 2C: Can you look at the top?

Video footage from Stage 2C shows Elizabeth with four children, Mikhail, Madison, Samuel and Carly, gathered around the table. Elizabeth discussed the activity and demonstrated how to fill one of the funnels with the different filtering materials. The children were invited to add materials to the filter, and Elizabeth then poured dirty water into the funnel and asked the children to observe:

Elizabeth:	Do you think this will go straight through or it might take a while?
Madison:	It might take a while.
Elizabeth:	It might take a while. OK. Look at this dirty water going in (pouring water into filter).
Madison/Mikhail:	It is going through.
Elizabeth:	Oh, what is that water like? Is it dirty or clean?
All:	It is clean!
Madison:	It is clean! Because all the dirt is staying out because it is too big.
Elizabeth:	What's too big?
Madison:	The dirt.
Elizabeth:	What is the water like?
Madison:	It is clean.
Elizabeth:	It is clean, isn't it? And can you look at the top? What is it like there?
Madison:	It is dirty.

Following her demonstration, Elizabeth invited the children to create their own filters. The children moved immediately to the table and began layering materials and pouring dirty water through their filters. Five minutes later Elizabeth returned to the activity. Mikhail held up his funnel to show Elizabeth, and sand fell through to the bottom. Elizabeth commented that he didn't have any big rocks in his funnel, and suggested that it would be interesting to see what would happen if rocks were added. Mikhail then added rocks to the top of his filter, while Carly and Madison poured water through theirs. Elizabeth and the children discussed how the water was seeping through the filtering layers. Mikhail emptied the entire contents of his filter into the trough and returned to the table. He announced to Elizabeth, *'I am doing rocks first.'* Mikhail finished putting rocks into his funnel and poured in handfuls of sand. He returned to the trough and poured water into his own and Samuel's filters. Clean water trickled from the bottom of Mikhail's filter. He caught the water in a smaller container. Mikhail then emptied the contents of the filter into the trough and returned to the table with an empty funnel. He tipped sand into his empty funnel, which immediately poured through the end. Mikhail grabbed handfuls of cotton wool and stuffed them into the bottom of the funnel. He poured more sand into the funnel and then placed rocks on top. Mikhail returned to the table with his re-filled funnel and poured dirty water into the top. He watched as clean water exited from the bottom of his filter. The children continued adding different layers to the funnels and pouring water through until they run out of dirty water. Elizabeth returned and provided more dirty water for the children, at which point the videoing ended.

Elizabeth recorded her reaction to the implementation of Stage 2C in her journal. Here Elizabeth noted the absence of the exploratory play that had characterized both Stage 2A, and Nathan's participation in the experience, during Stage 2B:

> I did more talking, made the sample in front of them. They were very quiet and I stayed with them for longer before leaving. They seemed to start getting involved. Didn't see the 'play' that was in the first session, or the way Nathan was in the second session. They seemed to remain on task. The group was certainly very focused. It was very involved play with purpose.

In a later journal entry, Elizabeth recorded her reaction to viewing footage of the children watching their own videoed play (Stage 3). During one of these interviews Toby, Thomas and Clayton indicated that the activity was 'better when Elizabeth showed us'. Elizabeth used this statement to support her belief that it might be best to go straight to the direct teaching. However, in saying this, Elizabeth also noted the need for children to participate in some open-ended play as a means of laying a conceptual foundation for later more directed play:

> I still don't know if I've answered my question – should they play first? When given the direct teaching, the play was certainly far more purposeful and focused on the task. I do think that there would be times when the children needed the free play first – with materials they haven't really had much experience with. However, from the children's comments I think I would go to the direct teaching/example first and let the children go from there – exploring for themselves as they would have some direction and

idea of where to start. This does fit in with the sociocultural theories as the teacher – me – is part of the peer/community group within which the children are working/playing/learning.

It is interesting to consider Mikhail's engagement with the play materials in light of these comments. Here, Mikhail engaged in some highly exploratory behaviour within the conceptual structure provided by Elizabeth's demonstration in her capacity as the teacher. Rather than engaging in the type of exploratory play exhibited in Stage 2A, Mikhail went about the process in an almost scientific manner. First he tested how the filter operated with sand only. When this failed, he added larger stones to the bottom of his filter, and then returned to test his 'sand-only' model. Finally Mikhail developed a working model similar to the one originally provided by Elizabeth's demonstration in which he layered cotton wool, sand and gravel in his own funnel to successfully filter the water. Elizabeth's movement towards more deliberate engagement with both the children, and the conceptual ideas embedded in the task, created a framework for Mikhail's activity and the construction of a working filter. This contrasts with the experience of the Stage 2A children who freely admitted at the time, and in later interviews, that they 'were making the water dirtier' and 'couldn't make it clean'.

Framing play provision

The restrictions of the intended methodology would not have allowed Elizabeth to fully examine and problematize her teaching and indeed the children's experiences. The researchers supported Elizabeth in challenging the research methodology, encouraging her to pose and explore critical pedagogical questions. As such, participation in the project allowed Elizabeth to examine how different aspects of her teaching related to the children's learning within each of the play-based experiences she implemented. Elizabeth reflected on the relationship between the ideas embedded in the experience, and the extent to which these ideas were emphasized in her teaching according to the way in which she utilized the children's play:

> It was interesting to watch my own journey. The first session, I was very brief with the introduction and instructions. 'Can you make the water clean? See if you can use the materials available to do this.' In the second session, I showed the sample, had a brief discussion and mentioned the filter. In the third session, there was more discussion about the materials and what was required – 'filtering the dirty water to get clean water'. There was

more direct teaching and the use of the more complex ideas and words. I was prepared to take the children to the next level with the words I used and the sample. I was prepared to let the children go from there and experience the concept for themselves. I feel in some ways that this has shown me that I underestimate what kindergarten children are actually capable of learning about and that I need to broaden, and extend my planning to encourage this learning potential.

Elizabeth was very clear that her focus on supporting the learning increased her own engagement with the scientific concepts embedded in the experience. This was associated with a more sophisticated use of language, and an increased awareness regarding the children's capacity to engage with complex ideas. This finding supports two recent advances in the field of early education, including: (1) research demonstrating the importance of sustained-shared thinking between children and adults during play to support learning (Siraj-Blatchford et al. 2008); and (2) research emphasizing the need for children's everyday understandings of scientific phenomena to be related to academic concepts during play to generate mature concepts (Fleer 2009). Elizabeth's reflections suggest that the more deliberately she focused on how to teach the content embedded in play, the more alert she became to the conceptual knowledge and language she wished the children to consider. Thus, both the sustained-shared thinking, and the realization of mature conceptual understandings were more readily achieved when the play itself was deliberately framed for learning in the first instance. For example, during Stage 2A, Elizabeth's interactions with the children were limited to prompts such as 'Have you worked it out yet?', whereas during Stage 2C she engaged in more deliberate and sustained discussion with the children. Here she pointed out what was happening to the water, asked questions that built on the children's responses and worked to help the children understand why and how the water was getting cleaner.

   This represented a significant outcome for Elizabeth, particularly given the emphasis her employer placed on the use of open-ended play within the kindergarten. Elizabeth's framing of the children's play helped her realize that she could activate conceptual learning in ways not necessarily enabled through open-ended play alone. In doing so, Elizabeth developed her pedagogy of play to the point that value was placed on the conscious realization of conceptual ideas using play, rather than the possible exploration of concepts within play (Fleer 2010). This shift from an open-ended to a purposefully framed pedagogy of play was consistent with Elizabeth's argument regarding the role of the teacher if children are 'to reach their potential and [achieve] a higher level of understanding or learning'. The importance of the teacher, the child and the situation is recognized in cultural-historical theory, which emphasizes the role joint collective activity has in generating, supporting and maintaining learning. The teacher's task in this situation is to 'know about the possibilities of his or her own pedagogical activity, to use these sensibly and thus raise to a new level the activity, consciousness [and personality] of his or her charges' (Davydov 1995: 17).

Throughout the project Elizabeth became increasingly aware of the 'possibilities of her own pedagogical activity' and began to see *that the type of play she used impacted the pedagogy she actually implemented.* Her more purposefully framed pedagogical strategies seemed more likely to allow her and the children to consciously engage with the filtration concepts than did the purely open-ended approach she implemented in the first instance. Elizabeth noted this when describing how she saw the relationship between teaching and learning in early childhood education: 'Our kindergarten environment is very fortunate because we as teachers can teach, and still let the children continue to learn through experimentation, so that their learning is consolidated, reinforced and continually built upon.'

Elizabeth's participation in the research process provided a supportive space for her to problematize her prior beliefs and practices. The methodology provoked a high level of reflection, in turn, guiding Elizabeth's professional learning and growth (Wood and Bennett 2000). Her contributions to the research methodology meant that she was able to implement pedagogical strategies associated with this reflection in ways that led her to enhance her practice and refine her beliefs about the pedagogy of play. While the benefits of reflection have been discused readily in the literature, the research process described in the chapter reveals that video-based methodologies that actively involve teachers (in the design and implementation of research projects) may also incite rich professional learning and growth that can support teachers to reflect on the relationship between play and pedagogy in early years education.

Acknowledgements

The research reported in this chapter was supported by a grant from the Faculty of Education, Monash University, Australia.

References

Ailwood, J. (2003) Governing early childhood education through play, *Contemporary Issues in Early Childhood*, 4(3): 286–99.

Cutter-Mackenzie, A. and Edwards, S. (2006) Everyday environmental education experiences: the role of content in early childhood education, *Australian Journal of Environmental Education*, 22(2): 13–19.

Cutter-Mackenzie, A., Edwards, S. and Fleer, M. (2009) Investigating the environmental scientific concepts in children's play: how do children and teachers interpret play-based learning? *Australian Journal of Research in Early Childhood Education*, 16(1): 49–63.

Davydov, V. and Kerr, S. (1995) The influence of L.S. Vygotsky on education theory, research and practice, *Educational Researcher*, 24(12).

Edwards, S. (2008) Images of childhood, early education and care: how do teachers' constructions of childhood influence pedagogy and practice?, in P.G. Grotewell and Y.R. Burton (eds) *Early Education: Issues and Developments*. New York: Nova Publishers.

Fleer, M. (2009) Understanding the dialectical relations between everyday concepts and scientific concepts within play-based programs, *Research in Science Education*, 39(2): 281–306.

Fleer, M. (2010) *Concepts in Play: A Cultural Historical View of Early Learning and Development*. Cambridge: Cambridge University Press.

Gaskins, S., Haight, W. and Lancy, D. (2006) The cultural construction of play, in A. Göncü and S. Gaskins (eds) *Play and Development: Evolutionary, Sociocultural and Functional Perspectives*. Mahwah, NJ: Lawrence Erlbaum.

Gibbons, A. (2007) The politics of processes and products in education: an early childhood meta-narrative in crisis? *Educational Philosophy and Theory*, 39(3): 300–11.

Goodfellow, J. (2005). Researching with/for whom? Stepping in and out of practitioner research, *Australian Journal of Early Childhood*, 30(4): 48–57.

Siraj-Blatchford, I., Taggart, B., Sylva, K., Sammons, P. and Melhuish, E. (2008) Towards the transformation of practice in early childhood education: the effective provision of pre-school education (EPPE) project, *Cambridge Journal of Education*, 38(1): 23–36.

Soto, L. and Swadener, B. (2002) Toward liberatory early childhood theory, research and praxis: decolonizing a field, *Contemporary Issues in Early Childhood*, 3(1): 38–66.

Taguchi, H. (2007) Deconstructing and transgressing the theory-practice dichotomy in early childhood education, *Educational Philosophy and Theory*, 39(3): 275–90.

White, J., O'Malley, A., Toso, M., Rockel, J., Stover, S. and Ellis, F. (2007) A contemporary glimpse of play and learning in Aotearoa New Zealand, *International Journal of Early Childhood*, 39(1): 93–105.

Wood, E. and Bennett, N. (2000) Changing theories, changing practice: exploring early childhood teachers' professional learning, *Teaching and Teacher Education*, 16: 635–47.

11 Powerful pedagogies and playful resistance

Role play in the early childhood classroom

Sue Rogers

Introduction

'Who would dare study play?' (Bruner et al. 1976: xii). It is by no means easy to find pathways through the vast literature on play. Its disparate elements testify to the enduring interest in play and the wide-ranging and multiple approaches to the subject. Bruner's rhetorical question is, I believe, an appropriate starting point for this chapter. It is posed at the beginning of his introduction to an anthology of play research, regarded as a seminal text in its day. Bruner goes on to note the 'many ways in which serious men [*sic*] have tried to grasp this antic topic [play] … historical, literary, clinical, introspective, anthropological, sociological, linguistic, ethological and via controlled experimental methods of the behavioural sciences' (Bruner et al. 1976: xii). His apparently deliberate juxtaposition of the 'serious' with the 'antic' invokes the way in which play is frequently trivialized in relation to its more serious counterpart, work. This polarizing tendency – play *versus* work – constitutes a persistent theme in the history of early childhood education. At the same time, early childhood discourse has been shaped by a very different perspective, suggested by the often made claim that 'play is the child's work', a phrase originally coined by that pivotal figure in early education's history, Frederick Froebel, and reiterated a century later by Susan Isaacs: 'play is indeed the child's work' (1929: 9). These words have inspired generations of educators to strive for a full and unqualified recognition of the value of play in early learning.

To complicate our understanding of play further, the field has been characterized by a quest for definitions. Definitions of play usually make some reference to the absence of rules, boundaries and extrinsic rewards. Thus play is described as free, aimless, amusing or diverting activities which are spontaneous and pursued for their own sake alone. So, on the one hand, we can distinguish play from the usual motivational contexts of work, learning and problem-solving, those activities that are normally associated with measurable outcomes and tangible achievement, while, on the other, play is harnessed precisely for this purpose in educational contexts.

More recently, reconceptualist agendas in early childhood research have offered alternatives to traditional ways of knowing the child and of understanding childhood activity including play (see, for example, Ailwood 2003; Gibbons 2007; Grieshaber 2008). Attempts to contest the discourses of developmentalism and individualism in early childhood education, which have tended to ignore the social and cultural diversity which shapes the lives of young children and their families, have offered alternative ways of viewing the paradigmatic child and, it follows, the paradigmatic teacher. Poststructuralist perspectives enable critical engagement about what it is that structures meanings, practices and bodies (Lind 2005). Ailwood (2003) and Cohen (2008) describe ideological commitment to subjects such as play as 'regimes of truth' in the Foucauldian sense, as a set of truths that generate an authoritative consensus about what needs to be done in that field and how it should be done (Cohen 2008). In practice, however, multiple perspectives and complexity characterize how play is enacted by children within the pedagogical orientations of their classrooms: these are places of tension, struggle and dilemmas (Sugrue 1997), not simply places where curriculum guidelines, educational theory, beliefs and ideals are put neatly into practice.

Walsh (2005) offers a cautionary note to the poststructural turn that has characterized much recent early childhood research, noting the danger in simply replacing one orthodox perspective with another, and preferring instead to look towards a contemporary developmental theory that recognizes how the child is located within culture: 'culture is both the context *within* which the child develops and the context *into* which the child develops' (2005: 45, original emphasis). We are left, then, with the possibility of understanding play from multiple perspectives, which acknowledge complexity and uncertainty.

Alongside the deployment of poststructural analytic concepts in early childhood education, there has been an increasing interest in researching children's perspectives on their experiences of education and care and in concomitant participatory and child-friendly data-collection methods. Studies which utilize poststructural concepts in research on children's perspectives are relatively rare, a point also made by Janzen (2008), who in a review of such studies asks 'Where is the (postmodern) child in early childhood education research?' More curious still, given its centrality to early childhood discourse, is the absence of a well-developed literature on play which takes the children's perspective. In this chapter, I will draw on my own recent study of children's perspectives on role play and, following

Powell et al. (2006), consider how children deal with, and experience, adults' regulatory practices in their everyday lives at school. Such considerations might, it is suggested, lead to more nuanced understandings of how play and pedagogy intersect in the early childhood classroom, and of the different ways in which play and pedagogy signal normalizing and controlling discourses within early childhood education.

Building on earlier work, then, I consider the intersection of play and pedagogy in early childhood classrooms through examples from a study of children's and teachers' perspectives on play, reported in Rogers and Evans (2008). I will examine the 'pedagogy of play' from the perspective of children, illustrating through examples from the research data the pedagogical factors that appear to either inhibit or support sustained and complex play in the classroom, and which at the same time lay bare some of the power relations that exist between children and adults, and between children. My aim in this chapter is to examine some of the tensions and possibilities that exist in popular conceptions of play pedagogy, and to argue that the relationship between play, on the one hand, and pedagogy, on the other, is under-theorized and under-developed in practice. What we are left with is the myth of a play-based curriculum grounded in an illusion of choice. I will try to justify why it is necessary to rethink the relationship between play and pedagogy as it is currently manifested in early childhood classrooms.

Powerful pedagogies

The coupling of play with pedagogy is in many ways a deeply problematic enterprise for at least three reasons: first, because traditionally, the concept of play has been positioned in marked opposition to its apparently more worthwhile counterpart, work. This division is marked not simply by the ways in which play is often relegated to specific times and places but also in the ways in which it is regarded in practice as a marginal and recreational activity removed from the real business of the early childhood classroom. Second, the *pedagogization* of play (pedagogy of play) has meant that play has increasingly become an instrument for learning adult competencies: 'real world things' (Strandell 2000: 146). Viewed in this way, play in early childhood education is valued mainly for the ways in which it reproduces and rehearses the expectations of society (Guss 2005; Rogers and Evans 2008). I have argued elsewhere that this compels us to judge play by particular standards, that is, what is good play or bad play? Such value judgements might not represent what children perceive to be of value in their play, but are rather rooted in adult perceptions and, moreover, politically prescribed notions of 'standards' and 'quality' (Rogers and Evans 2008). Play, then, is not only a supervised and curricularized activity, as Strandell contends (2000), but also an institutionalized and politicized activity. Finally, theorizing 'play as work' as Gibbons (2007: 303) argues simply obscures the ways in which play is 'a technique of social control and a means of transmitting assumptions and beliefs regarding the nature and purpose of childhood: the child must work at being a child' (see also Ailwood 2003; Cannella and Viruru 2004). Other critics have identified that approaches to play emphasize social realism rather than the transformative, mimetic and life-enhancing qualities (Guss 2005) which characterize not only children's play but human experience across the life span. The real value of play, then, is eclipsed by society's more pressing concerns engendered by serial legislation, policy initiatives, and the resultant culture of 'performativity' associated with early childhood and primary schooling (Ball 1998; Edwards 2001).

Turning our attention to the concept of 'play pedagogy', the literature gives little indication of what this might mean in practice. Moreover, play pedagogy/a pedagogy of play is described principally from the adults' perspective and with little, if any, reference to how and in what ways children might (and indeed do) participate in the making of pedagogy in classrooms, in shaping the pedagogical practices of which they are a part (Rogers and Evans 2008). Wood has described a pedagogy of play in broad terms as 'the ways in which early childhood professionals make provision for playful and play-based activities, how they design play/learning environments, and all the pedagogical techniques and strategies they use to support or enhance learning through play' (2009: 19). However, this definition emphasizes what adults do. It does not offer any explicit acknowledgement of the ways in which children exercise agency through their active participation in the making of pedagogy in early childhood classrooms (Rogers and Evans 2008). Wood's description does not account for the ways in which pedagogy is implicitly tied up with the exercise of power between teachers and pupils and how it is structured by adult-determined regulatory practices (Cannella and Viruru 2004; Powell et al. 2006) which may suppress the physical, social and affective qualities of play, and minimize the aesthetic and creative dispositions of play, in order to substitute in their place a highly prescribed, externally evaluated, purposeful play regime. Pedagogy is also, of course, bound up with the larger contexts and agendas of education and with the practical exigencies of classroom life. I want to suggest here an alternative conceptualization of a pedagogy of play, as a negotiated space in which participants' subjectivities and psychic and interpersonal relations are formed (see also Lind 2005). Clearly, early childhood classrooms are embedded contexts, which in turn operate within institutions that are culturally, historically and politically defined, and within which the practices of teaching and learning are mediated by the social and cultural identities of their participants, both children and teachers. Moreover, in the play between children, choice and agency are not simply associated with the individual child, but are mediated by and within the inter- actions between children, governed also by the pedagogical demands of the setting.

Researching children's experiences of role play in the reception class

I have selected three examples of empirical data taken from a year-long ethnographic study of children's and teachers' perspectives on role play. The study is reported more fully elsewhere (Rogers and Evans 2008), but for the purposes of this chapter a brief account of its methodology may be useful. The project was conceived within a socio-cultural framework in which children are seen as active agents (see, for example, Hill et al. 2004). 'Agency' is understood here as a person's way of being, seeing and responding in the world and as being embedded in contexts of activity and embedded practices (Edwards 2001). Data were gathered through participant and non-participant observations, photographs taken by children, and children's self-reports of play gathered through drawings and conversations. All children were either 4 or 5 years old and attended three reception classes. The 'reception class', a term with a particular currency in England, is the first class of primary school. It receives the new intake of children usually aged 4 or 5. In England, the statutory school starting age is the term after a child's fifth birthday, but in practice most children start school before the statutory age of 5. Play in reception classes is typically organized around uniform provision for constructive play (manipulative object play such as construction kits, sand and water), symbolic play (role play, small-world play) and increasingly as children mature, games with rules. However, alongside this provision for play are, typically, areas for work, tables at which chil- dren can sit to undertake more formal activities in preparation for school. So, even in its physical manifestation, the reception class incor- porates two contrasted pedagogies, one that is for play, the other for work. Though attempts to blur the boundaries between the two have occurred in light of new curricular guidance (the *Early Years Foundation Stage*, a statutory and avowedly play-based curricular framework for children from birth to the end of the reception year: Department for Children, Schools and Families 2007), divisions between play and work are likely to persist.

Who is the reception child: pupil or player?

Theorizing 'identity', Mozere (2006: 109) posits that 'a child in pre-school ... must conform to what is demanded, and be limited to that of the pre-schooler or day care child'. Similarly, I suggest that the reception child is constructed in a highly distinctive way which is markedly differ-ent to a child of a similar age and/or level of maturity in, say, a nursery class or kindergarten. Reception class children are constructed as pupils-in-waiting, and indeed quickly learn that they must conform to certain discursive practices associated with being and becoming a school pupil. I am not suggesting here that this is a uni-directional process, where chil-dren are passively moulded by the institution. Children also exercise agency and may desire to be school pupils. Children, like adults, operate within many different discourses, and as Grace (2008) notes, the non-unitary and shifting nature of subjectivity means that children occupy more than one social position at a time, though the tendency is to adopt the dominant discourse of a particular social situation. Children may, then, suppress other aspects of their lives in order to fit into the demands of the current context, in this instance the reception class.

Playful resistance, choice and control

Play and pedagogy, as I have suggested, intersect in a rather uneasy rela-tionship in the early childhood classroom. For the most part, play takes place in parallel with other work-like activities within the ubiquitous 'choosing time' offered to children as an alternative to, or reward for, work. Choice, however, is largely controlled by the teacher and other adults who select groups of children and direct them to specific areas of the play pro-vision, a pedagogical strategy which simultaneously offers the prospect of choice and exercises social control. Tobin (1995: 232) likens this approach to an 'auction', sketching a picture of the teacher (auctioneer) 'selling' the activities to the children (the bidders) as they sit in front of her at choos-ing time.

> Each time a child puts in a bid for dramatic play area, another one of the teacher's fingers goes down ... as higher and lower sta-tus children make their bids, the value of the dramatic area rises and falls like a commodity.

Tobin alludes here to the interplay of social relationships between children that underpins the surface pedagogy of the classroom. Children's position-ing in the social order also determines the outcome of the 'auction', in other words, where children play and with whom. This metaphor of choosing time as an 'auction', complicated by the social order of the classroom, highlights the complexity of play pedagogy for both children and teachers. Where children had choice, they were adept at engineering situations to ensure they could play with their friends. Children made 'pacts' with each other so that if they were chosen they would then choose their friend (Rogers and Evans 2008) and used social leverage to maintain the play.

> *Lucy*: (to Alice, trying to persuade her to be the patient) 'I'll be your best friend.'

Alice returns and Lucy says to her, 'Come on get into bed! I'll be your best friend ... you won't come to my party.' Alice agrees to be the patient but then asks to go to the toilet. Lucy then asks me if I will help her when Alice comes back.

> *Alice*: 'I'm going to a party today anyway.'

An alternative strategy for managing choice observed in this study was one which allowed children free choice from a range of activities, including role play. There was no auction. However, children's choices were subsequently controlled in other ways by adults' pedagogical assumptions and strategies, designed to deliver the prescribed curriculum. In the following example, Kevin negotiates entry into David's play.

> Kevin had been identified as a child with additional needs and is sometimes described by the adults around him as 'disruptive'. Kevin asks David if he can join in the play and David agrees. Both boys have waistcoats and peaked caps on and they start off as bus drivers walking around with clipboards, checking off their passengers.

> *Kevin*: I'm the Inspector, we're going to [the] beach.

> David is ahead of Kevin with a clipboard and pen.

> *Kevin*: Stop the train, let's open the doors.

> As the play develops, David is called away to do some work with the teacher. Kevin follows him. The teacher says to Kevin that David has to do his work. Kevin responds by saying 'I'm a policeman.' The teacher responds to Kevin, 'No, you're in the travel agents. There are no policemen in the travel shop.' Kevin responds with 'But David's a policeman.' The teacher replies rather tersely, 'just go [back] in there!'

There are a number of issues here. The role-play area has been constructed by the adult as the travel agency. This reflects the deliberate and instrumental intention that play will fulfil curriculum requirements. In turn, this carries with it certain expectations for what, and how, children will play and learn. The play is disrupted by the teacher's request that David engage in the more pressing task of work. David and Kevin pursue their collective desire to play a policeman game, but this is incompatible with the teacher's desire for travel agency play, and may not meet her curriculum objectives. Kevin and David's play both disrupts, and is disrupted by, the teacher's expectations that children should play in the ways expected by the teacher, and that David must do some work – even when the session has been represented to the children as 'choosing time for free play'.

Kevin is clearly disappointed, wanting the 'policeman' game to continue. The teacher's obvious frustration may be due to Kevin's challenge to her authority, or perhaps because his response exposed the absurdity of her comment that 'there are no policemen in the travel shop'. However, it may also be caused by her own lack of power to provide the play-based pedagogy she espouses. Nevertheless, the dominant discursive practice in this classroom is one of control, in which Kevin is learning what the teacher wants and is perhaps learning an instrumental attitude to play (Millei 2005). Such pedagogical control, I would suggest, limits the possible subject positions available to both teachers and children. Kevin cannot position himself as the policeman in the game. The teacher cannot fulfil her desire for children to engage in free play. Nor will she learn about Kevin's desire to be a policeman and what this might signify for him.

In the second example, the children have no choice. Rather, the teacher directs them to a specific play activity. Two children are to 'work' in the shop and two children are to be the customers. As the children make their way to the role play area it is clear that none is willing to play the 'customer'.

Kim says to the teacher: 'Me and Chloe don't want to be in the travel shop.'

The teacher says they have to stay in there. Chloe and Kim stand in the shop but won't join in the play. A few minutes later Kim starts to join in.

Chloe says to her 'We're not playing this are we? It's boring!'

Kim, having been reprimanded by Chloe, changes tack and says 'This is a baby's computer, we're five and we want 'five' things to do.'

Later, Lauren comes into the shop and Chloe says to her 'We don't want to be here, it's boring.'

Lauren responds: 'Well, come out then!'
Chloe: 'We're not allowed.'

We see here the asymmetrical power relations between children, where Chloe imposes her will to resist upon Kim, who might otherwise have complied with the teacher's directive to play. Chloe resists the teacher's directive and expresses her desire to be a pupil, to do 'five things'. This is not surprising as school is the way in which children attain the status of adults in contemporary society; however, the teacher has positioned Chloe as a child needing to play even when she had expressed her desire not to do so.

In the two preceding examples, we see how 'choice' is used as a mechanism for regulating play in early childhood pedagogy, and how this can create resistance for children in their interactions with adults and other children. In the following example, we see how pedagogical practices disrupt children's play to the extent that play is seen as less valuable, and thus becomes marginal rather than central to play-based pedagogy. A group of children begin to play in the 'hospital'.

After some persuasion from Molly, Cobi agrees to lie down and be the patient. At the same time, however, he is called away by an adult to 'change his books'.

Molly: There's no patient in yet he's just changing his books.

Cobi whilst changing his books and trying to read moves the barriers to the role play area and says 'You can't go in there, 'cos I'm the patient.'

On Cobi's return Molly is called away to undertake another activity and she says to Rhia, 'Don't let anyone in 'cos I've got to go somewhere.'

Hannah is then called away to do her book bag, and as she leaves she says to Rhia, 'Don't let anyone else in here.' Eliza arrives in the area and sits down at the computer. As agreed with Hannah, Rhia says: 'Eliza, you can't go there 'cos Hannah's playing.'

The numerous interruptions to play resulted in play operating as a holding task, fragmenting narratives, closing down opportunities for children to develop sustained social and imaginative interactions, and signalling that play was of less importance than the other more productive activity of school. Even the mundane and ubiquitous activity of 'changing books' observed in early childhood classrooms, held greater significance than the children's play activity. Children were creative in their responses, able both to resist and comply with the dominant pedagogical practices in the classroom, as Cobi did in his stalling techniques, and as Millie did by shouting 'take Rhia first!' when called away. In this way, the children adopted what may be defined as a 'balanced compliance' approach; balancing their own needs (wanting to be part of the play), while complying with adult requests to read, write or undertake other more formal classroom activity (Rogers and Evans 2008).

Two distinct positions are suggested by these examples: first, that play is viewed as the undisciplined activity of young children. Thus schools and other early childhood institutions are designed to control and sanitize play so that it reflects adult views of what is good play/bad play. Second, that play is viewed as less important than other activities in classrooms because of the way it is positioned at the margins of what counts as real and necessary activity such as reading with an adult and other literacy-related activity, including 'changing books'. From either perspective, play is used as a pedagogical device for delivering the demands of schooling and society, in other words, as an instrumental activity. My argument then is that play is regulated and controlled by more subtle forces of pedagogy, even when a pedagogy of play appears on the surface at least to prevail.

Set against this, opportunities for social pretend play offered children the possibility to explore identities within their relationships with others and in the process of navigating the dominant pedagogical practices of their classrooms. These identities are not fixed but rather shift with particular play events and social groupings. It is precisely because play allows for such social interactions and pretence (which enables also the exploration of pretend identities) that children are able to act and speak in ways that would not be possible in other social contexts. Within the formation of identities in play, children may also desire, and hence seek, acceptance from their peers, and membership of the play group. Part of the imperative to play witnessed in many children is tied up with this social recognition and acceptance within a social group. Play is also an occasion for children to demonstrate to their peers their autonomy from teachers, to display boundaries of inclusion and exclusion from shifting peer groups, and to experience power and control; friendships developed in and sustained by play are tied up with power and desire. In each of the examples we see the ways in which children exercise agency in trying to shape the play pedagogy of their settings.

The myth of free play and the illusion of choice

Can play in school ever be 'free'? Clearly the notion of free play, that is play which is intrinsically motivated, voluntary and free from externally imposed rules, is tempered in practice by the physical, conceptual and practical features of the school and the classroom setting. The concept of 'free' in our commonplace understandings of play pedagogy is closely linked to the notion 'freedom to choose'; hence the 'choosing' time characteristic of early childhood settings in England. Early childhood educators may interpret the notion of 'free play' in a variety of pedagogical ways. This in turn will influence the extent to which children make choices based on individual or collective peer group interests and/or desires, and to what extent they resist or comply with the dominant discursive practices. The concept of choice may operate on several levels in children's play in school (Bennett et al. 1997; Trawick-Smith 1998; Rogers and Evans 2008). As we have seen, choice can be applied to the process of selecting and combining materials, to the themes and content of play, to the time, place and duration of play and to the choice of play partners and groups. Each of these dimensions of choice will inevitably shape the nature of children's play experiences. At the same time, the ways in which individual teachers interpret choice will depend upon their particular situation, the practical exigencies of the school and classroom in which their work is located, but also (and this is a central point) how they interpret their particular situation. A summary of the dimensions of choice is presented in Table 11.1.

The centrality of friendship to social play, however fleeting it may be in some instances (Rogers and Evans 2008), suggests that children do not choose simply on the strength of their own individual and intrinsic interests. Rather their shifting and multiple identities and social relations influence how and with whom they want to play. As we can see in these examples, the pedagogical approach to play in terms of the ways in

Table 11.1 Dimensions of choice in play

Dimension	Choice
Materials and resources	What shall I play with?
Location	Where shall I play?
Playmates	With whom shall I play?
Outcome	What and how shall I play?
Temporal	When and for how long can I play?

which children were grouped, and of the material presentation of activities of play (temporal and thematic), militated against children exercising real choice in their play.

Rethinking the relationship between play and pedagogy

One of the main difficulties in recontextualizing play into pedagogical practice (what I have termed here as the *pedagogization* of play) is the resistance of play to categorization. What is the 'subject' matter of play? There are both conceptual and practical difficulties in fitting play into categories such as subject, discipline, pedagogy and curriculum since play transcends these artificial boundaries. Nevertheless, definitions of play proliferate in the literature. Attempts to locate and define play's ontological essence and to explain its primary function in human development have been the major preoccupations of scholars in the field. Yet play has proved to be a difficult and elusive concept to locate either empirically or conceptually, and for this reason it has been something of a commonplace to define play, not in terms of what it is, but rather in terms of what it is not (Bateson 1973). Rather than 'essence' we are offered 'difference'. Play has often been spoken of as 'not real', 'not serious', not productive' (Schwartzman 1978), 'of no material interest', 'not for profit' (Huizinga, cited in Sutton-Smith and Kelly-Byrne 1984).

I suggest that an alternative view of play pedagogy might be as a negotiated 'space', both physical and conceptual, for children and teachers to explore identities and desires, and evaluate questions of voice and power in the classroom. Play would not be viewed simply as a vehicle for delivering the curriculum, under the guise of 'play-based learning'. The starting point would be to see the value of play from the children's perspective, as a powerful context for understanding emerging and shifting subjectivities within classroom relationships. Play pedagogy as a negotiated practice, co-constructed between children and adults, may also help to overcome the play/work dualism that persists in early childhood classrooms (Cannella and Viruru 2004), which perpetuates the resistance evident in children's responses to the pedagogical structures surrounding their play.

This chapter opened with reference to Bruner's question, 'Who dares study play?' The research reported here suggests that it is not so much a matter of daring to study play, as it is to dare to study children's enactment of play when play is harnessed as a supposedly pedagogical tool for promoting 'learning'. For early childhood education, the question may well be 'Who dares study the pedagogization of play?'

References

Ailwood, J. (2003) Governing early childhood education through play, *Contemporary Issues in Early Childhood*, 4(3): 286–99.

Ball, S. (1998) Performativity and fragmentation in 'postmodern schooling', in J. Carter (ed.) *Postmodernity and the Fragmentation of Welfare*. London: Routledge.

Bateson, G. (1973) *Steps to an Ecology of Mind*. London: Paladin.

Bennett, N., Wood, L. and Rogers, S. (1997) *Teaching through Play*. Maidenhead: Open University Press.

Bruner, J., Jolly, A. and Sylva, K. (1976) *Play: Its Role in Development and Evolution*. Harmondsworth: Penguin.

Cannella, G. and Viruru, R. (2004) *Childhood and Postcolonization*. London: Routledge.

Cohen, L. (2008) Foucault and the early childhood classroom, *Educational Studies*, 44: 7–21.

Department for Education and Skills (2007) *The Early Years Foundation Stage*. http://standards.dfes.you.uk/primary/foundation_stage/eyfs/

Edwards, A. (2001) Researching pedagogy: a sociocultural agenda, *Pedagogy, Culture and Society*, 9(2): 161–86.

Gibbons, A. (2007) The politics and processes of education: an early childhood metanarrative crisis, *Educational Philosophy and Theory*, 39(3): 301–11.

Grieshaber, S. (2008) Interrupting stereotypes: teaching and the education of young children, *Early Childhood Education and Development*, 19(3): 505–18.

Grace, D.J. (2008) Interpreting children's constructions of their ethnicity, *Contemporary Issues in Early Childhood*, 9(2): 131–47.

Guss, F. (2005) Reconceptualizing play: aesthetic self-definitions, *Contemporary Issues in Early Childhood Education*, 6(3): 233–43.

Hill, M., Davis, J., Prout, A. and Tisdall, K. (2004) Moving the participation agenda forward, *Children and Society*, 18(2): 77–96.

Isaacs, S. (1929) *The Nursery Years*. London: Routledge.

Janzen, M. (2008) Where is the (postmodern) child in early childhood education research? *Early Years*, 28(3): 287–98.

Lind, U. (2005) Identity and power: 'meaning', gender and age: children's creative work as a signifying practice, *Contemporary Issues in Early Childhood*, 6(3): 256–68.

Millei, Z. (2005) The discourse of control: disruption and Foucault in an early childhood classroom, *Contemporary Issues in Early Childhood*, 6(2): 128–39.

Mozere, L. (2006) What's the trouble with identity?: practices and theories from France, *Contemporary Issues in Early Childhood*, 7(2): 109–19.

Powell, K., Danby, S. and Farrell, A. (2006) Investigating an account of children 'passing notes' in the classroom: how boys and girls operate differently in relation to an everyday, classroom regulatory practice, *Journal of Early Childhood Research*, 4(3): 257–75.

Rogers, S. and Evans, J. (2008) *Inside Role Play in Early Childhood Education: Researching Children's Perspectives*. London: Routledge.

Schwartzman, H.B. (1978) *Transformations: The Anthropology of Children's Play*. New York: Plenum Press.

Strandell, H. (2000) What is the use of children's play?: preparation or social participation, in H. Penn (ed.) *Early Childhood Services: Theory, Policy and Practice*. Buckingham: Open University Press.

Sugrue, C. (1997) *The Complexities of Teaching: Child-centred Perspectives*. London: Falmer.

Sutton-Smith, B. and Kelly-Byrne, K. (1984) The idealisation of play, in P.K. Smith (ed.) *Play in Animals and Humans*. Oxford: Blackwell.

Tobin, J. (1995) Post-structural research in early childhood settings, in J.A. Hatch (ed.) *Qualitative Research in Early Childhood Settings*. Santa Barbara, CA: Greenwood Publishing Group.

Trawick-Smith, J. (1998) School-based play and social interactions, in D.F. Fromberg and D. Bergen (eds) *Play from Birth to Twelve and Beyond*. New York: Garland Publishing.

Walsh, D. (2005) Developmental theory and early childhood education: necessary but not sufficient, in N. Yelland (ed.) *Critical Issues in Early Childhood Education*, Maidenhead: Open University Press.

Wood, E. (2009) Developing a pedagogy of play, in A. Anning, M. Fleer and J. Cullen (eds) *Early Childhood Education: Society and Culture*. London: Sage.

12 Using power on the playground

Brian Edmiston and Tim Taylor

> Children have the right to say what they think should happen and have their opinions taken into account.
>
> (United Nations Declaration
> of the Rights of the Child 1959)

Introduction

Advocates for children's right to play can be encouraged by a new policy in the United Kingdom: the British government's national *Play Strategy* for England now formally recognizes that play is essential to children's learning and development (Department for Children, Schools and Families 2008a). As education policy-makers champion play in public environments, including active adventure-seeking play, adults can anticipate how children's lives are likely to improve through changing the quality of play provision.

We argue that if children are to have play woven into their school lives, then teachers, parents and administrators must pay attention as much to how adults use power in response to children's behaviours, as to children's actual play. Children's playtime is always enmeshed with adult attitudes, assumptions, interpretations and actions towards children's energies and playful desires. Using Bakhtin's (1981) theory of dialogic interactions, we advocate that adults can use power *with* children to negotiate playground activities and expectations that aim to accommodate to the needs of everyone in a school. In this chapter we explore some of the complexities associated with this perspective in practice.

The following account by Tim Taylor could be read as an exemplar of the play strategy's implementation. A primary teacher for 15 years, Tim currently is assistant headteacher at Surlingham Community Primary School in England, which serves predominantly rural and suburban families with low to middle incomes. He shares teaching year 3–4 (children aged 7 to 9 years) with the headteacher, Catrin Parry-Jones.

> At break-time, Reception children [aged 4–5] trundle around on scooters and tricycles, weaving in-and-out of older children kicking

footballs, hitting balls against the wall, or playing games like Hide-and-Seek on the field. Others walk or sit in the garden talking.
(Tim, interview, 25 June 2008)

Promoting children's play is more complex than this description or the national strategy might suggest. Adults can easily romanticize happy, smiling, engaged children. But what if children's play seems to take a turn towards the dangerous or violent?

> In one corner of the field children run in and out of a den constructed, in the bushes and against the fence, out of eight-foot willow staves, rope, and camouflage netting. Older boys, with younger children in tow, are shouting orders. Some boys, and a few girls, carry pretend guns, made from blue plastic construction equipment, as they crouch, dash around the trees, or guard the entrances.
> (Tim, interview, 25 June 2008)

What are some of the challenges for adults' use of power in situations like this? Power is not simply the exercise of force. Foucault's theoretical framework (1984; cited in MacNaughton 2005) conceptualizes power as always relational, circulating among people in every discursive and physical interaction, and accumulating with those who use power both to control people's actions and the meaning of their activities. Adults have more power than children do in respect to how their play is interpreted and represented to others, and thus over what, and how, children are able to play. Adults can use power with, for and over others: how adults use power to support, undermine or engage with children's activities affects both the content, and the social interactions of, their play (Edmiston 2008).

I (Brian) was interested in learning more about how power circulates in schools, among children and adults, and in doing so, affects any moves to make schools more playful and interactions more dialogic. I wanted to gather examples of these dynamics in action, and so between June 2008 and March 2009 I interviewed Tim by email, phone and in person, about his experiences in relation to significant changes during playtime that occurred over the 18 months since he had first arrived at Surlingham Primary in September 2007. I did not have an opportunity to observe or interview at the school, though Tim and Catrin have both read and approved this manuscript.

Adults using power over children

Julia Smith,[1] the mother of a seven-year-old boy, Adam, came in unannounced one day [in October 2008] to watch her son at playtime. She was scared by what she saw. While some children, mostly girls, walked or sat and talked, over half of the children in the school were engaged in active play. Many were running, laughing and shouting in and around their dens. Some made loud shooting noises in noisy and boisterous attack-and-defending behaviour. Mrs Smith's initial response was to get angry and accusatory. She said to one of the adults on duty that the play was 'vicious and out of control' referring to one of the older boys as a 'little shit'. We [Catrin and Tim] invited her inside to discuss what she had seen: uncontrolled, dangerous behaviour with no rules. She was worried that a small group of 'vicious' boys were acting as role models for the younger children. She did not want to ban play but felt the adults should be more controlling. We stressed that she had not had the benefit of a member of staff to provide an alternative interpretation. We assured her that we took her reactions seriously, though as a staff we were committed to ensuring, as much as possible, every child's emotional and physical safety.

(Tim, email, 7 December 2008)

Though her response was understandable, Mrs Smith had largely misread the situation. Like many adults, she had difficulty distinguishing between actual and pretend violence (Paley 1984; Schaefer and Smith 1996; Katch 2001; Jones 2002). The children she had observed were playing. What Adam's mother feared was about to become physical violence, was in reality pretend aggression that was part of the children's verbal and often rough-and-tumble play (Pelligrini 1988). Activities that she believed demanded adult intervention had been broadly agreed upon in earlier adult–child discussions; children would require supervision and intervention only when necessary, to ensure physical safety or to help resolve difficulties.

Nor did Mrs Smith realize that the children's play, which had seemed to need adult control, was actually highly self-monitored and socially controlled by the children:

Their play is highly choreographed and predictable. Younger children mostly focus on chase whereas older children's play often centres on complex narratives. Boys of all ages join in, from aged four to eleven, along with one fully participating older girl and other girls who occasionally participate. Although children may describe the theme as 'war', there is no sign of real violence. There are sometimes disagreements about resources, which occasionally cause arguments, but what is remarkable is the level of spirited collaboration and wide-spread obvious enjoyment.

(Tim, email, 14 December 2008)

Tim and Catrin were concerned about any actual aggression and asked Mrs Smith to reflect more deeply about what was actually happening. Had any of the children been crying or been hurt? Had she noticed anyone being excluded? They explained how over the previous year the whole school, adults and children, had been involved in collaborative discussions that had established guidelines and rules for playtime with the aim that every child would have choices about which activities they would want to participate in, yet feel safe in the knowledge that caring adults were nearby. On reflection, she accepted that many of the children were joyful, that they were collaborating, and that apparently no one was being left out. But she still had serious reservations and advocated for a break-time organization like that in previous years.

Adults using power to control behaviour

In contrast with Mrs Smith's memory of playground order, Tim had had serious concerns about how previously adults had restricted the children's choices and behaviour.

> When I arrived [in September 2007], the children had a huge play area but few resources that engaged them. The infants [aged 4–7] had tricycles and a low-level climbing structure. The juniors [aged 8–11] had limited access to Physical Education equipment restricted to a daily option, for example, football on Thursdays. Decisions had been made with little reference to the children's desires and opinions. Knowing that children need firm and well-understood boundaries the previous head-teacher had made those boundaries clear but unequivocal, dealing fairly, and reasonably with those who exceeded them.
>
> (Tim, phone interview, 15 December 2008)

The Mid-day Supervisory Assistants (MSAs) whose job is to supervise the playground had been participating in a long-established rule-based power structure that preceded Catrin's appointment four years previously (Tim, email, 10 March 2009). For example, access to play materials could be restricted by an adult decision that was assumed would not be questioned by children. Catrin arrived intending to distribute power and change the school culture by sharing more authority for decision-making with staff and children (Catrin, email, 4 May 2009). However, she initially focused on changes in classrooms leaving the playground set-up largely unaltered. In the public space of the playground, the children were neither expected nor encouraged to take responsibility for their own actions, except in retrospect when judged to have transgressed rules imposed, monitored and enforced by watchful adults. From a Foucauldian viewpoint, adult surveillance was used to control behaviour, especially in regulating children's bodies. Play with violent themes and pretend guns was not allowed; physical contact games were disapproved. Rather than encouraging children's self-discipline, adults disciplined children by controlling their behaviour according to adult assumptions and decisions about appropriateness (Kohn 1996).

Adults using power for and with children

Tim proposed changes at playtime in response to the mood of the children, especially a group of older boys:

> I originally introduced [in November 2007] the staves, netting, and rope for den-making to engage a group of about a dozen older disaffected boys whom I felt were distrustful of me and who wandered around at playtime getting bored. Those boys instantly gravitated to the equipment and readily accepted the restriction that they not throw anything. Within days, over half of the children were building dens. The boys had been mostly invisible to the adults who paid attention to them only when causing problems; school seemed mostly a boring chore, mitigated by playground opportunities to spend time with friends.
>
> (Tim, email, 10 March 2009)

In contrast to the previous head-teacher, who it seemed had most often in relation to the playground used power *over* others by restricting options and deciding on rules with little meaningful discussion, Tim and Catrin wanted adults to use power as much as possible *for* all of the children by caring about their needs. Rather than impose specific rules prohibiting certain behaviours, or regard problems as residing in transgressive individuals, their intention was to shift more power to the children. They hoped to promote the sort of reciprocal, caring community that teachers ideally wanted for the school (Noddings 1992; Kohn 1996).

Tim and Catrin wanted to negotiate new arrangements that were acceptable to children as well as adults. Their intention was to have more dialogic interactions in which children's voices and views were heard by adults and vice versa (Bakhtin 1981). In other words, they wanted to use power *with* children and adults. They proposed that adults extend play options by introducing new materials. Tim led discussions with teacher colleagues, with the MSAs, and informally with the children, aimed at implementing changes to build a more inclusive school community.

The staff, MSAs and young people, in early 2008, all agreed in separate meetings that children should be more responsible on the playground; they would take shared responsibility for following two interrelated rules: (1) to make sure that everyone is having a good time; and (2) to ensure that everyone is safe. At a whole-school assembly the children were unanimous about ensuring that new arrangements would create 'win–win' equitable spaces, for adults as well as all of the children.

Several months later towards the end of the school year, as social patterns had established around equipment use, some adults raised questions in informal meetings with older children about how some of the younger ones were feeling excluded from dens and how some, especially girls, didn't want war play. The older boys negotiated and devised a solution that satisfied everyone when implemented. After that, nearly all younger children at times played in the dens both in parallel to, and with, older children. Tim discussed the plans outlined by the older boys:

> The boys proposed having three dens; one den would have nothing to do with war. Younger children [aged seven years or less] could go in any den they wanted, whenever they wanted. Each playtime older children [aged more than seven] had to choose one den and stay there.
>
> (Tim, email, 10 March 2009)

Additionally, some girls created a wish list for other adventure play activities, and using school funds, the School Council created a new garden with benches and an all-age shelter.

Since the initial decision to support more active play, Tim has seen significant cultural changes. Most adults recognized that boys were less bored and that those previously disaffected were highly motivated to use the equipment safely. Additionally, the relationship between adults and those boys improved:

> There is a much more cordial relationship and dialogue between all the children and adults. There is a consideration, on the adults' side, for interests and concerns of boys and girls. And an understanding, on the boys' side, that they are a contributory part of the school community, deserving of respect and beholden to respect the rights and interests of others.
>
> (Tim, email, 10 March 2009)

As Tim and Catrin have drawn on all children's energies and ideas in their year 3–4 classroom, a playful overlap has developed between curriculum study, playground games and classroom activities:

> A month or so after introducing the staves, rooting around in the sheds outside I found a box of blue plastic construction pieces from which children made vehicles they used inside and outside. When we studied medieval life some boys, with some help from me, created a functioning trebuchet with weights at one end and a swing used by all to throw rags and teddies. Increasingly elaborate machines created by children were incorporated in games about storming and defending castles. In the classroom, Catrin and I participated in dramatizations of some stories that continued at playtime, some of which were incorporated in an open house for parents and younger children.
>
> (Tim, interview, 25 June 2008)

Challenges when shifting power

As changes were introduced at the school, Tim began to realize that he was challenging a deeply seated status quo.

Adults' stance towards children's responsibilities

As well as agreeing to shift more responsibility to all of the children, the staff agreed that their stance should change from monitoring, controlling and intervening with an assumption that adults need to fix perceived problems to watching, supporting and assisting children who ask for, or clearly need, help in working through difficulties or disagreements:

> Children of any age are inevitably going to fall out from time to time and, if necessary, adults can help children talk with one another to clarify a resolution that meets everyone's needs. For example, teachers have agreed to start from the premise that everybody makes mistakes and that these are an opportunity to learn.
>
> (Tim, email, 10 March 2009)

Changing patterns of behaviour, along with their underlying assumptions, has not been simple for the adults who have continued to meet and informally talk about the new approach:

It is a challenge to all of us, as we have to shift our default position from 'putting things right' to supporting children in finding their own solutions.

(Tim, email, 10 March 2009)

Moving from controlling options and implementing adult-created rules to negotiating with and supporting children in play that is safe has been much more challenging for adults than for children. All children, with adult support, have been prepared to address problems, change rules and alter playground space. As those most consistently and directly involved in implementing new approaches, it is MSAs who have faced most change. Though they have shared some of the concerns voiced by Adam's mother, like all adults they are motivated by concerns over the children's welfare:

Their great fear is that something awful will happen so they are reluctant to allow anything that they see as dangerous. Mostly they've maintained a watchful but distrustful distance, as have some of the boys.

(Tim, phone interview, 15 December 2008)

Adult fear, accompanied by a tendency to restrict rather than open up play options, can unintentionally undermine negotiations and the caring relationships that adults need to develop with children if school play is to become more responsive to all children's energies and interests. Kindlon and Thompson (2000) argue that boys, as much as girls, need emotional relationships with adults. Further, they believe that adults, without realizing it, begin to undermine their relationships with children when they don't trust them to follow their energies and desires but rather disallow, for example, boys' hunt-and-chase play. As Thompson (2008) puts it, 'If you start to fear boys' play, and begin to fear them, then all they feel is that you dislike them. If boys feel that you dislike them they are going to write you off' (n.p.). The 'disaffected boys' that Tim had observed on his arrival at the school tended towards writing off the adults who restricted their play. Such distrust is unlikely to begin to dissipate without the sort of genuine dialogue that became possible in the caring relationships developing at Surlingham.

Safety concerns within caring relationships

Providing more play opportunities for children means adults use power on behalf of, and with, children. But doing so may not be easy for adults previously assuming a controlling use of power *over* children. Learning to

manage fears of putting children at risk is likely to be easier in relationships grounded by an ethic of care and an assumption that children can
negotiate with adults about their actions.

Despite understandable adult reservations, risk-taking in play has been
recognized as an integral part of children's adventure play that has an
element of danger. The British government's consultative document, *Fair
Play* (Department for Children, Schools and Families 2008b), both recognizes that safe play unavoidably often incorporates risk and that adults
have to recognize that they can be over-protective. Josie Gleave (2008),
of the organization Play England which consults on the implementation
of the Play Strategy, summarizes the research on risk and play:

> Children often crave risk when playing; they want challenge,
> excitement, and uncertainty in their play and they learn from it.
> The research shows that children need to experience challenging
> play in order to develop important life skills and to better man-
> age risk and challenge in their daily lives. However, opportuni-
> ties for children to take such risks are limited. This is due to our
> risk-averse culture and an increase in health and safety con-
> straints. It is clear that we need to address the current 'cotton
> wool culture' and provide children with more opportunities for
> adventurous play.
>
> (n.p.)

The fact that the recently published *The Dangerous Book for Boys* (Iggulden
and Iggulden 2007) has been a best seller on both sides of the Atlantic
suggests that, despite the academic critique of its gendered assumptions,
many adults recognize how appealing self-chosen physical danger and its
accompanying feelings of exhilaration and fear can be to children. The
book, drawing on two brothers' memories of their own joyful adventurous childhood play, advocates active games, as well as possibly risky playful activities, such as making a bow and arrow. The authors stress the
need for supportive adults who make such play available to all children
to help them challenge themselves in extending their feelings of security.

Attitudes towards pretending to be aggressive

Encouraging adventurous play is often most difficult for adults when it
involves pretend aggression. As Tim recounted:

> Many parents have expressed, though in a less forthright way
> than Mrs Smith, their unhappiness with the boys 'violent' play,
> in particular using the construction equipment to make guns.
> Some parents of younger children felt it was making boys more

aggressive. 'Well, he didn't learn that at home' was a frequent comment.

(Tim, email, 14 December 2008)

It is vital to recognize that pretending to be aggressive is an activity universally shared by humans and other mammals (Huizinga 1955). Many early childhood educators have realized (e.g. Paley 1984; Holland 2003) that pretending to be violent, including using a weapon, just cannot be suppressed. For example, they pretend to attack, defend and escape. Children will use fingers to invent guns just as they'll cradle a blanket to imagine an infant. They may also use aggressive language with an intensity that would be quite inappropriate in a classroom. Human games of chase, hide-and-seek, chess and fantasy role-play, are all formalized versions of play aggression where children can shift how they use power from pretending to be oppressive to being chased, captured or imagining themselves as victims.

Recognizing play

One easy way to determine whether children are playing with aggressive behaviour, or actually being aggressive, is to observe non-judgementally and resist any desire to intervene. If, as Julia Smith noticed, all children are smiling and not crying, moving in-and-out of pretending, and not seeking adult help, they are likely to be enjoying pretend play rather than actually being aggressive. By looking more closely an observer can notice how players continually signal to each other that they are playing. As Bateson (1956) recognized, like the playful nips of wolf pups that signal to each other they could bite each other but are choosing not to, young children's laughter, mock aggression and parodied actions, are examples of how they signal their intentions not to hurt one another, including when they chase each other or roll around.

Sometimes children overtly signal an intention to others to join a play space. For example, when a child holding a doll asks her mother to hold the baby. Similarly, when a boy points a finger saying 'I've got you' this can be interpreted as an invitation to enter an imagined space and initiate a playful exchange with a response such as, 'You missed!'

Problems may arise when one person pretends to be elsewhere but another is not imagining the same fictional situation. However, when one person's imagined space physically intrudes on others' spaces, as Paley discovered, rather than censor activity rules can be renegotiated so that parallel play may continue (Paley 1984). Tim concurred:

> I think it's particularly important for adults to help younger children to realize that their actions can disrupt others and, like the

children in the dens, learn to share space. Occasionally, when things go wrong adults can assist the children in their negotiations.

(Tim, email, 10 March 2009)

Violence and pretending to be violent

I (Brian) have described elsewhere occasions when my 5-year-old son's imagined actions were uncomfortable for me (Edmiston 2008). It took me well over a year to be able to reinterpret my concerns that by pretending to be violent I might promote a love for actual violence. Initially, I had worries like those of parents at Surlingham:

> There was a problem when children who arrived early would 'shoot' at parents and children. Many parents felt that the school was encouraging (by not banning) a love of guns, violence, and death.
>
> (Tim, email, 7 December 2008)

Only after many months of playing in mythic worlds, like the landscape of *The Tale of Dr. Jekyll and Mr. Hyde*, did I come to understand that when my son, Michael, pretended to kick or shoot as Hyde he was exploring possibilities for acting in evil ways that complemented his imagined goodness to patients as the altruistic Jekyll. Unlike when we pretended to cook or be firefighters, this play was not a 'rehearsal' for a future social life (Erikson 1963) but was rather what I call a 'workshop for life' where highly antisocial, hateful possible ways of being could be explored alongside being kind. I came to realize that, ironically, through pretending to be violent Michael was becoming more, not less, committed to peaceful resolutions in everyday life.

Mrs Smith was worried that her son might become violent by pretending to be violent with older boys. But pretending to be violent does not create violent people, just as gorillas' play fighting does not create violent gorillas. When children play together, whether or not they pretend to be aggressive, they collaboratively create an imagined space where their social relationships can be different. Between the ages of 3 and 8 my son pretended to attack or kill thousands of monsters and people, yet aged 13 he protested during the run-up to the Iraq War. In a similar spirit, one of the 10-year-old den-making boys at Surlingham was adamant: 'There's actually no point to war. It's the people who start it who are on the wrong side. They may think they are on the right side but they're on the wrong side.'

Adam's mother was wise to be concerned about actual aggression. When children stop pretending together and start arguing, then actual disagreements may erupt into real aggression that needs to be confronted directly. Ironically, the teachers at Surlingham discovered, like Paley (1984), that quiet girls may be more aggressive than boisterous boys:

> There are few physical arguments among the girls. They tend to use words as their weapons, for example, name-calling, put-downs, social-exclusion, and refusing to play with one individual or other. Last year there were a lot of arguments that caused unhappiness. Parents were concerned about bullying.
> (Tim, phone interview, 15 December 2008)

Just as they do when they are reading or watching movies, children know that playing with how the world could be does not mean wanting to become what they imagine. As Peter, another 10-year-old boy at the school who enjoyed war play, put it, 'I want to be a dentist when I grow up, not a mass murderer.' When Tim interviewed a group of his peers, including some of those who were disaffected at times, the children were unanimous that they were not actually being aggressive, unsafe or hurtful:

> We might be playing it but it doesn't mean we actually mean it ... actually hurt people.

> You may think it makes us violent, but it doesn't because boys usually like battering games ... since I was 5 I've been obsessed with guns.

> It's just playing a game. We're not going to effect real life. We're always playing against imaginary people ... us playing war is just for excitement and fun.
> (Tim, Quicktime movie attachment
> to email, 14 December 2008)

Powerful challenges

Vygotsky (1967) stressed that children's experiences of playing are likely to be very different from the apparent meaning of their behaviours. When children play, they imaginatively, and intentionally transform objects, for example, waving sticks become parrying swords, or dolls represent crying babies. And, what may appear to a watching adult to be dangerous behaviours, or uncontrolled energies, like running, yelling or climbing, are much most likely to be self-chosen actions with enjoyable risks that children take in challenging themselves. Children playing are actually self-monitoring, developing the ability to choose appropriate action and control behaviour within the rules of any imagined situation.

As Vygotsky stressed, when children pretend, activities are bound by largely implicit cultural rules and social expectations; it is pleasurable to accept and play within the constraints created by implicit rules. For example, boys chasing and pretending to be in an army platoon would likely protect each other just as a cluster of girls pretending to be in a family would want to keep babies safe. Further, like the children at Surlingham, children want to negotiate with one another, or with adults, to agree on overt rules to keep play safe and enjoyable for everyone.

Rational discussions about why children need to engage in risk-taking play and why pretend violence is different from actual violence may not be sufficient to resolve adults' instinctive feelings of antipathy to playful aggression as well as actual aggression (Freud 1933; Erikson 1963; Reynolds and Jones 1997). Tim acknowledged that despite the desire to support children's choices, he shares with his colleagues a sense of unease about war play. A socio-cultural explanation for resistance to changing the status quo is that adults are being asked to challenge views that are less personal opinions than shared discursive frameworks, or discourses (Bakhtin 1981), that have acquired cultural meaning over time through social interactions.

Foucault's discursive theory of how power accumulates with, and is applied by, those in positions of authority helps illuminate how power will not be used equally, even in a school where children and staff intend to create win–win situations. When discursive frameworks make them feel justified, adults may apply pressure to impose an outcome but in doing so they run the risk of ignoring, diminishing or silencing children's voices. Yet, teachers who desire to use power with children rather than oppress them, as much as possible can move to accommodate children's views and mitigate the effects of adults' actions as well as explain, listen and negotiate. For example, as Tim described:

> Matters reached a head [in December 2008] when a [5-year-old] child in Reception had been injured by another Reception child who was playing with the construction equipment. It was irrelevant that neither child was actually using the equipment as a weapon and that the incident was a complete accident. The response of the parent was to remove her child from school for two days. There were rumours of a petition to have the construction equipment banned and concerns were voiced by a school governor about a perception of permissiveness damaging the school's reputation. Under such pressure there was a growing feeling of unrest among the staff. We decided that for the new term it would be tactically astute to put the construction equipment away for several months. Not to ban it, but to give it a rest.

We discussed things with the boys and explained as best as we could the position. They were understanding, if disappointed. A set of new construction equipment was bought for each age group by the parent association and made available inside. At break-times in addition to the outside play areas all children now have staff-supervised free access to space inside the school.

(Tim, email, 10 March 2009).

Conclusion

Examining assumptions about children's play on one playground has revealed facets of how power can operate in schools. Adults may use power to assist children to negotiate, to create play spaces for all children, and to formulate policy. Power may also be used to shape constraints, to restrict and control children's play. How adults balance such uses of power is an open question that has complex consequences for everyone in a school. Though changing playground practices at Surlingham proved to be challenging, the process has shown adults more of children's desires and capabilities:

Those things that were covert and marginalised, such as the boys' great interest in fantasy war play on the playground, are now out in the open with opportunities in classroom time for all children to explore their interests through writing, art, and ICT.

(Tim, email, 10 March 2009)

At Surlingham Primary, recognizing that disagreements most often arose when resources were limited, over misunderstandings, or from feelings of unfairness, but not from play itself, the staff developed a conflict resolution policy that distinguishes between everyday disagreements and bullying. Adults used their power both to make institutional change and to create more dialogic spaces where all sides may be heard whether or not children are playing. Tim stressed the advantages:

We can interpret incidents more accurately with children, staff, and parents. Problems no longer escalate as they did.

(Tim, email, 10 March 2009)

The Surlingham teachers are now planning to write a formal statement about the school ethos. One idea is to make central the universal rights of children that include the right to play enshrined in the United Nations Declaration of the Rights of the Child. In parallel with a right to play is the right to be protected from physical and mental harm, that by implication includes situations when other children play, or where adults organize playtimes. Implicitly rejecting a belief that unfettered power can be used *over* children to impose behaviour control, or that some children's play can dominate others, the UN Charter clearly regards children as people whose views about their lives should be included in any decision-making process.

Power can be used *for* children when adults give substance to the spirit of policy documents. Framing play both as a universal right and as sanctioned by the British government brings the authority of international law and national policy to considerations of the power relationships that shape discussions among staff, the governing body, parents and children, about who should decide what happens on the playground. The UN principles make the goal of discussions clear:

> The best interests of children must be the primary concern in making decisions that may affect them. All adults should do what is best for children. When adults make decisions, they should think about how their decisions will affect children.
>
> (United Nations Declaration
> of the Rights of the Child 1959)

Adults can share power more equitably *with* young people when they talk and play with children. Adults who care for children at play can hear their voices, allow their views to shape adult assumptions and decisions, and create respectful spaces where everyone's dignity is maintained in a community of genuine dialogue.

Note

1. Names of parents and children are all pseudonyms.

References

Bakhtin, M.M. (1981) *The Dialogic Imagination*, ed. M. Holquist, trans. C. Emerson and M. Holquist. Austin, TX: Texas University Press.

Bateson, G. (1956) The message 'This is play', in B. Schaffner (ed.) *Group Process*. New York: Josiah Macy, pp. 145–242.

Department for Children, Schools and Families (2008a) *The Play Strategy*. Retrieved on 12 December 2008 from http://www.dcsf.gov.uk/play/.

Department for Children, Schools and Families (2008b) *Fair Play*. Retrieved on 12 December 2008 from http://www.dcsf.gov.uk/play/.

Edmiston, B. (2008) *Forming Ethical Identities in Early Childhood Play*. London: Routledge.

Erikson, E. (1963) *Childhood and Society*. London: Routledge & Kegan Paul.

Freud, S. (1933) *New Introductory Lectures on Psychoanalysis*, trans. W.J.H. Sprott. New York: Norton & Company.

Holland, P. (2003) *We Don't Play with Guns Here: War, Weapon, and Superhero Play in the Early Years*. Maidenhead: Open University Press.

Huizinga, J. (1955) *Homo Ludens: A Study of the Play-Element in Culture*. Boston: Beacon Press.

Iggulden, C. and Iggulden, H. (2007) *The Dangerous Book for Boys*. New York: William Morrow.

Jones, G. (2002) *Killing Monsters: Why Children Need Fantasy, Superheroes, and Make-Believe Violence*. New York: Basic Books.

Katch, J. (2001) *Under Deadman's Skin: Discovering the Meaning of Children's Violent Play*. Boston, MA: Beacon Press.

Kindlon, D. and Thompson, M. (2000) *Raising Cain: Protecting the Emotional Life of Boys*. New York: Ballantine Books.

Kohn, A. (1996) *Beyond Discipline: From Compliance to Community*. Alexander, VA: Association for Supervision and Curriculum Development.

MacNaughton, G. (2005) *Doing Foucault in Early Childhood Studies*. London: Routledge.

Noddings, N. (1992) *The Challenge to Care in Schools: An Alternate Approach to Education*. New York: Teachers College Press.

Paley, V.G. (1984) *Boys and Girls: Superheroes in the Doll Corner*. Chicago: University of Chicago Press.

Pelligrini, A.D. (1988) Rough-and-tumble play from childhood through adolescence, in D. Fromberg and D. Bergen (eds) *Play from Birth to Twelve and Beyond: Contexts, Perspectives, and Meanings*. New York: Garland, pp. 401–8.

Reynolds, G. and Jones, E. (1997) *Master Players: Learning from Children at Play*. New York: Teachers College Press.

Schaefer, M. and Smith, P.K. (1996) Teachers' perception of play fighting and real fighting in primary school, *Educational Research*, 38: 173–81.

Thompson, M. (2008) Interview on Wisconsin Public Radio's *To the Best of Our Knowledge*, 7 December.

United Nations (1959) Declaration of the Rights of the Child. Retrieved on 21 March 2009 from http://www.unhchr.ch/html/menu3/b/25.htm

Vygotsky, L. (1967) Play and its role in the mental development of the child, *Soviet Psychology*, 5: 6–18.

13 Let the wild rumpus begin!

The radical possibilities of play for young children with disabilities

Leigh M. O'Brien

Introduction

The focus of this chapter is on how young children with disabilities[1] can be supported in discovering who they are in the world through play. First, for young children to be empowered by play opportunities, adults have to take play seriously.[2] Moreover, in a liberatory model such as this (e.g. Freire 1970), adults also must see all children as competent, strong and rich in potential (Edwards et al. 1993), and all children as deserving of autonomy and freedom.[3] In addition, teachers must view these things as integral to a just and democratic society which needs and expects all children to become active, responsible and caring citizens (O'Brien 2001). Further, teachers and others working in early care and education (ECE) have to move beyond a deficit view of children with disabilities wherein 'fixing' their perceived problems takes precedence over providing the kinds of child-centred experiences that have been argued as appropriate and desirable for young children (e.g. Mallory 1994).

For too long and far too often, children with identified disabilities have been taught isolated skills, designed to address their designated areas of weakness, in isolated settings (O'Brien 2001, 2006a, 2006b). This limited and limiting education has made it difficult to provide young children with disabilities with the kinds of play-based learning opportunities their typically developing peers [are supposed to] have in 'developmentally appropriate' settings (Bredekamp and Copple 1997). Broadening the educational frame to include all children in a positive, strength-based way can maximize the potential of child-initiated, open-ended experiences like play.

Free play in particular, that is, play that is pleasurable, self-motivated and child-initiated/directed, imaginative, non-goal-directed, spontaneous, active and free of adult-imposed rules (Johnson et al. 1987; White and Stoecklin 1998), offers children the freedom to find out who they are, to make their own choices, to develop their strengths and their creativity. Through free play, especially outdoor, nature-based play, children can both explore and find their places in the world. Even if we focus primarily on academics, there is a growing body of evidence (Louv 2005) that unstructured, outdoor free play can enhance children's concentration and school performance.

Interesting, but what does this mean for young children with disabilities? Can *all* children play? *Should* all children play? Do all children *learn* from play? And if they do learn, *what* do they learn? *Must* all children play in order to develop fully? Is, in fact, access to play one of children's *rights*? And, if many of the most prominent researchers in the field of child psychology (Piaget, James, Freud, Jung, Vygotsky, etc.) have viewed play as endemic to the human species, why did they so rarely address children who appear to be outside the parameters of typical development?

The right to play is explicitly recognized in Article 31 of the Convention on the Rights of the Child (adopted by the General Assembly of the United Nations in 1989). Although many believe this to be a minimal statement of rights, the United States has not yet ratified the document because there has been opposition by some conservative groups. I find this both fascinating and troubling. Could this be because we *don't* really want to empower all children? That we *don't* see all children as capable, strong and rich in potential? We *don't* believe all children are deserving of autonomy and freedom? That, despite the rhetoric, we *don't* take play seriously as a way in which all children can learn? That access to play is, in fact, *not* believed to be one of children's rights? My hunch is some worry that opening the door to free play might lead to an undue and inappropriate focus on freedom and autonomy – in conservative parlance, a lack of structure, even *wildness* – as in Sendak's (1963) call to 'let the wild rumpus begin!'

For me, these questions lead to another: Do young children with disabilities get to play in the same way those without disabilities do? The short answer is *sometimes*. However, play is more typically used for therapy, to teach discrete academic and social skills, and to reward children for completing a task or doing the 'right' thing (Frost 1992).[4] In my experience, children with disabilities may *lose* play time or 'privileges' when they 'misbehave' or cannot finish work within the allotted time frame. This situation is doubly egregious in that these are the children who may most need to and benefit from play (Allen 1975). To me, this is just short of a crime. Findings about how play influences brain growth suggest that playing, though it might look silly and purposeless to adults, warrants a place in *every* child's day. Not too overblown a place, not too sanctimonious a place, but a place that embraces all styles of play and that recognizes play as essential to healthy neurological development (Henig 2008).

This is not to say that there are no questions to be raised about children's play, that it is an unalloyed good (see, for example, Sutton-Smith 2001). In fact, children's play can be cruel and devastating to children who are left out or made fun of, and this must be addressed. Play has also been reified in ECE to the point that it is often presented uncritically as a good thing for all children, at all times, in all settings. Additionally, the use of play as a way to learn about the self and the world, as I will address below, poses some dilemmas for teachers of young children with disabilities. My point here is that we ought to give play the attention it deserves.

If we did so, we might learn more about children's strengths in areas not typically addressed in school and thereby support more children's development in more caring and thoughtful ways. If we believe play to be an important factor in children's development, then the adults who are with the children might ask, what kinds of play experiences are 'high quality'? How can we ensure play is beneficial for *all* children? How can we best address issues pertaining to age, race, class, gender, ability, language and other dimensions of diversity in the context of play? What kinds of negative experiences are occurring and how can we thoughtfully address them? How can we capitalize on outdoor experiences in terms of connecting children to the natural world? Attending closely to, and valuing, young children's play may be one way to address these questions.

Intersecting theoretical frames

I frame my thinking about this in a number of overlapping critical perspectives. First, I believe in an approach to disability that leads to an emancipatory agenda and autonomy (Skrtic 1995). The principles of self-determination and human agency are important if people are to be subjects of their own lives (O'Brien 2006b). Valuing these principles means we must believe and act on the premise that individuals want to – and can – exert control over their own lives. Abery argues that, 'A sense of self-determination is necessary for the development of individual identity, a crucial catalyst of independence and autonomy' (1994: 34). The ability of a person to make his or her own decisions has a significant effect on that person's self-esteem and sense of efficacy, and hence quality of life. If this is important for all children, how do we develop self-determination? Play, freely chosen by each child, is certainly one avenue. Free play in particular can be emancipatory because it is about 'dialogic being' (Bingham 2000: 431).

Second, I believe in education structures and practices that support fully inclusive school communities (e.g. Lipsky and Gartner 2001). Inclusion is about belonging and hence about adults providing a framework within which *all* children are valued, treated with respect, and provided with real opportunities (Thomas and Loxley 2007). To get to this place, educators need to work for the inclusion of young children with disabilities, and at the same time be passionate advocates for a meaningful, relevant curriculum that helps them learn about themselves and their world (O'Brien 2001). Play is important to the curriculum for young children for just these reasons.

However, in US schools today, the all-too-typical practice is to put 'different children' in regular classes and then ignore them (Hamovitch 2003) *or* to categorize and then segregate them in resource rooms, self-contained classes or special schools. How, then, can we educate children about their dynamic and multiple identities? What are the implications of segregation around ability (or any other characteristic) for the education of the young on the foundations of democracy and a sense of community?

What we need to counter this deficit approach is greater attention to liberatory, dialogic education (Freire 1970). In this approach to education, learners of all ages and abilities are seen as complex individuals who need to be supported in their knowledge construction. Given that starting point, we can frame the purpose of 'special education' as minimizing the impact of disability by giving children the supports, skills and opportunities to live as full a life as possible and maximizing the opportunities to fully and meaningfully participate in schooling and the community.

Building on the foregoing is the traditional moral imperative of schools in purportedly democratic societies: to create a public capable of sustaining the life of a democracy. Democratic citizens must be able to make decisions, analyze social situations, frame purposes, debate outcomes – in short, feel enfranchised with the power to effect change. A free democratic state calls for the education of critical, thoughtful citizens who can define their own purposes and are able and willing to act upon their ideas (Dewey 1966). 'Only by being true to the full growth of the individuals who make it up, can society by any chance be true to itself' (Dewey [1902] 1990: 7).

Thus, in a democracy, we need education that helps children find their own voices and communicate their own messages. We should help children to be gloriously different individuals who will enrich our world by posing and solving problems in ways we have never tried. Again, we ought to support education that liberates humans rather than domesticates them (Freire 1970); that will, to paraphrase Frederick Douglass, unfit them to be slaves. This is where free play, with its imaginative, non-goal-directed, spontaneous and active nature, offers liberatory, and hence radical, opportunities for young children with disabilities.

The role of adults in children's play

As noted earlier, the extant body of play literature supports and acknowledges the importance of researching and understanding play for typically
developing children, but there has been far less research focused on the
play of children with disabilities and, consequently, our knowledge of
how they play is limited. However, early childhood educators are increasingly focusing on the value of play when developing programmes for
children with disabilities (Bray and Cooper 2007). As they do so, it is
important to think about how play environments support or restrict children's play (O'Brien 2003).

From a Vygotskian perspective, play that is optimal for development
reflects or slightly stretches the current social or cognitive abilities of the
child. To contribute to children's development and education, then, play
opportunities must be both appropriate and challenging. Careful adult
involvement in play benefits the level of children's play as well as children's social and intellectual development; this is especially so for young
children with disabilities. Sutton-Smith (2001) has suggested a sequence
for adult participation in play:

1. Observe carefully to determine children's interests and skills.
2. Join in and play with the children.
3. Back away and observe again.

The emphasis here is clearly on observation and, in fact, mere teacher
presence in an activity appears to encourage children's involvement
(Johnson et al. 1987). However, if observation reveals that some children
are not playing at all, exhibit low levels of play, or are 'bogged down' in
repetitive play episodes, the adult may want to intervene. Furthermore,
children with disabilities may fail to play because their environment is
not stimulating and doesn't take into account varied developmental abilities, or because the regimen of group care provides little or no opportunity for play. However, given opportunities, materials and adult support,
as needed, children with disabilities do play and learn from doing so
(Quinn and Rubin 1984, cited in Frost 1992). This cycle, then, can be
extended for children with disabilities if adults, as appropriate and necessary, also model play behaviours, describe what is happening and make
suggestions, and otherwise support and guide children's play (Johnson
et al. 1987).

Consistent with Vygotsky's theory that certain kinds of play serve as
a context for the development of self-regulation, Krafft and Berk (1998)
found that the incidence of private speech was much higher during
open-ended activities, especially fantasy play, that require *children* to

determine the task. In line with previous research, the more direct involvement by teachers, the lower the rate of children's private speech. Conversely, engagement with peers, in the form of associative play, predicted greater self-directed language. This obviously provides a dilemma for teachers who believe certain children need their play scaffolded by adults: How does one ensure that children are engaged with peers during open-ended activities without being intrusive or overly directive?

Many believe that the goal for teachers in inclusive classrooms is to use the least intrusive strategies possible to help children reach their learning goals (Winter 2007). Winter suggests that a core set of strategies for teaching in an inclusive classroom would include *naturalistic strategies* such as play and activity-based intervention. These are implicit strategies and practices that naturally occur within the typical context of early childhood settings. Naturalistic strategies respect a child's way of learning, value play as a catalyst for learning, are unobtrusive, and foster learning in a relevant context.

Naturalistic strategies permit teachers to increase the opportunities for children to learn without adding undue pressure. Key strategies include scheduling time for children to play indoors and out; observing children during play to find opportune moments to intervene and stimulate learning; scaffolding learning in thoughtful, unobtrusive ways; and embedding interventions or therapy into daily contexts. The power of naturalistic strategies is that children are learning in a meaningful context that is relevant to them (Winter 2007). For children who are used to having their every movement and utterance chronicled, assessed and corrected, this is radical, indeed!

Outdoor play

Outdoor areas lend themselves to meeting children's individual needs. Natural environments allow for investigation and discovery by children with different learning styles (Moore and Hong 1997). Research consistently shows that children have a strong preference to play outdoors in natural landscapes, and that parents generally support this kind of play (White and Stoecklin 1998). More than 100 studies of outdoor experiences in natural areas show that natural outdoor environments produce positive psychological and physiological responses, including reduced stress and a general feeling of well-being (Lewis 1996). We could do more to capitalize on this time out-of-doors to help children develop environmental values, a basic respect for and appreciation of nature. Outdoor play experiences can enhance learning and shape lifelong attitudes, values and patterns of behaviour towards nature (Louv 2005).

Louv (2009) says we also need to articulate the underlying 'first principle': a meaningful connection to the natural world is fundamental to our survival and spirit. Louv asks, does a child have a right to a walk in the woods? The answer, he contends, is yes, if we can agree that the right at issue is fundamental to our humanity, to our being. Further, he argues, if E.O. Wilson's biophilia hypothesis is right – that human beings are hard-wired to get their hands wet and their feet muddy in the natural world – then we must do more than talk about the importance of nature; we must ensure that all children have everyday access to natural spaces, places and experiences.

Based on my research on recess at a suburban elementary school (O'Brien 2003), I argue that outside play can provide the freedom to explore, to let imaginations loose, and so provides a welcome break from the daily routines of school. Recess provides one of the few opportunities available for children to speak and act relatively unfettered by adult expectations (Kieff 2001). Some have argued for a 'third space' (Soja 1996) or 'third discourse', where those who are marginalized can act and speak freely. Sidorkin contends that 'third discourse [polyphony] is clearly and openly in opposition to the first discourse [teacher-dominated monologue]' and as such happens mainly in places like playgrounds and other sites not dominated by teachers (cited in Bingham 2000: 431). In this space, school is made familiar and students feel a sense of ownership over a part of it.

It is that non-adult-directed, counter-cultural 'stuff' that is so rewarding for children – and so threatening to those who would maintain control at all costs. That is why I found it so disturbing that most of the adults monitoring recess at this site quickly shut down any play that even hinted at danger or 'wildness'.[5] In one study (Maxwell et al. 1999), school children noted that recess was the *only* time of the day when they could make choices and that to be able to choose made them feel respected. I think here of the third-grade boy who charged up the steps to the playground, threw both arms in the air, and shouted 'Freedom!' Shouldn't all children get to experience this feeling?

It may well be that unstructured time, plenty of physical and psychological roaming space, and lack of adult-imposed rules are needed to open doors and minds. Michaels (2000) contends we will lose our free thinkers, sensitive communicators, and safe outlets for self-expression if we continue to eliminate recess or severely curtail freedom during this time. Educators who agree might ask, how many and what kinds of choices can and should be provided? If restrictions are needed, how many, what kind, and to what end are they needed? How can we make play areas safe without stifling children's choices, creativity, imagination and need to be powerful?

A few suggestions for ways to help children start the wild rumpus

With a deficit model (applied to, in this case, ability), our conception of education becomes one of narrow, technical rationality. I am calling, instead, for a view of schooling which says life ought to feel infinitely open; one which says happiness is crucial, exploration and curiosity are learning tools, and growth is variable but integral to each person's life (O'Brien 2001). The shift that needs to be made is towards the healthy development of all young children's innate and multifaceted potentials. I believe true education, for all children, begins and ends in the perpetual uncovering and unfolding of self in the world. We need to move towards a school culture that attends to developing each individual's capacity to act as a free and thoughtful agent striving to master his or her world (Kohn 1998). In this model, teachers guide and encourage children to be all that they can be, not necessarily what adults think they should be.

To make this ideal a reality, we must keep – or reinsert, in most cases – the joy in education, especially for children with disabilities. We shouldn't be so concerned with specific goals and outcomes, narrow academic tasks, behaviour modification, and the like. Rather we must attend to each child's development of autonomy, individual needs and successes, sense of wonder, and happiness (O'Brien 2006a).

What would happen to early care and education if we viewed children with disabilities as capable rather than needy? If we saw them as autonomous and competent, with varying strengths and challenges? As deserving of wonder and happiness in their lives? As able to play with wild abandon? If our vision was based on the foregoing, we might move in the direction of making sure *all* children are able to learn through self-initiated experience. We can maintain an 'us/them' society wherein some children get one kind of school experience and those labelled disabled get another, or we can create communities where all are valued and included (Snow 2007).

Related to this is the notion of local understanding, which Kliewer and Biklen (2007) describe as an educational dialogue in which the values, intelligence and imagination of *all* children are recognized, and responsive settings are created that foster increasingly sophisticated citizenship. In this kind of school, purpose, capacity, competence and potential are ascribed to members' actions and fostered across school contexts. This dialogic approach is a reflection of Freire's (1970) *conscientização*, wherein all children are constructed as capable.[6] If we worked from the premise that *all* young children are capable, we would begin moving towards inclusive democratic communities.

Unfortunately, the school exists largely as an instrument of social and economic power for the most influential elite groups (e.g. Karier 1973). Therefore, many children experience a constrained and impoverished view of future possibilities because educators are bound by systems that extinguish imagination (Ware 2001). Further, for many reasons, it can be difficult for societies used to segregated schooling to move towards more inclusive education (O'Brien 2007). It is my hope that parents and educators, working on the edges (Bateson 1989), can help push our societal paradigm in a different direction, a more humanistic and inclusive one. Lipsky and Gartner put it succinctly: 'How a society treats its youngest children, including those with disabilities, is critical both for its future and as a measure of the society's values' (2001: 46).

If the purpose of schooling is to educate responsible and democratic citizens, as most Western societies aver, then we must make sure all children receive the kind of education outlined in the preceding. This inclusive vision of democracy welcomes plurality and diversity and rejects barriers that exclude and divide (Sapon-Shevin 2007). Our ethical responsibility and moral imperative is this: We must strive to see every child as a unique human being with hopes, dreams, aspirations, skills and capacities. We must assume each has the capacity for full human feeling, for deep reflection and thought (Ayers 1996). What we need, then, is a system that views all children as 'of promise', and that builds on their interests and strengths (Swadener 1990). Eisner contends, 'We ought to be providing environments that enable each youngster in our schools to find a place in the educational sun' (2001: 372).

So, to answer the questions I posed in the Introduction: Can all children play? Should all children play? Do all children learn from play? Must all children play in order to develop fully? And, is access to play one of children's rights? I say yes! We must resist the trend towards limiting or 'directing' play and instead be tireless advocates for the radical possibilities to be found in play. Free, open-ended – sometimes even wild – play is the right of *every* child. And our advocacy for this kind of play is one very important way we can support the 'irrepressible possibility of humans' (Booth 2001).

Notes

1. How we describe or name children with disabilities reflects our views and beliefs. The term 'special needs', commonly used in the US, has been critiqued for many reasons including its dishonesty (Snow 2002–06). I use the term 'children with disabilities' because I find it to be the most forthright and hence the most useful. This chapter describes the situation in the United States unless otherwise noted.

2. In sum, empowerment is the process that allows one to gain the knowledge, skill-sets and attitude needed to cope with the changing world and the circumstances in which one lives.
3. See O'Brien (2006a), for more on how I define these terms; basically, I am arguing that children should have power and a sense of control over their lives.
4. For example, a Google search of 'play and special education' revealed the most relevant link as 'Special Education Instrument Set' which is designed for therapists to use in early intervention. In the ERIC [Education Resources Information Center] system, I did find a (very) few articles about play and children with disabilities, but most were about *assessing* children's play or *using* children's play to teach something.
5. This situation reminds me of Foucault's notion of the panoptic (1977), the all-seeing eye capable of – or, more importantly, *thought* to be capable of – watching all areas at once, thus ensuring compliance and control. This surveillance by an all-powerful adult 'gaze' often regulates what is arguably the only time during the entire school day the children can truthfully call their own.
6. See also the pre-schools of Reggio Emilia and the Golden Key schools in Russia (Kratsov and Kratsova 2009).

References

Abery, B. (1994) A conceptual framework for enhancing self-determination, in M. Hayden and B. Abery (eds) *Challenges for a Service System in Transition*. Baltimore, MD: Paul H. Brookes, pp. 345–80.

Allen, M. (1975) *Adventure Playgrounds for Handicapped Children*. London: James Galt.

Ayers, W. (1996) Commencement speech given at Nazareth College, Rochester, New York, May.

Bateson, M.C. (1989) *Composing a Life*. New York: Penguin Press.

Bingham, C. (2000) Review of the book *Beyond Discourse: Education, the Self, and Dialogue. Educational Studies*, 31(4): 427–32.

Booth, E. (2001) The John Washburn Memorial Lecture, paper presented at the Memorial Art Gallery, Rochester, New York, July.

Bray, P. and Cooper, R. (2007) The play of children with special needs in mainstream and special needs settings, *Australian Journal of Early Childhood*, 32(2): 37–42.

Bredekamp, S. and Copple, C. (1997) *Developmentally Appropriate Practice for Children: Birth through Age Eight*. Washington, DC: National Association for the Education of Young Children.

Dewey, J. ([1902] 1990) *The Child and the Curriculum.* Chicago: University of Chicago Press.

Dewey, J. (1966) *Democracy and Education: An Introduction to the Philosophy of Education.* New York: The Free Press.

Edwards, C., Gandini, L. and Forman, G. (eds) (1993) *The Hundred Languages of Children: The Reggio Emilia Approach to Early Childhood Education.* New York: Ablex.

Eisner, E. (2001) What does it mean to say a school is doing well? *Phi Delta Kappan,* 82(5): 367–72.

Foucault, M. (1977) *Discipline and Punish: The Birth of the Prison.* New York: Pantheon Books.

Freire, P. (1970) *Pedagogy of the Oppressed.* New York: Continuum.

Frost, J.L. (1992) *Play and Playscapes.* Albany, NY: Delmar Publishers, Inc.

Hamovitch, B. (2003) Hoping for the best: 'inclusion' and stigmatization in a middle school, in S. Books (ed.) *Invisible Children in the Society and its Schools.* London: Routledge.

Henig, R.M. (2008) Taking play seriously: what can science tell us about why kids run and jump? Retrieved from http://www.blueridgenow.com/, 3 January 2009.

Johnson, J.E., Christie, J.F. and Yawkey, T.D. (1987) *Play and Early Childhood Development.* New York: HarperCollins Publishers.

Karier, C.J. (1973) Business values and the educational state, in C.J. Karier, P. Violas and J. Spring (eds) *Roots of Crisis: American Education in the Twentieth Century.* Chicago: Rand McNally, pp. 6–29.

Kieff, J. (2001) The silencing of recess bells, *Childhood Education,* 77(5): 319–20.

Kohn, A. (1998) *What to look for in a classroom ... and other essays.* San Francisco: Jossey-Bass.

Kliewer, C. and Biklen, D. (2007) Enacting literacy: local understanding, significant disability, and a new frame for educational opportunity, *Teachers College Record,* 109(12): 2579–600.

Krafft, K.C. and Berk, L.E. (1998) Private speech in two preschools: significance of open-ended activities and make-believe play for verbal self-regulation, *Early Childhood Research Quarterly,* 13(4): 637–58.

Kravtsov, G. and Kravtsova, E. (2009) Cultural-historical psychology in the practice of education, in M. Fleer, M. Hedegaard and J. Tudge (eds) *Childhood Studies and the Impact of Globalization: Policies and Practices at Global and Local Levels.* New York: Routledge, pp. 199–210.

Lewis, C.A. (1996) *Green Nature, Human Nature: The Meaning of Plants in Our Lives.* Chicago: University of Chicago Press.

Lipsky, D.K. and Gartner, A. (2001) Education reform and early childhood inclusion, in M.J. Guralnick (ed.) *Early Childhood Inclusion.* Baltimore, MD: Brookes Publishing Co., pp. 39–48.

Louv, R. (2005) *Last Child in the Woods: Saving Our Children from Nature–Deficit Disorder*. Chapel Hill, NC: Algonquin Books.

Louv, R. (2009) A walk in the woods: right or privilege? *Orion* magazine, March, April. Retrieved 17 March 2009 from www.orionmagazine. org/index.php/articles/article/4401/.

Mallory, B. (1994) Inclusive policy, practice, and theory for young children with developmental differences, in B.L. Mallory and R.S. New (eds) *Diversity and Developmentally Appropriate Practices: Challenges for Early Childhood Education*. New York: Teachers College Press, pp. 44–62.

Maxwell, D.M., Jarrett, O.S. and Roetger, C.D. (1999) Recess through the children's eyes, paper presented at the Conference on Qualitative Research in Education, University of Georgia, January.

Michaels, B. (2000) Art and recess, in R.L. Clements (ed.) *Elementary School Recess: Selected Readings, Games, and Activities for Teachers and Parents*. New York: American Press, pp. 70–4.

Moore, R.C. and Hong, H.H. (1997) *Natural Learning: Creating Environments for Rediscovering Nature's Way of Teaching*. Berkeley, CA: MIG Communications.

O'Brien, L.M. (2001) Juggling scarves or inclusion for what? Young children with special needs in an era of school 'reform', *Contemporary Issues in Early Childhood*, 2(3): 309–20.

O'Brien, L.M. (2003) The rewards and restrictions of recess: reflections on being a playground volunteer, *Childhood Education*, 79(3): 161–6.

O'Brien, L.M. (2006a) My daughter, myself: mother as early childhood teacher educator, in L.M. O'Brien and B.B. Swadener (eds) *Writing the Motherline: Mothers, Daughters, and Education*. Lanham, MD: Rowman & Littlefield, pp. 3–24.

O'Brien, L.M. (2006b) Being bent over backward: a mother and teacher educator challenges the positioning of her daughter with disabilities, *Disability Studies Quarterly*, 26(2). Available at: http://www.dsq–sds. org/_articles_html/2006/spring/obrien.asp.

O'Brien, L.M. (2007) A school for everyone? The Swedish school system's struggles to reconcile societal goals with school and classroom practices, *Childhood Education*, 83(6): 374–9.

Sapon-Shevin, M. (2007) *Widening the Circle: The Power of Inclusive Classrooms*. Boston: Beacon Press.

Sendak, M. (1963) *Where the Wild Things Are*. New York: Harper and Row.

Skrtic, T.M. (1995) *Disability and Democracy: Reconstructing (Special) Education for Postmodernity*. New York: Teachers College Press.

Snow, K. (2002–06) The case against 'special needs'. Retrieved 24 October 2007, from www.disabilityisnatural.com.

Snow, K. (2007) Presume competence: challenging conventional wisdom about people with disabilities. Retrieved 14 September 2007, from www.disabilityisnatural.com.

Soja, E. (1996) *Thirdspace: Journeys to Los Angeles and Other Real-and-Imagined Places.* Cambridge, MA: Harvard University Press.

Sutton-Smith, B. (2001) *The Ambiguity of Play.* Cambridge, MA: Harvard University Press.

Swadener, B.B. (1990) Children and families 'at risk': etiology, critique, and alternative paradigms, *Educational Foundations*, 4(4): 17–39.

Thomas, G. and Loxley, A. (2007) *Deconstructing Special Education and Constructing Inclusion*, 2nd edn. Maidenhead: Open University Press.

Ware, L.P. (2001) Writing, identity, and the other: dare we do disability studies? *Journal of Teacher Education*, 52(2): 107–23.

White, R. and Stoecklin, V.L. (1998) Children's outdoor play and learning environments: returning to nature, *Early Childhood News*, 10(2): 24–30.

Winter, S. (2007) *Inclusive Early Childhood Education: A Collaborative Approach.* Upper Saddle River, NJ: Pearson.

14 Children's enculturation through play

Bert van Oers

Introduction: play and culture

Since the 1980s, education, and particularly schools, have increasingly been conceived of as sites for the production of decent, loyal, responsible and well-informed citizens. With the growing emphasis on the outcomes of schools in relation to societal needs and costs, a modern school culture is emerging with a strong obligation for results and accountability. It can be expected that this tendency will be further reinforced by the recent trends towards the knowledge economy (van Oers 2009).

In this cultural-economic climate, discussions about the relevance of play for school learning are still going on with increasing intensity, without reaching consensus. As several authors have already pointed out, opportunities for playing have been reduced in schools in recent decades. Play has been mostly reserved to the early grades (until the age of 6) and is almost completely replaced by 'real learning', when children grow older. But even in the early grades play seems to be more and more in danger (e.g. Moyles 1989; Michnick Golinkoff et al. 2006). Obviously, the cultural value attributed to playing in our Western societies is changing. In this chapter, I will argue that play can be rehabilitated as a productive and meaningful context for learning and development. A critical reconsideration of the concept of play is therefore necessary.

Towards a cultural-historical approach to playing

In his critical overview and appraisal of play theories, Sutton-Smith (1997) didn't provide (the beginning of) a solution for the inconsistent picture that emerged, because he didn't thoroughly deconstruct the very notion of play itself. In my view, in the past century the discussion of the relevance of play for human development has suffered from two basic but false assumptions, which were not rigorously criticized, nor replaced by another conception:

1. Play is seen as *a natural behavioural type*, which is inherent in human nature. Basically, this view is grounded in a naturalistic interpretation of human development that was romanticized in the eighteenth century, for example, by Rousseau and his followers. This naturalistic conception attributes the capacity for playing to human nature, which is especially manifest during childhood. A basic assumption of this perspective is that free and uncultivated ('wild') fantasy is the origin of play.
2. Play is seen as *a special type of activity 'sui generis', in distinction to other activities like learning and work*. Many theories of play assume a distinction between play and work (e.g. Hughes 1999: 3–5). Play is often conceived of as a preparation stage for adulthood, where children can learn and practise important skills for later adult life (work).

Both assumptions underpin the *naturalistic and romantic conception of play* that has dominated research, discussions and implementations of play during the nineteenth and twentieth centuries. An important consequence of this conception was the moral ban on adults' interference in children's (natural) play. Both assumptions and their pedagogical implications, however, are inappropriate for understanding the cultural dimensions of play, and for linking play with culture, as educators try to do. Bruner (1976) already pointed out that human beings (unlike animals) have very few natural means for instinctive compensation of the immaturity of the newborn. Immaturity in human beings has to be compensated by cultural artefacts, care and education. Socio-cultural studies in recent decades have demonstrated that there is a strong and intrinsic relation between culture and play, both with regard to the content of play, and to the frequency of its occurrence (Göncü et al. 1999; Rogoff 2003).

On the basis of this view, we can conceive of play as one of the means for adjusting the process of enculturation to children's physical and psychological characteristics. Following a cultural-historical point of view, El'konin (1978: 39–64; 1989: 67–8) pointed out that play depends on the historical conception of the position of the child in society, with regard to cultural activities, peers and adults. The conception of play changes across history and cultures in compliance with specific historical, ideological and economic conditions. From this point of view, we can see play indeed as a cultural invention to give children access to important cultural experiences, in a way that is not risky and gives room to explore new combinations of actions (Bruner 1976: 38).

Following Vygotsky, Leont'ev (1981a) elaborates the cultural-historical conception of play by articulating that play does not originate from fantasy, but emerges as a way to accomplish activities wherein the child participates. Leont'ev proposes to analyze play in terms of play *activities*, and to focus on the play motive, children's actions, the child's interpretations of the situation (and its affordances), the child's role, and the perceived rules and tools (Leont'ev 1981a: 481–508). Fantasy, according to Vygotsky and Leont'ev, is a product of playing and not the origin.

In most analyses of play from a cultural-historical point of view, however, researchers are not very specific about the characteristics of play in relation to cultural activities (including work and learning activities). In order to better understand the possibilities for enculturation in the context of play, we need to have a more specific understanding of the characteristics of *play* as a specimen of the abstract category of *activity*.

Play as activity format

Leont'ev (1975, 1981b) distinguishes a number of fundamental constituents in his theory of activity. He characterizes an activity as a cultural-historical category for the qualification of object-focused action patterns. Activity originates from a motive and is directed to a (mental, verbal or concrete) object. Basically, the motive (or motivating object) defines the nature of an activity. An activity where a ball is the object, is essentially different from an activity that takes a book or vegetables as an object, because they call for different rules, different instruments, different goals, etc. At a specific moment, an activity is always embodied in a series of goal-oriented actions. To give a simplified example: to perform a mathematical activity like addition (596 + 785 = _), we have to follow different steps in the right order, for example, add up the units, tens and hundreds separately, write the resulting outcomes in columns as units, tens and hundreds, then repeat the procedure with these intermediate outcomes until each column only contains either units, tens, hundreds or thousands.

In distinction to one-dimensional activities, practices can be conceived of as functionally integrated composites of different object-oriented activities. Although activities and practices should be distinguished at least for conceptual reasons, they are closely related and share some basic characteristics. For instance, the temporary order (based on a step-wise series of sub-goals) we identified in (mathematical) activities can also be seen in everyday practices. We can see this organization also in cultural practices, as, for example, cooking. In the practice of cooking a meal, different steps have to be taken. Every step is a particular sub-goal-directed action, which has to be realized at the right moment in order to reach the final goal (an edible meal on the table). For cooking, people often have, for instance, to take a pan first (action 1), then fill it with water (action 2), put the pan on the stove (action 3), turn on the stove (action 4), record the time (step 5), and so on. Depending on your specific goal, some actions may be different from the one described here, some may be omitted (e.g. action 5), and some may be carried out in parallel.

The Leont'ev approach to human activity provides a powerful instrument for the analysis and understanding of human actions. Although different critical appraisals have elaborated this work considerably (Brušlinskij and Polikarpov 1990; Engeström 2005), for the present purpose, it is not possible to deal with those extensions. Starting from Leont'ev's original activity theory, my analyses of cultural activities over the past decade have led to the conclusion that the way an activity or practice is carried out (i.e. the activity *format*), is highly important for its developmental effect (van Oers 2003b, 2009).

In many cases, the order of the actions within a practice is regulated by rules (of cooking or otherwise). Taking the cooking example above again: if, for instance, you want to save energy (for environmental reasons), there is a rule that says: don't switch on the stove before the pan is on it. It is important to notice here that a realization of an activity/practice at a certain moment is always a *rule-governed pattern of actions* that may differ across situations or persons, or even across time (dependent on new cultural insights). Whether the actor is in the position to vary the actions depends on many different (situational, institutional or personal) factors, such as the tools available, conventions regarding the ways activities should be carried out, expertise, moral-ethical point of view, and so on.

Following Vygotsky, we maintain that the quality of an activity/practice also depends on the *degrees of freedom* that an actor is allowed in choosing or changing actions, tools, rules, goals. Furthermore, the *level of personal involvement* of the actor in an activity/practice, also strongly determines the quality of that activity/practice.

Any activity/practice can be characterized by these three dimensions: (1) the nature of the *rules*; (2) the *degrees of freedom* allowed to the actors; and (3) the *level of involvement* of the actor. These three dimensions can vary, according to the nature of the situation, the moral-ethical stance of the participants, or the theoretical understandings of supervisors. The three dimensions constitute the format of activities and practices. The format with the highest developmental potential for human beings is, in my view, the format that is characterized by explicit rules, high levels of involvement, and degrees of freedom for the participants.

With the help of this format and its specific values we can now define the nature of play and relate it to activities or practices (like most types of work). Play is concretely characterized by the following activity format:

- There are explicit or implicit *rules*; for example, in children's role play there are often implicit rules, although in some instances children can specify the rules when needed. In manipulative play, a hidden rule is, for example, manifest in the repetition of specific actions. A well-known rule in children's role play is the 'as-if rule'. Children can start a role play with the call 'let's do as if we were pilots' and then start playing. Often children start with implicit rules embedded in the play-script. As Bateson (1972) and Garvey (1990) pointed out, children spontaneously adopt special behavioural signals to communicate the status of their participation and their compliance (or not) with certain tacit rules. A smile, for example, may signal 'I am joking', or a change in verb tense may signal that one steps out of the play momentarily for comments, reflection and revision of the rules. We can witness explicit rules in games like hopscotch, but also in role play, for example, when a child initiates play by making the roles and script explicit: 'I am the doctor and I will give all the babies an injection. All the parents have to draw a number ticket.'
- Players have some *degrees of freedom* in the choice of actions, instruments and goals. This is an essential element for an activity to be playful. The degrees of freedom give the players the right to make their own (idiosyncratic) versions of a socio-cultural activity. In a doctor play, that I once observed, one child put the stethoscope on the patient's knee, and ended up eating the medicine he had prescribed (sweets). Most certainly he has never seen this before in a doctor's practice, but he makes his own version of the activity, and nobody protested against it. A play would be seriously threatened as being play if the degrees of freedom were minimized.
- The conditions of the play activity are such that the players can build up *personal involvement* in the play. 'Personal involvement' means intrinsic willingness to participate in an activity or practice out of personal engagement with this practice, its contents, tools, roles and outcomes, and to enjoy it for its own sake. In order to achieve this, certain requirements in the situation must be met: for example, that participants have the right to voluntarily decide if they participate and when they quit. The play activity must contain elements (such as roles, tools, peers) that make participation attractive and raise emotional or affective reactions in the participants. Note that in this view, involvement always implies high-quality participation, but not every form of participation also meets the required conditions for involvement.

It is evident now why play should not be seen as another activity *sui generis*, alongside activities like learning and working. It is clear that play has no object of its own, but always borrows its object from other cultural activities or practices. To put it in yet another way: cultural activities and practices can be carried out in playful ways, if specific conditions are met in the way the activity or practice can and may be accomplished. There is no play apart from practices/activities such as building, routine, rituals, reading, mathematizing, singing, cooking, and so on. *Play is basically a specific format of an activity or practice*, in other words a way that an activity (or practice) is carried out by its participants. Any activity or practice can be carried out (if permitted by circumstances) in a playful way. Even work and learning!

A brief note is in order here regarding the combination of the format characteristics just described. There is significant interdependence among them. As Vygotsky (1978: 99, 103) already pointed out, there is an irreducible tension between rules and freedom. Rules are indeed essential for any activity or practice, but they unavoidably restrict to some extent the freedom of the actors (in the same way as reality itself restricts absolute freedom; absolute freedom, according to Vygotsky, is an illusion). That is why I speak of *degrees* of freedom that are necessary for the play format.

A final note concerns the position of games. When the rules become more explicit and sanctioned, the play becomes more of a regular game, according to Leont'ev (1981a: 498–500). In contrast to playful activities, games (such as chess) have often adopted their own object, while still retaining the quality of play. That is why games can eventually evolve into a kind of work (see professional chess players, tennis players). Basically, this can also be seen as an argument for the idea that any activity can be carried out in playful ways, as long as it abides by the format of play.

Enculturation through (playful) participation in cultural practices

Recent cultural-historical understandings of learning acknowledge a strong relation between learning and participation in cultural practices (see, for example, Lave and Wenger 1991; Wenger 1999; Rogoff 2003). Most modern practices are complex systems making permanent progress through the integration of new sophisticated instruments and techniques. As a result, cultural practices themselves permanently generate the need for new learning. These circumstances render practices difficult to access for newcomers (such as children). Cultures, therefore, have invented different institutions and artefacts for giving children access to cultural practices. For a long time in history, schools were primarily seen as cultural institutions for preparing children to take part in future adult practices. Hence, for a long time, the school's core business was mainly defined by the training of children on isolated prerequisites of activities (such as the alphabet, technical reading abilities or counting) that were supposed to be relevant for cultural practices. The main assumption underlying this relationship between school learning and practice is the transfer hypothesis that holds that learning in one context (school) can be applied to another context (e.g. adult cultural practices). This assumption, however, has been criticized as being invalid (Tuomi-Gröhn et al. 2003). Whatever is learned in the classroom, tends to vanish outside school. The alternative now is to get children more directly involved in cultural practices, and bring practices (or practice simulations) into the classrooms. However, we must still take into account that practices in the classroom have to be appropriately reconstructed in order to make them accessible and productive for children's learning and development.

El'konin (1978) has pointed out that play is the cultural invention that makes adult practices accessible for young children. Following his activity-theoretical approach to playing, I will generalize this position by hypothesizing that the play format opens activities and practices for novices (young and old), and creates opportunities for meaningful learning that can promote the quality and willingness for participation. Activities formatted in a playful way embody the optimal conditions (rules, degrees of freedom and involvement) for transferable learning and for the subsequent promotion of development.

In our Dutch Developmental Education project we follow this view and implement a Vygotskian cultural-historical activity theory in classroom practices. In recent decades we have been designing, in collaboration with teachers, curriculum designers and teacher trainers (see van Oers 2009) a play-based curriculum for primary education, using the ideas explained above. Reasoning from the theory of play as an *activity format*, teachers try to establish the following conditions for achieving Development-Promoting-Learning (DPL) in pupils:

1. *Get children involved in meaningful socio-cultural activities*: basically, this maxim implies that teachers should invite or encourage children to participate in cultural activities that make sense to them, which they are eager to get engaged in, and that are made accessible for them by arranging them according to the play format. There are several ways to spark involvement in pupils:
   (a) It is important to start off from the pupils' *interests and questions* and to try to capture these in cultural practices. Like the teacher who noticed that her pupils were interested in

dinosaurs. She went to a museum for natural history with them and suggested setting up a museum with dinosaurs in their own classroom. The children started collecting things related to dinosaurs, like little toys, pictures, books, but step by step extending the collection with other things from the past. All the children participated enthusiastically in this project.

(b) On the basis of this enthusiasm, the teacher could suggest certain *roles* (as in the real museum): someone who sells the tickets, someone who writes the descriptions, someone who designs the announcements and invitations, someone who makes the shelves for the exhibits, and so on. It is important to realize that every role can only be accomplished by using (cultural) tools. For writing descriptions, one needs to have information, to read books, and to be able to write. So, all roles need specific instruments (often including reading and writing). Getting young children engaged in certain roles, creates a 'natural' stepping stone for getting them authentically engaged in the appropriation of cultural tools.

2. *Guarantee awareness of significant rules*: this maxim implies that the teacher should pay attention to relevant rules for the accomplishment of the ongoing practice and for the proper use of tools. Sometimes children themselves are eager to imitate adult practices as closely as possible, and make agreements on the rules in their play. The rules may be moral-ethical (dos and don'ts) or more technical-informative. In our experience, the accomplishments of roles more often than not raise the need for new tools and information about how to use them properly. This is one of the most important ways of using playful activities as a meaningful context for learning! The main source for this kind of information is the participating teacher or more knowledgeable peers.

3. Allow pupils *degrees of freedom* necessary for exploring the activity and its possible *outcomes*, as far as possible taking into account safety, pedagogical responsibility and educational goals. *Give children the right to do it their own way*: this is important to make cultural practices accessible for them. When they feel that their personal efforts are taken seriously, it will keep them motivated. This does not mean that everything is allowed. Sometimes children will set high standards for their own and others' work, but still diverge from societal standards. When they make announcements, they will probably make drawings according to their own abilities, rather than using the sophisticated graphic

techniques, usually employed in advertisements in the adult world. When they decide that a ticket for the museum should be five cents, it differs from the usual prices for museums. Who cares?

It should be obvious from these characteristics of DPL that education in Developmental Education classrooms is definitely not a matter of *'laissez-faire'*. The teachers participate in children's play and take a role. From this position, the teacher can ask questions, give help, suggest solutions, but also spot new teaching opportunities for assisting pupils with the appropriation and employment of relevant cultural tools and improving pupils' participation abilities in the current practice (see van Oers 1999).

In our own classroom observations in Developmental Education schools, we witnessed teachers implementing these maxims interactively with their pupils in their own practice, and with remarkable outcomes. In the next section, I will briefly summarize some of the research that we did in early grade classrooms within our play-based curriculum.

Cultural learning in a play-based curriculum: examples from the Developmental Education Approach

In the Netherlands we have been able to initiate an educational movement with teachers, teacher trainers, curriculum developers and researchers that implements a play-based (early years) curriculum drawing on the assumptions described above (see, for example, van Oers 2003a, part 2; 2008). The curriculum development started in the 1980s and has developed along with the primary school curriculum. Although the curriculum development process is far from being completed, we have collected practical and empirical evidence over the past decades, which demonstrates the value and productivity of the activity-theoretical interpretation of playing. Our first empirical evidence of the potentials of this approach was based on observational studies and case studies (see van Oers 1994, 2003b, 2007). In the past decade we have supplemented this evidence by a number of quasi-experimental studies on a larger scale in the lower grades in primary school (pupils aged 4–8 years old).

The teachers in our studies all took care to realize the above-mentioned conditions in their classrooms to initiate and maintain Development-Promoting-Learning (DPL). Some of the relevant projects and empirical studies will be briefly summarized below.

Literacy development

In one of our research projects (Duijkers 2005) we studied *vocabulary acquisition* in a quasi-experimental design. In this research we compared a Developmental Education early years classroom (4–5-year-olds), with a classroom where the teacher worked with the children at vocabulary acquisition according to the 'mapping strategy' (Bloom 2001), wherein children were exposed to new object–word combinations, and had to learn these new words in an instruction session (here called the Mapping Strategy approach, further called the MS-approach). In the Developmental Education approach (the DE-approach) children were involved in a project on 'The Kitchen', where they were playing with water, washing dishes, and so on. During this kitchen-practice, the need for new words emerged, and appropriate new words were introduced and practised during conversations. Both projects took place in the same period of the year, lasted about eight weeks, and were focused on the same topic (water). Pupils from both projects were pre- and post-tested (on active and passive vocabulary) with the same vocabulary test, composed of project-based words related to water (like soap, rinsing, sponge, wring out, etc). The test was proved to be reliable (i.e. the individual measurements with this test were statistically proven to be stable and trustworthy). Moreover, the children were observed by the researcher in different situations inside the classroom and outside. The main outcomes of this study were:

- 4–5-year-old pupils in a DE classroom learned significantly more theme-related words than pupils in MS classrooms.
- Children who learned the new words in a meaningful way (in the DE-approach) frequently used their newly learned words outside the classroom, whereas this rarely happened in the MS-classrooms.

In a recent evaluation study of the language outcomes of four Developmental Education schools (some of them with considerable proportions of ethnic minority children), we tested pupils from grade 1 to grade 4 (ages 4–7) in three consecutive years on vocabulary, comprehensive reading, and reading proficiency (Poland 2007a). For each of these areas we constructed a high-level criterion, based on national norms, or based on a criterion of 65 per cent mastery. The performances of the children on these tests were compared with these criterion standards. Looking at the results we found:

- All pupils progressed over the years in terms of percentages that reach the criterion (when we compared the last year of the study with the first year).

- Some 60–70 per cent of the pupils scored above the criterion on comprehensive reading on a nationally standardized test (which is actually very high on a national scale).
- Some 65–78 per cent of the pupils scored above the criterion on the reading proficiency test (this was also a nationally standardized test).
- The situation with regard to vocabulary was a bit more complex. In grade 1 (4-year-olds) 50–55 per cent of the children scored higher than the criterion. In the other grades 30–40 per cent outperformed the criterion (against 8–22 per cent in the first year of the study).

Other recent empirical studies confirm this general picture (van Oers 2007). Developmental Education where the play format is the basis for the children's activity-based learning is a promising way of bringing young children to appropriate literacy competence.

Schematizing ability and mathematics learning

In her dissertation project Poland (2007b; Poland and van Oers 2007) elaborated my previous studies on schematizing in young children (see van Oers 1994, 1996, 2002). Within our cultural-historical perspective, schematizing was defined as a cognitive activity for the production of structured symbolic representations (such as maps, diagrams, pictograms, construction plans, brief instructions, etc.) that could be used for the organization of real-world activities or practices.

Poland (2007b) followed up on these observational studies with a more controlled investigation. Using a quasi-experimental design (pre-test and post-test in three experimental and three control schools; N = 137; all Developmental Education schools), she worked with experimental schools for a whole year in grade 2 (on average 5-year-olds). All schools were working with a play-based curriculum, but the experimental schools were assisted in introducing schematizing whenever possible and relevant in a meaningful way. At the beginning of the experiment, there was a slightly and significantly higher performance of the control children with regard to early mathematical abilities such as counting.

Children in the experimental schools frequently produced schematic representations (such as maps, construction plans, symbolic signs, etc.) and reflected on the meaning of these representations with the help of the teacher. At the end of grade 2, pupils in the experimental group outperformed the pupils from the non-experimental group on schematizing. But that was not our final goal, because that would have been a trivial result (pupils who never learned or practised schematizing will obviously not demonstrate high abilities on such tasks). Poland did the final test in grade 3 (6-year-olds) in the context of these pupils' mathematics development. She followed both the experimental and control pupils in their mathematics performances in the next year (grade 3). The main results of her study were:

- In a play-based curriculum it is possible to assist young children in developing schematizing abilities in a meaningful way.
- The playful mastery of schematizing abilities is an important prerequisite for early mathematics learning that brings about significantly better performances on mathematizing a year later, when compared to a control group.
- However, when meaningful schematizing is not continued and practised, the advantage of the experimental pupils will disappear in six months.

Again this large-scale experiment produces positive evidence for the potentials of the play-based curriculum.

Conclusion

Our theoretical analyses argued for a play concept that refutes the idea of play as an activity *sui generis,* as young children's natural way of existence. From a cultural-historical point of view, I argued for a conception that defines play as a special *format* of the way socio-cultural practices are carried out. On the basis of this starting point, we elaborated a play-based curriculum, which has been implemented in a number of primary schools in the Netherlands since the early 1980s. In our classroom practices we could witness that this is not a *laissez-faire* curriculum: the teacher has an important stimulating, supporting and co-operative role. The empirical evidence until now confirms the potentials of the play-based curriculum as conceived here.

A final interesting consequence must be mentioned here only briefly. Extrapolating from our findings so far, we believe that the play-based curriculum for the younger grades of primary school can easily be projected onto the curriculum in the higher grades. Teaching and learning in the upper grades can also be embedded in meaningful cultural practices: these practices can also be formatted in a way that articulates *rules* (stricter and more sophisticated rules than in the early grades), endorses the importance of *involvement* (by using pupils' own questions as starting points), and emphasizes pupils' relative *degrees of freedom*. At the moment we are cautiously exploring the learning perspectives of older pupils when participating in a playfully organized cultural practice that could be called 'research', actually leading to an inquiry-based curriculum. There is no space to dwell longer on these experiments. Hopefully, for now, this outlook may add to the core of our general argument: play – as a specific format of accomplishing cultural practices and activities – is a powerful and rich context for enculturation, i.e. for meaningfully learning cultural competences.

References

Bateson, G. (1972) Theory of play and fantasy, in G. Bateson, *Steps to an Ecology of Mind*. Chicago: University of Chicago Press, pp. 177–93.

Bloom. P. (2001) *How Children Learn the Meaning of Words*. Cambridge, MA: MIT Press.

Bruner, J.S. (1976) Nature and uses of immaturity, in J.S. Bruner, A. Jolly and K. Sylva (eds) *Play: Its Role in Development and Evolution*. Harmondsworth: Penguin.

Brušlinskij, A.V. and Polikarpov, V.A. (1990) *Myšlenie i obščenie* [Thinking and Communicating]. Minsk: Universitetskoe Izd-vo.

Duijkers, D. (2005) Spelenderwijs naar een rijke woordenschat: [Towards a rich vocabulary in a playful way], *De wereld van het jonge kind*, 32: 10 (June): 328–31.

El'konin, D.B. (1978) *Psichologija igry* [The Psychology of Play]. Moscow: Pedagogika.

El'konin, D.B. (1989) K probleme periodizacii psichiceskogo razvitija v detskom vozraste [The Problem of Periodization of the Psychological Development of the Child], in D.B. El'konin, *Izbrannye Psichologiceskie Trudy* [Collected Psychological Works]. Moscow: Pedagogika, pp. 60–77.

Engeström, Y. (2005) *Developmental Work Research: Expanding Activity Theory in Practice*. Berlin: Lehmanns Media.

Garvey, C. (1990) *Play* (enlarged edn). Cambridge, MA: Harvard University Press.

Göncü, A., Tuermer, U., Jain, J. and Johnson, D. (1999) Children's play as cultural activity, in A. Göncü (ed.) *Children's Engagement in the World: Sociocultural Perspectives*. Cambridge: Cambridge University Press, pp. 148–70.

Hughes, F.P. (1999) *Children, Play, and Development*, 3rd edn. Boston: Allyn & Bacon.

Lave, J. and Wenger, E. (1991) *Situated Learning: Legitimate Peripheral Participation*. Cambridge: Cambridge University Press.

Leont'ev, A.N. (1975) *Dejatel'nost', soznanie, licnost'* [Activity, Consciousness, Personality]. Moscow: Politizdat (English translation, 1978, Prentice Hall, Englewood Cliffs, NJ).

Leont'ev, A.N. (1981a) *Problemy razvitija psichiki* [Problems of Psychological Development]. Moscow: Izd-vo Moskovskogo Universiteta.

Leont'ev, A.N. (1981b) The problem of activity in psychology, in J.V. Wertsch (ed.) *The Concept of Activity in Soviet Psychology.* Armonk, NY: M.E. Sharpe, pp. 37–71.

Michnick Golinkoff, R., Hirsh-Pasek, K. and Singer, D.G. (2006) Why play = Learning: a challenge for parents and educators, in D.G. Singer, R. Michnick Golinkoff and K. Hirsh-Pasek (eds) *Play = Learning: How Play Motivates and Enhances Children's Cognitive and Social-emotional Growth.* New York: Oxford University Press, pp. 3–12.

Moyles, J. (1989) *Just Playing? The Role and Status of Play in Early Childhood Education.* Milton Keynes: Open University Press.

Poland, M. (2007a) Bergopwaarts in taalontwikkeling [Reaching Higher in Language Development], *De wereld van het jonge kind*, 35(3): 79–84.

Poland, M. (2007b) The treasures of schematising: the effects of schematising in early childhood on the learning processes and outcomes in later mathematical understanding, dissertation. Enschede, Ipskamp.

Poland M. and van Oers, B. (2007) The effects of schematising on mathematical development, *European Early Childhood Education Research Journal*, 15(2): 269–93.

Rogoff, B. (2003) *The Cultural Nature of Human Development.* New York: Oxford University Press.

Sutton-Smith, B. (1997) *The Ambiguity of Play.* Cambridge, MA: Harvard University Press.

Tuomi-Gröhn, T., Engeström, Y. and Young, M. (2003) Conceptualizing transfer: from standard notions to developmental perspectives, in T. Tuomi-Gröhn and Y. Engeström (eds) *Between School and Work: New Perspectives on Transfer and Boundary Crossing.* Bingley, UK: Emerald, pp. 19–38.

van Oers, B. (1994) Semiotic activity of young children in play: the construction and use of schematic representations, *European Early Childhood Education Research Journal*, 2(1): 19–34.

van Oers, B. (1996) Are you sure? The promotion of mathematical thinking in the play activities of young children, *European Early Childhood Education Research Journal*, 4(1): 71–89.

van Oers, B. (1999) Teaching opportunities in play, in M. Hedegaard and J. Lompscher (eds) *Learning Activity and Development.* Aarhus: Aarhus University Press, pp. 268–89.

van Oers, B. (2002) The mathematization of young children's language, in K. Gravemeijer, R. Lehrer, B. van Oers and L. Verschaffel, (eds) *Symbolizing and Modeling in Mathematics Education.* Dordrecht: Kluwer, pp. 29–57.

van Oers, B. (2003a) *Narratives of Childhood.* Amsterdam: VU Press.

van Oers, B. (2003b) Learning resources in the context of play: promoting effective learning in early childhood, *European Early Childhood Education Journal*, 11(1): 7–26.

van Oers, B. (2007) Helping young children to become literate: the relevance of narrative competence for developmental education, *European Early Childhood Education Research Journal*, 15(3): 299–312.

van Oers, B. (2008) Inscripting predicates: dealing with meanings in play, in B. van Oers, W. Wardekker, E. Elbers and R. van der Veer (eds) *The Transformation of Learning: Advances in Activity Theory*. Cambridge: Cambridge University Press, pp. 370–80.

van Oers, B. (2009) Developmental education: improving participation in cultural practices, in M. Fleer, M. Hedegaard and J. Tudge (eds) *Childhood Studies and the Impact of Globalization: Policies and Practices at Global and Local Levels – World Yearbook of Education 2009*. New York: Routledge, pp. 293–317.

Vygotsky, L.S. (1978) The role of play in development, in L.S. Vygotsky, *Mind in Society: The Development of Higher Psychological Processes*. Cambridge, MA: Harvard University Press, pp. 92–104.

Wenger, E. (1999) *Communities of Practice: Learning, Meaning, and Identity*. Cambridge: Cambridge University Press.

15 Playing with some tensions

Poststructuralism, Foucault and early childhood education

Jo Ailwood

Introduction

While this chapter does not report on a research project about play, or indeed focus specifically on play alone, I take the perspective that play is everywhere in early childhood education. Play has long been at the heart of Western ideas about early childhood education with all the glories, thrills, chills and despairs that involves. It has been an integral part of the idea of a universal child, just as it is now an integral part of the examination and decommissioning of the idea of a universal child. Almost all of the early childhood research discussed in this chapter has play content of some kind, and since play is not just for, or about, children I am instead taking the opportunity to begin playing with some theoretical ideas.

In her keynote speech at the annual meeting of the European Early Childhood Education Research Association, Berit Bae (2008) suggested, among other things, that we in early childhood educational research need to take a critical stance towards play. This chapter is an attempt to take up, and play with, that challenge. To do this I will first say a little about poststructuralism, then I will briefly outline the growth of feminist poststructural research in early childhood education, especially in Australia. I then play with these ideas, keeping in mind Foucault's (1977: 230) suggestion that 'to imagine another system is to extend our participation in the present system', in other words we are in and of social systems, even as we may resist them.

Poststructuralism and Foucault

Poststructuralism is not, strictly speaking, a *position*, but rather a critical interrogation of the exclusionary operations by which 'positions' are established. In this sense, a feminist poststructuralism does not designate a position from which one operates, a point of view or standpoint which might be usefully compared with other 'positions' within the theoretical field.

(Butler and Scott 1992: xiv)

It is widely accepted that poststructuralism, especially when developed through the ideas of Foucault, is a body of thought that enables scholars to question universal truths and metanarratives. It is a means, as Butler and Scott suggest above, of theorizing 'exclusionary operations', often through investigating functions of power, discourse and knowledge. Foucault is not the only thinker to contribute to the ideas that circulate through poststructuralism; others include Gilles Deleuze, Félix Guattari and Jacques Derrida. Given the range of thinkers contributing to the field of thought, conflict is an inherent component of poststructuralism, often even within the analysis of one scholar. Foucault is, however, a dominant reference point among these thinkers in the context of poststructuralism in Australian early childhood educational research. Interestingly, like many others credited as influential 'poststructuralists', Foucault never referred to himself as a poststructuralist. Indeed, he generally refused to define himself or his intellectual project. Perhaps the closest he came was to name his position at the *Collège de France* as the Professor of the History of Systems of Thought. This title also points towards the task of history in making the present problematic, a key poststructural process.

That there is little in the way of a 'Foucauldian template' is both terribly seductive and terribly frustrating. As Clare O'Farrell (2005: 53) suggests, 'one does not simply "apply" Foucault's method in the same way that one applies ethnomethodology and other sociological methods'. It should also be remembered that Foucault's body of work is 'an immense monument to discipline and order in the historical analysis of ideas and thought' (O'Farrell 2005: 52). Remembering history can displace us and remind us of our location in the present, and that 'things' have not always been as they are (e.g. Cannella 1997; Ailwood 2003). It can remind us that we are not the first to critique play (see, for example, Scott 1969; Stubbs 1969) nor are we the first to 'reconceptualize' early childhood education. In their own times and places, figures such as Froebel, Dewey or Montessori all reconceptualized 'who' children were, and what sort of education was appropriate. In the 1970s, sociologists such as Ronald King (1978) investigated children and early years education, arguing for social understandings and analyses. Remembering our place and our moment reminds us to be reflexive, careful and humble about our own claims to 'truth'.

Poststructuralism, education and Foucault

There are many researchers internationally who have engaged with Foucauldian ideas across the broad fields of children, childhood and education – a few examples include O'Farrell (1997), Baker (1998), and Popkewitz and Bloch (2001). Many of these researchers (and those in their edited collections) have been interested in investigating the historical and systemic processes – the conditions of possibility – that have enabled and constrained the ways in which we currently produce discourses of childhood and education. The key ideas of poststructural research include analyses of discourses, power and knowledge. All of these have been influential in Australian educational research, especially within the field of gender. Feminists in Australian educational research have engaged quite widely with poststructural theories as a framework for investigating, and understanding gender in schools, especially during the 1990s (e.g. Davies 1989; Gilbert and Taylor 1991; Luke 1991; Gore 1992).

Alongside this growth of feminist poststructural research in education more generally during the 1990s, there also emerged work focusing on young children and their teachers in early childhood settings. This research is usually also aligned with the 'reconceptualizing early childhood' movement in the US and the growing critique of developmental psychology as the basis for early childhood practice . Given its prominent position in Australian feminist and educational research, it is unsurprising that the engagement with feminist poststructuralism is reflected in Australian early childhood education research (e.g. Ailwood 2003; Blaise 2005; MacNaughton 2005; Sumsion 2005; Saltmarsh 2009). Feminist poststructural theories, particularly those using the work of Foucault, have frequently been proposed as an alternative to developmentally appropriate practice in early childhood education. The use of poststructural theoretical frameworks has, therefore, been a key means for resistance to 'traditional' early childhood educational practices in Australia. Over the same period, parallel developments in Europe (Dahlberg et al. 1999; Jones 2001) and the US (Cannella 1997; Ryan 2005) have also contributed to the body of work.

This body of research has made use of poststructuralism in different ways – not all of them deal directly with play. Sumsion (2005), for example, makes an analysis of pre-school children's drawings and talk regarding their male teacher. Fenech et al. (2008) analyze Australia's regulatory framework for child care settings as a form of governance. Others using governmentality include Popkewitz and Bloch (2001), Hultqvist and Dahlberg (2001) and Ailwood (2008). A serious and common concern among many of these poststructural researchers in early childhood, however, has been play, and in particular gender and play (e.g. Davies 1989; MacNaughton 2000; Giugni 2003).

Playing with ideas: remembering that everything is 'dangerous'

Moving forward from this brief overview, I want to play with McLeod's (2001) point that while many researchers have argued the 'virtues' of poststructuralism, very few have investigated our own claims to truth as poststructuralists. In this chapter, I am working alongside the body of research that has investigated ways of putting poststructuralism to work in interactions in early years settings. Much of this work has aimed to challenge 'traditional' practices (i.e. those based in developmental psychology) producing alternative pathways for thinking about early childhood educational practices. I want to suggest, however, that it is time to hesitate, to investigate how the use of the term poststructualism and the name of Foucault have come to be markers of an alternative to the traditional – and what the effects of this may be – an activity that can only happen with hindsight and in retrospect. This investigation is tentative for I have no wish to devalue the political work that can potentially be achieved; however, I do want to pursue some reflection on what new claims to 'truth' we create through poststructural theories.

When talking of 'truth' in this chapter, I do not mean an inexorable truth, which would of course be the antithesis of poststructural research. I mean that when we discuss gender, play and childhood we create our own (perhaps small 't'?) versions of 'truths'. I am seeking the space to wonder if the 'feminist poststructural moment' requires its own critique. For, while I would consider feminist poststructuralism as undoubtedly useful, it may produce its own version of good teacher and good child. Reflecting the quote from Foucault in the introduction of this chapter, Sawicki (1991: 10) has suggested that, 'Our discourses can extend relations of domination at the same time that they are critical of them, and ... any emancipatory theory bears the traces of its origins in specific historical relations of power/knowledge.' Let me be clear here, I am not playing with this line of thought in order to discredit or immobilize. Rather, I aim to contribute to the further development of the ideas in question. As a sometime 'feminist poststructuralist' who has become exceedingly wary of such labels, I am asking questions of my own work, as well as the work of others. In reflecting on the potential dangers of playing within Foucault's toolbox, I follow other feminists who have reminded us of the need to be alert to the regulatory effects of our own discourses; for example, Gore's (1992) engagement with feminism, poststructuralism and critical pedagogy or McLeod's (2001) questioning of the truth effects of poststructuralism. In this chapter, I am insisting on the reminder 'not that everything is bad, but everything is dangerous, which is not exactly the same as bad' (Foucault 2004: 104).

I am exploring the idea that poststructural analysis and 'doing Foucault' are in themselves regulatory tools – ways and means of producing and managing early childhood subjectivities. The question that comes to mind is how thinking about play and early childhood education in a 'poststructural' way is any more or less regulatory than thinking about it in terms of developmentally appropriate practice, the Reggio Emilia Approach or other ideas in early childhood education.

Gender and play

Many researchers in early childhood education have used feminist post-structuralism to engage with the notion that subjects are constituted, in gendered ways, through discourses. From here it seems to follow that changing the discourses of gender and childhood will enable children, particularly girls, to change the gendered ways in which they operate. However, attempts to shift from a position of analysis, critique or resistance to a position of practice and pedagogy have often (sometimes by an author's own admission) ended by offering relatively simple readings of classroom situations and of poststructuralism. The most common reading is of the individual child and teacher being in a position to pick and chose from a smorgasbord of gendered discourses. This gendered smorgasbord is usually optimistically free of negative implications and the material consequences such 'choices' might produce. Such a position negates the embodiment of gendered discourses; the pleasures, pains, investments and dangers of being a 'boy' or of being a 'girl', and indeed of being a 'teacher' in an early childhood setting. A focus on choices with little reference to consequences or social location elides deeper understanding of the 'complex interplay of choice, action and constraint' (O'Farrell 2005: 110) in Foucault's analyses of the ethics and politics of the self.

Some early childhood education research using feminist poststructuralism emphasizes the positive implications of poststructural theories, while silencing and marginalizing the regulatory frameworks that are also produced through poststructuralism. For example, it has been suggested that feminist poststructuralist ideas 'seek ways of being gendered that do not regulate but are full of possibilities for girls, for boys and for their teachers' (MacNaughton 2000: 3). In that same text MacNaughton does raise Foucault's point that all discourses are dangerous, however, this point is set aside in the search for a 'non-regulatory' ideal of gender.

While hope and possibility are unarguably worthy of pursuit, freedom from regulation and relations of power is impossible; certainly from a poststructural perspective. As Foucault (2000: 343) pointed out, 'a society without power relations can only be an abstraction', a point supported by Walkerdine (1984: 196) who showed us the 'impossibility of setting the "individual" free' within early childhood education.

McLeod (2001: 276) suggests that some feminist poststructural early childhood research, although

> deeply critical of developmentalism ... nevertheless govern[s] childhood subjectivity through making gender reflexivity part of the necessary protocol of growing up. Gender identity is not imposed by social forces beyond one's control. Nor is gender the result of intrinsic disposition or essence ... Gender identity is an individual project.

Poststructural accounts of gendered childhood, particularly those that position gender as 'an individual project' that each child and teacher takes on, could be identified as forms of regulation in themselves. Foucault (1978: 27), when discussing shifting discourses of sexuality, stated that

> [there] was a new regime of discourses. Not any less was said about [sex]; on the contrary. But things were said in a different way; it was different people who said them, from different points of view, and in order to obtain different results.

Following this point, I would suggest that the poststructural feminist influence in early childhood education is but another discursive regime, that not any less is being said about young children (and gender), but it is being said in different ways, by different people, for different purposes and with different results.

There is a slippage between the poststructural early childhood teacher's thinking, and children's construction of their identities, whereby the limits and acceptabilities, constraints and relations are too easily elided. There are many reasons why the suggestion that children make 'choices' about identity, especially gendered identity, is potentially problematic. For an individual child to make choices that resist and refuse dominant discourses of gender, they need to engage with ways of being that are potentially confrontational, perhaps even violent, and require a great deal of emotional courage and maturity to maintain in any ongoing way, especially beyond the classroom environment. Danby (1998) clearly shows the potential for violence when 'being a boy' in the block area and feminists have regularly argued that gender is constituted via exclusions and erasures (Butler 1993). This is not to say the choices are beyond children – it is to wonder if we are asking children to make choices that many adults do not have the courage and maturity to make. It needs to be remembered and made clear that choices have real consequences, both positive and negative, for children.

Walkerdine (1984: 190) suggested that a 'system of regulation and normalization' produces what counts as 'good pedagogy'. It produces, therefore, what counts as a 'good teacher'. While feminist poststructuralism is a long way from being 'normal' in early childhood education, it does need to be remembered that the pedagogies encouraged in its name are also regulatory. For example, MacNaughton (2000: 23) suggests in her research with teachers on gender and poststructuralism, that 'Edna's tensions might have been fewer and her failures avoided if she had had access to an alternative theory of young children's identity formation, such as feminist poststructuralism.' To argue that feminist poststructuralism can produce good teaching, that it can correct 'bad habits' or prevent 'failures' is of course not 'bad'; but it *is* potentially dangerous in the Foucauldian sense that it becomes another form of regulation. The question becomes then, how our exhortation to act as an early childhood teacher in a poststructural and/or feminist 'way' is less regulatory, less tension inducing and more successful than adhering to developmentally appropriate practices. Or indeed, making use of any other theoretical frame for early childhood education? After all, the observational gaze of the adult teacher remains, it is the focus that shifts. Rather than the powerful teacher gaze of PIES (physical, intellectual, emotional and social development), there is the powerful teacher gaze of gender, and possibly class or race. Of course with such changes teachers and researchers can see differently – and that can be useful and political. However, a feminist poststructural gaze remains a disciplinary gaze, it is in itself another form of disciplinary power, a power that includes surveillance and managing conduct.

Beyond the 'choices' … children manipulating power relationships

Within the networks and relations of power in early years settings, children are rarely in a position to challenge stubborn and deeply embedded discourses, such as those of gender. Indeed, many adults struggle to challenge these discourses. A feminist poststructuralist teacher can invite children to challenge, give space and time to pause, to think, to ask questions. However, there tends to be little analysis of what happens after this invitation to challenge and resist dominant discourses and practices. What are we asking of children when we encourage them to 'choose' a different way of, for example, 'being a girl'? What relationships of power – in terms of class or race for example – cut through this 'choice'? What are the potential consequences? What are the potential violences? Pleasures? Investigating the intricate and sometimes unexpected consequences of engaging with difference in terms of children's friends, families and communities is important. The example of Kim, an Asian child described by MacNaughton (2005) who when asked to choose an anti-bias persona doll that she identifies with, unexpectedly chooses not an Asian doll, but a white doll, serves as a potent reminder that relationships of power are entwined not only with gender, but with other social categories that are arranged to manage us, such as class, race or religion.

Further in-depth analysis of the relations of power, the capillaries and networks that work to produce the available 'choices' is an important aspect of the ongoing work of poststructural research in early childhood education. In our work with young children in education settings, the power relationships between adults and children are often taken as common sense, and therefore easily ignored, marginalized or forgotten in the pace of daily life. However, in discounting the fact that children do operate in a world where all adults have greater access to political, social and economic relations of power, we fail to recognize that children (and particularly very young children) continue to live in a world produced and managed by adults. We thereby marginalize the impact of factors such as class, race, religion, sexuality or geographical location that also slice through more nuanced understandings of gender.

One of the limits we necessarily face as adults in the early years are the unwritten and largely hidden social codes of behaviour and inclusion/ exclusion in play that children negotiate and establish among themselves (e.g. Danby 1998; Giugni 2003; Campbell 2005; Ryan 2005). Children hold a significant body of knowledge about the functioning of their social world; a knowledge to which most adults do not have access. Children are adept at 'playing the system'. Questions about, for example, power, knowledge and gender, may be discussed and negotiated between adults and children in one way (e.g. a poststructural feminist way), but in very different, and perhaps distinctly '*un*feminist' and '*un*poststructural' ways once the adult has left the scene. Once an adult has departed, the power relationships change, the context and consequences change and children may return to their very effective policing of each other's behaviours within their own social negotiations and their own codes of conduct.

One example of children's ability to 'play the system' is presented by Theobald (2009). While it is an example produced out of ethnomethodology and conversation analysis, in the context of this chapter it serves to reveal children's astute and political usage of adults in pursuit of their own codes of conduct while playing at school. Theobald presents a video-recorded scene in which girls and boys are playing together, negotiating materials and the direction of the play; but the boys begin to 'break the rules'. The girls use the 'I'm telling' tactic, leaving the play space to tell the teacher about the boys' behaviour. While the girls are away, the boys take the opportunity to lead the play and take the materials they require. The girls, on the other hand, return and strategically make use of the teacher's responses to their tale to attempt to manage the boys and the play situation. The girls 'told on' the boys four times in all – sometimes they returned to replay the teacher's words and sometimes they manipulated or ignored the teacher's advice.

This scenario is interesting on many levels, but for the purposes of this chapter it illustrates the powerful – and deeply gendered – political work children do without direct adult interference or supervision. This work children do through negotiating and manipulating their way around their deep knowledge of the power relationships in school and accessing and making use of 'powerful' adult advice in an attempt to gain a desired outcome. As a bystander without access to the repeated viewing of the video, the teacher did not (and could not) have access to the complex power relationships the children were negotiating within. The girls knew, for example, that it would be much more powerful to 'tell on' the boys to the actual classroom teacher, rather than to the researcher.

As Giugni (2003) and Campbell (2005) have both argued, there is 'secret children's business' in early childhood settings.[1] In the case of Campbell, this secret business meant that staff 'watched as our discourse of social justice was displaced and reconfigured by how children practiced their gender' (2005: 155). These examples indicate that children do not just 'choose' what we as teachers in early childhood would want them to choose, they engage in their own political decision making and negotiations. To a large degree, we as adults do not have access to this secret play world – and children will continue to strategically use and manipulate their understanding of social networks in their play in early childhood settings to navigate through circuits and relations of power.

Conclusion

I would again like to emphasize that it has not been my intention in this chapter to dismiss feminist poststructural work in early childhood, which I am certain has made a powerful difference to the lives of some early childhood teachers and the children they work with. Instead I would like to play with the idea that we could be acknowledging more clearly that the activity of producing, managing, watching and regulating relationships is inherent in every early childhood teacher's daily practice. The ways in which we go about that 'producing, managing, watching and regulating' reflect our ethico-political choices – and the actions, consequences and constraints that they in turn create must be acknowledged. For, in Foucault's words, 'the ethico-political choice we have to make every day is to determine which is the main danger' (2004: 104–5).

Poststructural theories, and the work of Foucault in particular, have been the catalyst for a great deal of positive engagement with ideas providing a significant challenge to 'traditional' early years theories and practices. Poststructural and feminist theories provide us with powerful and valuable ways of thinking. Various versions and combinations have helped us challenge common sense and ask political questions in particular ways; for example about power, knowledge, relationships, space, ethics and bodies – all of which are fundamental to education at any level. In early childhood education this is evident in a range of research about children's play and investigations of, for example, power and gender (Danby 1998; Ryan 2005), race (Rossholt 2006) or children's perceptions of their teacher (Sumsion 2005).

Regardless of their usefulness, as tools of thought they remain regulatory in and of themselves. In and of themselves, they are not a remedy for girls playing 'school' and boys playing blocks. Theory should be put to work to improve practice; but we also need to be reflective and careful about the new claims to truth these 'poststructural' practices produce; that is, the new regulatory frameworks and new exhortations to govern oneself as a feminist poststructural teacher and child in early childhood educational settings. One way of grappling with these tensions may be to maintain our sense of humility coupled with a renewed focus on the historicity of our own work both within and beyond early childhood. We need to be able to sustain our political and ethical debates, ideas and practices without losing sight of the ways in which children and adults need each other to build a respectful and ethical social world. I suggest that a 'poststructural challenge' is to remember that as we do this we are in and of our systems, and the relationships we build are always regulatory – even as we hope that they may be liberatory.

Note

1. It should be noted here, as Giugni also notes, that the idea of 'secret business' will have particular resonances for Australian audiences as it has come to signify aspects of the reconciliation processes between Indigenous and non-Indigenous Australians, in particular with regard to secret Indigenous knowledges and the relationships of power and politics that potentially circulate around these.

References

Ailwood, J. (2003) Governing early childhood through play, *Contemporary Issues in Early Childhood*, 4(3): 286–9.

Ailwood, J. (2008) Earning or learning in the Smart State: changing tactics for governing early childhood, *Childhood*, 15(4): 535–51.

Bae, B. (2008) Children's right to participate – pitfalls and possibilities, keynote address, European Early Childhood Education Research Association annual conference, Stavanger, Norway, 3–6 September.

Baker, B. (1998) Childhood-as-rescue in the emergence and spread of the U.S. public school, in T. Popkewitz and M. Brennan (eds) *Foucault's Challenge: Discourse, Knowledge and Power in Education*. New York: Teachers College Press.

Blaise, M. (2005) A feminist poststructuralist study of children 'doing' gender in an urban kindergarten classroom, *Early Childhood Research Quarterly*, 20(1): 85–108.

Butler, J. (1993) *Bodies That Matter: On the Discursive Limits of 'Sex'*. New York: Routledge.

Butler, J. and Scott, J.W. (eds) (1992) *Feminists Theorize the Political*. New York: Routledge.

Campbell, S. (2005) Secret children's business: resisting and redefining access to learning in the early childhood classroom, in N. Yelland (ed.) *Critical Issues in Early Childhood*. Maidenhead: Open University Press.

Cannella, G.S. (1997) *Deconstructing Early Childhood Education: Social Justice and Revolution*. New York: Peter Lang.

Dahlberg, G., Moss, P. and Pence, A. (1999) *Beyond Quality in Early Childhood Education and Care: Postmodern Perspectives*. London: Falmer.

Danby, S. (1998) How to be masculine in the block area, *Childhood*, 5(2): 151–75.

Davies, B. (1989) *Frogs and Snails and Feminist Tales: Preschool Children and Gender*. Sydney: Allen & Unwin.

Fenech, M., Sumsion, J. and Goodfellow, J. (2008) Regulation and risk: early childhood education and care services as sites where the 'laugh of Foucault' resounds, *Journal of Educational Policy*, 23(1): 35–48.

Foucault, M. (1977) Revolutionary action: 'until now', in D. Bouchard (ed.) *Language, Counter-Memory, Practice*. Oxford: Basil Blackwell.

Foucault, M. (1978) *The History of Sexuality*, vol. 1, *The Will to Knowledge*. London: Penguin.

Foucault, M. (2000) The subject and power, in J.D. Faubion (ed.) *Michel Foucault, Power, The Essential Works*, vol. 3. London: Penguin Books.

Foucault, M. (2004) On the genealogy of ethics: an overview of work in progress, in P. Rabinow and N. Rose (eds) *The Essential Foucault*. New York: The New Press.

Gilbert, P. and Taylor, S. (1991) *Fashioning the Feminine: Girls, Popular Culture and Schooling*. Sydney: Allen & Unwin.

Giugni, M. (2003) 'Adults only': secret children's business, *International Journal of Equity and Innovation in Early Childhood*, 1(1): 47–58.

Gore, J. (1992) What can we do for you! What *can* 'we' do for 'you'?: Struggling over empowerment in critical and feminist pedagogy, in C. Luke and J. Gore (eds) *Feminisms and Critical Pedagogy*. New York: Routledge.

Hultqvist, K. and Dahlberg, G. (eds) (2001) *Governing the Child in the New Millennium*. London: RoutledgeFalmer.

Jones, L. (2001) Trying to break bad habits in practice by engaging with poststructuralist theories, *Early Years*, 21(1): 25–32.

King, R. (1978) *All Things Bright and Beautiful? A Sociological Study of Infants' Classrooms*. Chichester: John Wiley & Sons Ltd.

Luke, C. (1991) On reading the child: a feminist poststructuralist perspective, *Australian Journal of Reading*, 14(2): 109–16.

MacNaughton, G. (2000) *Rethinking Gender in Early Childhood Education*. London: Sage.

MacNaughton, G. (2005) *Doing Foucault in Early Childhood Studies: Applying Poststructural Ideas*. London: Routledge.

McLeod, J. (2001) When gender meets poststructuralism, in K. Hultqvist and G. Dahlberg (eds) *Governing the Child in the New Millennium*. London: RoutledgeFalmer.

O'Farrell, C. (1997) (ed.) *Foucault: the Legacy*. Kelvin Grove, Queensland University of Technology.

O'Farrell, C. (2005) *Michel Foucault*. London: Sage.

Popkewitz, T. and Bloch, M. (2001) Administering freedom: a history of the present – rescuing the parent to rescue the child for society, in K. Hultqvist and G. Dahlberg (eds) *Governing the Child in the New Millennium*. London: RoutledgeFalmer.

Rossholt, N. (2006) Inscribing the body: 'black', 'white' and gender in early childhood education and complexity, *Journal of Australian Research in Early Childhood Education*, 13(1): 112–24.

Ryan, S. (2005) Freedom to choose, examining children's experiences in choice time, in N. Yelland (ed.) *Critical Issues in Early Childhood Education*. Maidenhead: Open University Press.

Saltmarsh, S. (2009) Becoming economic subjects: agency, consumption and popular culture in early childhood, *Discourse: Studies in the Cultural Politics of Education*, 30(1): 47–59.

Sawicki, J. (1991) *Disciplining Foucault: Feminism, Power and the Body*. New York: Routledge.

Scott, P. (1969) For or against play: is this the issue?, *Australian Pre-School Quarterly*, 10(1): 20–33.

Stubbs, B. (1969) Resisting pressures in the pre-school centre, a place to play and grow, *Australian Pre-School Quarterly*, 10(1): 13–19.

Sumsion, J. (2005) Preschool children's portrayals of their male teacher; a poststructuralist analysis, in N. Yelland (ed.) *Critical Issues in Early Childhood*. Maidenhead: Open University Press.

Theobald, M. (2009) Participation and social order in the playground, unpublished PhD, Queensland University of Technology, Australia.

Walkerdine, V. (1984) Developmental psychology and the child-centred pedagogy: the insertion of Piaget into early education, in J. Henriques, W. Hollway, C. Urwin, C. Venn and V. Walkerdine (eds) *Changing the Subject*. London: Methuen & Co. Ltd.

Afterword

Susan Edwards and Liz Brooker

In the Introduction to this book we outlined our reasons for moving from the concept of challenging play to engaging play. We talked about how we saw the notion of engaging play as allowing us to respond in a meaningful way to the complexity of today's world, and as a way of thinking about what the world might be like 35 years from today, when the children currently enrolled in our pre-schools will be taking responsibility for the lives of future generations. In doing so, we drew on arguments derived from the philosophy of science regarding knowledge production and the genesis, and role, of knowledge production in twenty-first-century communities.

The emergence of Mode 2 knowledge from Mode 1 knowledge, identified by Gibbons et al. (1994), perhaps mirrors a similar trend in early childhood educational research in which an increasing range of theoretical ideas, arguments and perspectives have been used to investigate play and the relationships between play and pedagogy in early years settings. In developing this book we have been able to think about the various chapters, and what they offer early childhood scholarship, by shifting our focus from how the chapters might have challenged conventional notions of play, to considering the various 'contexts of application' with which each chapter engages. Thus, we have been able to see links between chapters which draw on a range of theoretical perspectives while focusing on similar problem situations, or contexts of application. The contributions to this book suggest three such directions, each of which has its own focus on how knowledge about (and through) play might evolve. The first of these focuses on attempts to explore conventional notions of play in early years settings from practical and theoretical perspectives, as described, for instance, by Elizabeth Wood, Jo Ailwood and Annica Löfdahl. The second attempts to show the ways in which children engage with, and respond to, the pedagogical uses of play within particular contexts, as exemplified, for instance, by Liz Brooker, Helen Hedges and Bert van Oers; and finally, there are illustrations of the ways in which reflective teachers engage with their own practice trying to understand the play/pedagogy relationship, as shown, for instance, by Barbara Jordan, and Brian Edmiston and Tim Taylor.

Identifying these directions suggests that the movement from challenging to engaging play has been useful because it has allowed us to think about play in relation to the concept of knowledge production, rather than continuing debate around existing discourses about play and the various available definitions of play. We find this an important shift for our own thinking as it frees us to consider the many ways in which play contributes to the production of knowledge, for and by children and within the field of early childhood education. This means that, rather than trying to determine the nature of play, the book has been able to consider the many ways play is represented and enacted in early childhood settings. Enabled by a focus on the context of application, this means thinking instead about the ways in which play relates to the production of knowledge across multiple settings for a range of purposes and for different stakeholders. Thus, we can think about how play produces (or perhaps limits) knowledge for researchers, children and teachers. For researchers this could mean considering the production of empirical and theoretical knowledge about play and its pedagogical applications in early childhood settings (through a range of theoretical lenses, and in collaboration with a range of different stakeholders). For children, this might involve the ways in which knowledge is produced through and within their play in order to achieve their own intentions, and with multiple and unpredictable outcomes. For teachers, this suggests thinking about the interface between play and pedagogy in practice. Several examples of each of these spring to mind, including, for example, Fleer's demonstration of the need for children and teachers to establish contextual and conceptual intersubjectivity to support learning; Löfdahl's examination of girls' strategies for excluding each other from play experiences; and finally, Edmiston and Taylor's analysis of the ways in which a school explored, and responded to, the play experiences and needs of the children during break times.

Each of these examples shows individuals working together in a specific, local, social and cultural context to develop and share meanings. This work may involve creating new knowledge (as the child at the centre of Blaise's study is doing), or appropriating the cultural knowledge which is part of each setting's heritage (as the children in van Oers' study are seen to do). And each offers a perspective on play which contributes to how we might, more broadly, read and understand play and pedagogy in early childhood settings. Seeing these contributions in terms of knowledge production *about* play or (in the case of the children) *through* play means we have not had to focus on challenging play at all. Rather we have been able to work towards understanding the many dimensions of play in particular contexts and situations. Like the movement from Mode 1 towards Mode 2 knowledge production this has allowed us to stop thinking about challenging universal understandings of play, and move towards thinking about how play is enacted, experienced and interpreted by children and adults for differing, and sometimes wildly contradictory, reasons. Collectively, the chapters in this book move beyond contributing knowledge that is seen to support certainty about universal perspectives on play, to understanding the contexts and situations that draw on and use play in particular ways with particular results (for example, O'Brien's discussion of the ways in which play can be harnessed from a deficit perspective to 'help' children with disabilities).

We are reminded here of the many children, teachers and researchers peopling the pages of this book, and the many and various activities they are engaged in. There is the problem of Humpty Dumpty and his medication (Chapter 5), and the mystery of the hot toast located in the distance between the teacher's and children's perspectives on the activity (Chapter 3); there is Madison the boy puppy insisting on her production of boyness (Chapter 6); and there are the policemen creating their own responses to the activities of the 'travel agent' (Chapter 11). There are also the groups of adults comparing their own play experiences to those of today's children, suggesting as they do so that play has lost its imaginative force for the children of the twenty-first century (Chapter 4); and finally there is Elizabeth constructing a research methodology for investigating the implications of her own pedagogical stance on play (Chapter 10). Each of these children, teachers and situations shows us the many ways in which play is engaged in early childhood settings, and how it contributes to the production of knowledge about how and what children learn, particularly when play is used as a basis for pedagogical activity. We therefore see the contributions to this volume as offering important insights into the ways in which play might be thought about now and into the future. As a collective endeavour, we also see the book as a stimulus for thinking more broadly about play, so that instead of focusing on endless definitions of play and pedagogy, we are able to think about engaging with the many ways play is understood, experienced and theorized, by children, teachers and researchers alike.

Reference

Gibbons, M., Limoges, C., Nowotny, H., Schwartzman, S., Scott, P. and Trow, M. (1994) *The New Production of Knowledge: The Dynamics of Science and Research in Contemporary Societies.* London: Sage.

Index